# Postsecondary Educational Opportunities for Students with Special Education Needs

The decision to go to college is a big one. It signifies a transition into young adulthood and the increasing expectations for independence that can feel exciting, liberating, and daunting! For students with disabilities, this transition may be even more challenging. Despite the challenges, more and more students with disabilities are attending postsecondary colleges and universities. While this is certainly encouraging, students with disabilities are less likely to successfully complete their postsecondary programs when compared with their general population peers. So, what do we do? We can learn from our successes during early education and from successful postsecondary programs, taking what we have learned and bringing these lessons to scale so that fully inclusive postsecondary programs are available for all students with special education needs.

This book was originally published as a special issue of the *European Journal of Special Needs Education*.

**Mary Ruth Coleman**, PhD, is a Senior Scientist, Emeritus, at the FPG Child Development Institute at the University of North Carolina at Chapel Hill, USA. She directs Project U-STAR~PLUS (Using Science, Talents and Abilities to Recognize Students – Promoting Learning in Underrepresented Students).

**Michael Shevlin** is Professor in Inclusive Education in the School of Education, Trinity College Dublin, Republic of Ireland, and Director of the Trinity Centre for People with Intellectual Disabilities. He has researched widely in the area of inclusive education with a strong focus on establishing inclusive learning environments and facilitating pupil voice within schools.

# Postsecondary Educational Opportunities for Students with Special Education Needs

*Edited by*
Mary Ruth Coleman and Michael Shevlin

LONDON AND NEW YORK

First published 2018
by Routledge
2 Park Square, Milton Park, Abingdon, Oxon, OX14 4RN, UK

and by Routledge
711 Third Avenue, New York, NY 10017, USA

*Routledge is an imprint of the Taylor & Francis Group, an informa business*

© 2018 Taylor & Francis

All rights reserved. No part of this book may be reprinted or reproduced or utilised in any form or by any electronic, mechanical, or other means, now known or hereafter invented, including photocopying and recording, or in any information storage or retrieval system, without permission in writing from the publishers.

*Trademark notice*: Product or corporate names may be trademarks or registered trademarks, and are used only for identification and explanation without intent to infringe.

*British Library Cataloguing-in-Publication Data*
A catalogue record for this book is available from the British Library

ISBN13: 978-0-8153-6406-1

Typeset in Myriad Pro
by codeMantra

**Publisher's Note**
The publisher accepts responsibility for any inconsistencies that may have arisen during the conversion of this book from journal articles to book chapters, namely the possible inclusion of journal terminology.

**Disclaimer**
Every effort has been made to contact copyright holders for their permission to reprint material in this book. The publishers would be grateful to hear from any copyright holder who is not here acknowledged and will undertake to rectify any errors or omissions in future editions of this book.

# Contents

*Citation Information* vii
*Notes on Contributors* ix

Guest Editor's comments 1
*Mary Ruth Coleman and Michael Shevlin*

1 Inclusive education in higher education: challenges and opportunities 3
   *Anabel Moriña*

2 Academic self-efficacy, sense of coherence, hope and tiredness among college students with learning disabilities 18
   *Shiri Ben-Naim, Roni Laslo-Roth, Michal Einav, Hadar Biran and Malka Margalit*

3 Functioning and participation problems of students with ADHD in higher education: which reasonable accommodations are effective? 35
   *Dorien Jansen, Katja Petry, Eva Ceulemans, Saskia van der Oord, Ilse Noens and Dieter Baeyens*

4 Making the transition to post-secondary education: opportunities and challenges experienced by students with ASD in the Republic of Ireland 55
   *Sheena Bell, Cristina Devecchi, Conor Mc Guckin and Michael Shevlin*

5 Functioning and participation problems of students with ASD in higher education: which reasonable accommodations are effective? 72
   *Dorien Jansen, Katja Petry, Eva Ceulemans, Ilse Noens and Dieter Baeyens*

6 Developing an inclusive learning environment for students with visual impairment in higher education: progressive mutual accommodation and learner experiences in the United Kingdom 90
   *Rachel Hewett, Graeme Douglas, Michael McLinden and Sue Keil*

7 Responding to the needs of students with mental health difficulties in higher education: an Irish perspective 111
   *Esther Murphy*

## CONTENTS

8  Belonging to higher education: inclusive education for students with intellectual disabilities  126
   *Kristín Björnsdóttir*

9  Re-visiting the role of disability coordinators: the changing needs of disabled students and current support strategies from a UK university  138
   *Mujde Koca-Atabey*

10 Dual PowerPoint presentation approach for students with special educational needs and note-takers  147
   *Nitin Naik*

11 From the voice of a 'socratic gadfly': a call for more academic activism in the researching of disability in postsecondary education  154
   *Jane Seale*

   *Index*  171

# Citation Information

The chapters in this book were originally published in the *European Journal of Special Needs Education*, volume 32, issue 1–2 (2017). When citing this material, please use the original page numbering for each article, as follows:

## Guest Editorial
*Guest Editor's comments*
Mary Ruth Coleman and Michael Shevlin
*European Journal of Special Needs Education*, volume 32, issue 1–2 (2017) pp. 1–2

## Chapter 1
*Inclusive education in higher education: challenges and opportunities*
Anabel Moriña
*European Journal of Special Needs Education*, volume 32, issue 1–2 (2017) pp. 3–17

## Chapter 2
*Academic self-efficacy, sense of coherence, hope and tiredness among college students with learning disabilities*
Shiri Ben-Naim, Roni Laslo-Roth, Michal Einav, Hadar Biran and Malka Margalit
*European Journal of Special Needs Education*, volume 32, issue 1–2 (2017) pp. 18–34

## Chapter 3
*Functioning and participation problems of students with ADHD in higher education: which reasonable accommodations are effective?*
Dorien Jansen, Katja Petry, Eva Ceulemans, Saskia van der Oord, Ilse Noens and Dieter Baeyens
*European Journal of Special Needs Education*, volume 32, issue 1–2 (2017) pp. 35–53

## Chapter 4
*Making the transition to post-secondary education: opportunities and challenges experienced by students with ASD in the Republic of Ireland*
Sheena Bell, Cristina Devecchi, Conor Mc Guckin and Michael Shevlin
*European Journal of Special Needs Education*, volume 32, issue 1–2 (2017) pp. 54–70

## Chapter 5
*Functioning and participation problems of students with ASD in higher education: which reasonable accommodations are effective?*
Dorien Jansen, Katja Petry, Eva Ceulemans, Ilse Noens and Dieter Baeyens
*European Journal of Special Needs Education*, volume 32, issue 1–2 (2017) pp. 71–88

## Chapter 6
*Developing an inclusive learning environment for students with visual impairment in higher education: progressive mutual accommodation and learner experiences in the United Kingdom*
Rachel Hewett, Graeme Douglas, Michael McLinden and Sue Keil
*European Journal of Special Needs Education*, volume 32, issue 1–2 (2017) pp. 89–109

## Chapter 7
*Responding to the needs of students with mental health difficulties in higher education: an Irish perspective*
Esther Murphy
*European Journal of Special Needs Education*, volume 32, issue 1–2 (2017) pp. 110–124

## Chapter 8
*Belonging to higher education: inclusive education for students with intellectual disabilities*
Kristín Björnsdóttir
*European Journal of Special Needs Education*, volume 32, issue 1–2 (2017) pp. 125–136

## Chapter 9
*Re-visiting the role of disability coordinators: the changing needs of disabled students and current support strategies from a UK university*
Mujde Koca-Atabey
*European Journal of Special Needs Education*, volume 32, issue 1–2 (2017) pp. 137–145

## Chapter 10
*Dual PowerPoint presentation approach for students with special educational needs and note-takers*
Nitin Naik
*European Journal of Special Needs Education*, volume 32, issue 1–2 (2017) pp. 146–152

## Chapter 11
*From the voice of a 'socratic gadfly': a call for more academic activism in the researching of disability in postsecondary education*
Jane Seale
*European Journal of Special Needs Education*, volume 32, issue 1–2 (2017) pp. 153–169

For any permission-related enquiries please visit:
http://www.tandfonline.com/page/help/permissions

# Notes on Contributors

**Dieter Baeyens** is an Associate Professor at the Department of Special Education at the University of Leuven, Belgium, and a member of the Leuven Autism Research. He specializes in ADHD and inclusive higher education.

**Sheena Bell**, PhD, is a Senior Lecturer in SEN and Inclusion at the University of Northampton, UK, teaching on a range of undergraduate and master's level courses. She is a member of the research group CeSNER: Centre for Special Needs Education and Research.

**Shiri Ben-Naim**, PhD, Rehabilitation Psychologist, is a Senior Lecturer in the School of Behavioural Sciences, Peres Academic Centre, Rechovot, Israel, and Director of the Neuropsychiatric Clinic, Hadassah Medical Centre, Jerusalem, Israel.

**Hadar Biran** is an MA Student in the Educational Psychology Program at the School of Behavioural Sciences, Peres Academic Centre, Rechovot, Israel.

**Kristín Björnsdóttir** is an Associate Professor in Disability Studies, Faculty of Education Studies, School of Education, University of Iceland, Iceland.

**Eva Ceulemans** is a Professor at the Methodology of Educational Sciences Research Unit of the University of Leuven, Belgium, and specializes in methodology in Educational Sciences and Psychology.

**Mary Ruth Coleman**, PhD, is a Senior Scientist, Emeritus, at the FPG Child Development Institute at the University of North Carolina at Chapel Hill, USA. She directs Project U-STAR~PLUS (Using Science, Talents and Abilities to Recognize Students – Promoting Learning in Underrepresented Students).

**Cristina Devecchi**, PhD, is an Associate Professor (Education) in the University of Northampton, UK, and is a member of the research group CeSNER: Centre for Special Needs Education and Research.

**Graeme Douglas** is a Professor of Disability and Special Educational Needs, and the Head of the Department of Disability, Inclusion and Special Needs at the University of Birmingham, UK.

**Michal Einav**, PhD, Clinical Psychologist, is a Senior Lecturer in the School of Behavioural Sciences, Peres Academic Centre, Rechovot, Israel.

**Rachel Hewett** is a Research Fellow in the Department of Disability, Inclusion and Special Needs at the University of Birmingham, UK.

## NOTES ON CONTRIBUTORS

**Dorien Jansen** is a Research Fellow at the Parenting and Special Education Research Unit of the University of Leuven, Belgium, and a member of Leuven Autism Research.

**Sue Keil** is a Research Officer in the Children, Young People and Families team at the Royal National Institute of Blind People (RNIB), UK.

**Mujde Koca-Atabey** was an Assistant Professor at the Department of Psychology, Ipek University, Ankara, Turkey.

**Roni Laslo-Roth**, PhD, Organizational Psychologist, is a Lecturer in the School of Behavioural Sciences, Peres Academic Centre, Rechovot, Israel, and Adjunct Lecturer in the Shamoon College of Engineering, Ashdod, Israel.

**Malka Margalit**, PhD, is an Educational and Rehabilitational Psychologist and Dean of the School of Behavioural Sciences, Peres Academic Centre, Rechovot, Israel. She is also Professor Emeritus of the School of Education, Tel-Aviv University, Israel.

**Conor Mc Guckin**, PhD, is an Assistant Professor in the School of Education, Trinity College Dublin, Republic of Ireland.

**Michael McLinden** is a Professor of Education and Deputy Head of the School of Education at the University of Birmingham, UK.

**Anabel Moriña** is an Associated Professor in Inclusive Education. Her research interests are inclusive education, disability, higher education, teacher/faculty training, and qualitative methods.

**Esther Murphy** works as Senior Research Officer with Mental Health Reform, Ireland's coalition organization for mental health. She is also a Visiting Research Fellow at Trinity College Dublin's School of Education, Republic of Ireland.

**Nitin Naik** is an Associate Professor and Head of Cyber Security at the Defence School of Communications and Information Systems at the Ministry of Defence, UK.

**Ilse Noens** is an Associate Professor at the Department of Special Education at the University of Leuven, Belgium.

**Katja Petry** is an Associate Professor at the Parenting and Special Education Research Unit of the University of Leuven, Belgium, and specializes in inclusive higher education.

**Jane Seale** is Professor of Education at the Open University, UK. Her research operates at the intersection between disability, technology, and education.

**Michael Shevlin** is Professor in Inclusive Education in the School of Education, Trinity College Dublin, Republic of Ireland, and Director of the Trinity Centre for People with Intellectual Disabilities.

**Saskia van der Oord** is an Associate Professor at the Department of Clinical Psychology at the University of Leuven, Belgium, and is associated with the Department of Developmental Psychology and the Centre for Cognitive Science of the University of Amsterdam, The Netherlands.

GUEST EDITORIAL

# Guest Editor's comments

This special issue, *Postsecondary Educational Opportunities for Students with Special Education Needs*, was a team eff ort. We would like to thank Seamus Hegarty, *EJSNE* editor, for inviting us to serve as guest editors and for his generous support throughout this process. We also thank the *EJSNE* Editorial Board for sharing their thoughts on this work and especially Jane Seale and Jean Jacques Detraux for their dedication and insight which helped bring this to fruition.

The purpose of this special issue is to provide current information on higher educational opportunities and challenges for students with special educational needs. To achieve this, we have gathered an outstanding set of articles and short reports that reflect some of the best thinking from around the world: exploring the strengths and needs of students with disabilities and examining the infrastructure (i.e. policies, practices and personnel preparation) required to support their success within higher education.

The special issue opens with a comprehensive review, 'Inclusive Education in Higher Education: Challenges and Opportunities' by Anabel Moriña, followed by an investigation of some of the special issues faced by students with special educational needs, 'Academic Self-efficacy, Sense of Coherence, Hope, and Tiredness among College Students with Disabilities' by Shiri Ben-Naim, Roni Laslo-Roth, Michal Einav, Hadar Biran, and Malka Margalit.

The next set of papers explores the experiences of students within the higher education system opening with Dorien Jansen, Katja Petry, Eva Ceulemans, Saskia van der Oord, Ilse Noens, and Dieter Baeyens contribution, 'Functioning and Participation Problems of Students with ADHD in Higher Education: Which Reasonable Accommodations are Effective?' This is followed by two papers that address students with ASD, 'Making the Transaction to Post-secondary Education: Opportunities and Challenges Experienced by Students with ASD in the Republic of Ireland' by Sheena Bell, Cristina Devecchi, Conor Mc Guckin, Michael Shevlin and 'Functioning and Participation Problems of Students with ASD in Higher Education: Which Reasonable Accommodations are Effective?' by Dorien Jansen, Katja Petry, Eva Ceulemans, Ilse Noens and Dieter Baeyens. While it is unusual to find two articles by the same lead author (i.e. Dorien Jansen) in the same issue, we chose to include both as we believe that this kind of nuanced replication is essential in building a comprehensive understanding of effective practices for different groups of students under a variety of conditions.

Rachel Hewett, Graeme Douglas, Michael McLinden and Sue Keil's paper, 'Developing an Inclusive Learning Environment for Students with Visual Impairment in Higher Education: Progressive Mutual Accommodation and Learner Experiences in the United Kingdom' shares the unique experiences of students with visual impairments. The next two papers address emerging areas within higher education. First a look at mental health with 'Responding to the Needs of Students with Mental Health Difficulties in Higher Education: An Irish Perspective' by Esther Murphy and second, an examination of programming for students with intellectual challenges with Kristín Björnsdóttir paper 'Belonging to Higher Education: Inclusive Education for Students with Intellectual Disabilities'.

Two short reports shift the focus to institutional practices of staff and faculty. 'Re-visiting the Issue of Disability Coordinators: The Changing Needs of Disabled Students and Current Support Strategies from a UK University' by Mujde Koca-Atabey and 'NDual PowerPoint Presentation

Approach for Students with Special Education Needs and Note-takers' by Nitin Naik share best practices to support student success. In the final paper, 'From the Voice of a "Socratic Gadfly": A Call for More Academic Activism in the Researching of Disability in Postsecondary Education', Jane Seale offers a clarion call for progressive and inclusive approaches to research and policy as we continue to improve practice so that *all* students can find the support they need to be successful within our institutes for higher education.

Thank you,

Mary Ruth Coleman
FPG Child Development Institute, University of North Carolina, Chapel Hill, NC, USA
maryruth.coleman@unc.edu

Michael Shevlin
Inclusive and Education and Society Research Group, School of Education,
Trinity College, Dublin, Republic of Ireland

# Inclusive education in higher education: challenges and opportunities

Anabel Moriña

**ABSTRACT**
Implementing the principles of inclusive education within higher education can be challenging. Inclusive education was originally developed for younger students, prior to its application within higher education. However, as more students with disabilities successfully complete their early schooling, the need to move towards inclusive practices within higher education has increased. The purpose of this article is to offer thoughts on inclusive practices within higher education. The paper is organised into three sections: a description of the current situation of inclusive education in relation to students with disabilities in higher education; a review of the literature focused on students with disabilities and on faculty members within higher education; and a discussion of how moving the university towards an inclusive setting requires designing policies, strategies, processes and actions that contribute to ensuring the success of all the students.

## Introduction: the context for inclusion within institutes of higher education

Inclusive education can be defined as an educational approach proposing schools in which all the students can participate and all are treated like valuable school members. It is an educational philosophy and practice that aims to improve the learning and active participation of all the students in a common educational context. Inclusive education is conceived of as an unfinished process and a belief system that poses a challenge to any situation of exclusion (Ainscow 1998; Sapon-Shevin 2003).

Inclusive education is recognised as a basic human right and the basis for a fair and equitable society (European Agency for Development in Special Needs Education 2012; Forlin 2013). An ethical component is also considered (Reindal 2016). Inclusive education focuses on the need to provide a high-quality educational response for all students, increasing the practices that lead to full participation (Ainscow 2015; Messiou et al. 2016). Within the inclusive philosophy, diversity is conceived in a broad sense comprising the different capabilities, gender differences and differences in social and cultural origin. These differences are seen as a benefit rather than as a problem. The belief is that all students, without exception, should benefit from high-quality learning and enjoy full participation in the educational system.

Inclusive education was developed and implemented within educational settings prior to higher education. However, for some years, inclusive principles and practices have been making inroads into university agendas, policies, and teaching and learning practices. In the context of higher education, there is still a long way to go before we can claim full inclusion, and many challenges must be addressed to align educational practices with the principles of inclusive education.

The purpose of this article is to address the current state of inclusion in higher education with regard to students with special educational needs, specifically students with disabilities. The work is organised around three sections. First, an introduction to the topic considering: the increase of the students with disabilities in the university with an examination of policies, a discussion of the principles of inclusive education and an overview of the social model of disability. This section helps to contextualise how higher education is currently responding to students with disabilities. The second section reviews the literature on higher education, inclusive education and disabilities. The studies in these sections are organised around the findings regarding students and faculty. The third section discusses the social and educational impacts of inclusion within the university. The paper concludes by exploring the policies, strategies, processes and actions that contribute to ensuring the success of all the students.

## Inclusive education in higher education: ensuring students' access, participation and success

Many have called for increased inclusivity within universities, claiming that it should be the university's responsibility to respond to the needs of all students (Fuller, Bradley, and Healey 2004; Doughty and Allan 2008; Prowse 2009). Indeed, Gairín and Suárez (2014) conclude that inclusivity is a hallmark of a quality university.

Yet, moving towards the principles of inclusive education is a challenge in higher education. We only need to go back a decade to verify that the contemporary higher education classroom is very different from its predecessors; and while we cannot explain this simply by the fact that today's students are different a common trait in the current university is the increasing diversity among students. Thomas (2016) proposed that participation in the university is broader due to the progressive incorporation of collectives that were traditionally marginalised from higher education including students of different nationalities, ages, cultures, socio-economic situations or capabilities. This growing diversity, which is transforming the classrooms, has gained increasing scientific protagonism and there are more investigations examining how higher education is responding to this new situation. Many of these studies focus on non-traditional groups, including students who need additional support, who, depending on the country, may be students with disabilities, students from minority cultural groups and/or students from a low socio-economic origin (Weedon and Riddell 2016). A growing number of studies focus on the analysis of the experiences of students with disabilities at the university (Claiborne et al. 2010; Leyser et al. 2011; Gibson 2012; Moriña, Cortés-Vega, and Molina 2015).

With regard to this collective, the number of students with disabilities within higher education continues to increase year after year (Pumfrey 2008; Liasidou 2014; Seale et al. 2015). The approval of statements and regulations aimed at promoting inclusion may have influenced this increase in students. The Convention of the Rights of People with Disabilities

(UN 2006) pointed out the obligation to ensure that people with disabilities have access – without discrimination and within the same conditions as the rest – to higher education, professional training, adult education and lifelong learning. The European Union is committed to inclusive education within the framework of higher education. For this purpose, the creation of support plans and services that improve access and educational inclusion of non-traditional students was proposed in the *European Strategy 2010–2020* (European Commission 2010). In other countries, such as Australia, the United States or the United Kingdom, proceedings of discrimination have been approved to guarantee the right to education in the university for persons with disabilities.

A significant number of countries have launched actions to make universities more accessible for people with disabilities, becoming progressively more committed to the processes of inclusion (Barnes 2007; Jacklin et al. 2007). In response to these laws and policies, many universities have established offices to support the educational needs of students with disabilities, have incorporated the use of new technologies and/or have implemented inclusive educational practices. However, the existence of these actions is insufficient to ensure the right of the students to quality education, without discrimination and based on the principles of inclusive education. Recently, several studies (Quinn 2013; Gibson 2015; Thomas 2016; Wilson et al. 2016) concluded that it is not enough to guarantee diverse students access to education, it is also necessary to provide appropriate support to ensure their inclusion. As has been reported (Wessel et al. 2009; Quinn 2013; Lombardi, Murray, and Kowitt 2016), students with disabilities are at greater risk of prematurely dropping out of universities in comparison to students without disabilities. Therefore, it is necessary to design policies and strategies that encourage students to remain in the university and complete their degree courses successfully.

In order to guarantee equal opportunities and facilitate the inclusion of students with disabilities, it is necessary to incorporate the principles of inclusive education and universal design for learning into university policies and practices based on the social model of disability. Inclusive education postulates the right to full participation and quality education guaranteed to all university students. Diversity is valued in inclusive educational contexts, which foresees design of accessible educational projects, taking into account the different ways of learning and anticipating possible needs that may arise.

The social model, postulates that society, and in this case the university, generates the barriers that hinder the inclusion of university students with disabilities; arguing that the practices, attitudes and policies of the social context generate the barriers and/or supports that influence access and participation (Oliver 1990). According to the social model, disability is not a personal tragedy or an abnormality and there is no need to cure the 'disease'. Barriers to success are a form of discrimination and oppression and universities should avoid the use of medical labels to identify students with disabilities and they should make efforts to establish inclusive teaching strategies to support student success (Matthews 2009). In contrast, the medical model considers disability as an 'individual problem' (Armstrong and Barton 1999). From the perspective of the social model, higher education must restructure the educational experience so that all the students can participate.

## Current research on higher education, inclusive education and disability

At present, research on higher education, disabilities and inclusive education is focused mainly on two areas: students with disabilities and faculty members. For this review, the studies were selected from relevant professional journals of higher education (e.g. *Higher Education, Studies in Special Education, Teaching in Higher Education*) and specific journals of special educational needs (e.g. *Disability and Society, European Journal of Special Need Education, International Journal of Inclusive Education*). Key words for the search were 'higher education', 'disability', 'students with disability' and 'inclusive education'. The review looked at investigations after the year 2000.

The works that are cited in this article do not represent all the existing ones in this line of research. To keep the focus of the article, I selected only those investigations that were most relevant for the analysis, and often selected a single representative study for a given topic. Finally, some cited works are not research but are theoretical in nature.

Most of studies revolve around the students themselves. Three primary areas have been examined: the barriers and aids identified by students with disabilities; the transitions from educational stages prior to higher education towards this formative stage; and students' concern about whether or not disclose their disability if it is 'invisible'. Many of these studies were qualitative that sought to hear amplify student voices.

Studies about faculty members, although not as numerous, address three topics: analysing the attitudes of the faculty members towards students with disabilities; the faculty members' need for training; and the use of universal design for learning.

## *Students with disabilities*

The largest group of research studies examined the voice of the students (see Table 1) as they identify both the barriers and the supports in their university experiences (Shevlin, Kenny, and Mcneela 2004; Jacklin et al. 2007; Claiborne et al. 2010; Hopkins 2011; Mullins and Preyde 2013; Moriña, López, and Molina 2015). In this summary, we have chosen to look at the experiences of students with disabilities as a whole, rather than examining individual disability areas. Regarding the barriers, the most important obstacle identified was the negative attitudes displayed by faculty members. In many cases, the students stated that the professor doubted they had a disability, did not adapt the teaching projects and questioned their capacity to study in the university. Additional challenges reported by students with disabilities included: architectural barriers; inaccessible information and technology; rules and policies that are not actually enforced (e.g. the exam schedules and formats were not adapted, class attendance was not facilitated for students with difficulties derived from their disability); or methodologies that do not favour inclusion (e.g. only providing master classes without any interaction between the students and the faculty, technological resources – identified as an aid – were not used) (Mullins and Preyde 2013; Strnadová, Hájková, and Květoňová 2015).

These students' paths are frequently very difficult, somewhat like an obstacle course and students even define themselves as survivors and long-distance runners (Moriña 2015). Their eventual performance is similar to that of the rest of the students, but in all cases, they reported that this implies a greater investment of effort and time (Skinner 2004). Students with disabilities commonly report that they feel they have to work harder than other students because they have to manage both their disability and their studies (Seale et al. 2015).

It is interesting to note that many of the barriers identified by students with disabilities are also shared by other students (e.g. the difficulties with learning when faculty are inflexible or not empathetic; when the professor uses exclusively master classes to teach, without any kind of additional resources or personal interaction) (Madriaga et al. 2010). Nevertheless,

**Table 1.** Students' voice (barriers and facilitators).

| Article citations | Target populations | Key research findings |
| --- | --- | --- |
| Claiborne et al. (2010) | Four students with disabilities; 7 faculty members; 3 staff; 3 students without disabilities | Barriers to access and resources; non-accessible technology, negative attitudes of the faculty |
| Gibson (2012) | 5 students with disabilities | Facilitators: Positive impact of friendships, peer support networks, significant education contacts and studying |
| Jacklin et al. (2007) | 192 students with disabilities | Mostly positive experiences<br>Negative experiences: lack of support |
| Hopkins (2011) | 6 students with disabilities | Physical, attitudinal, social, cultural and political barriers |
| Madriaga et al. (2010) | 172 students with disabilities<br>312 students without disabilities | Students with disabilities confront barriers of access in their learning and assessment, there are similar difficulties they share with non-disabled students |
| Moriña (2015) | 44 students with disabilities | Barriers: fear of disclosing the disability, doing twice as much to get half as far<br>Facilitator: personal skills |
| Moriña, López, and Molina (2015) | 44 students with disabilities | Barriers: Faculty and staff's negative attitude, inadequate use of PowerPoint, ruling on disability is not enforced, professor is not informed about or trained in disabilities<br>Facilitator: curricular adaptations |
| Mullins and Preyde (2013) | 10 students with invisible disabilities | Barriers: negative social culture, negative attitudes; organisational aspects, desire to have a visible manifestation of their disability (reduce public questions about the validity of their disability) |
| Prowse (2009) | 44 students with disabilities | Higher education as an opportunity; need to replace labels |
| Riddell, Tinklin, and Wilson (2004) | 56 students with disabilities | Barriers: teaching methodologies, assessment and professional development of the faculty |
| Seale et al. (2015) | 175 students with disabilities | Barriers: technological resources are not appropriate or effective<br>Students have to manage both their disability and their studies |
| Shevlin, Kenny, and Mcneela (2004) | 32 students with disabilities | Barriers: physical in nature, negative attitudes, assessment not adapted<br>Facilitator: disability support office |
| Skinner (2004) | 20 students with learning disabilities | Facilitators: support from family, friends, instructors, and/or academic support personnel; Importance of perseverance; academic accommodations |
| Strnadová, Hájková, and Květoňová (2015) | 34 students with disabilities | Barriers: institutional, negative attitudinal, and disability-specific barriers<br>Facilitators: family support, peer support, support provided by assistants, personal strategies (assertiveness, self-determination, etc.) |

for people with disabilities, these issues may be even more complex and may need additional support to solve.

Although less present in the literature, there are also studies describing a series of facilitators to support students with disabilities within the university. Among the supportive factors are: family support to study in the university (Riddell, Tinklin, and Wilson 2004; Skinner 2004), friendships and peer support networks, counting on close people who encourage them and assist them in their studies (Riddell, Tinklin, and Wilson 2004; Gibson 2012); help from certain faculty and staff who believe in them, facilitating the necessary adjustments, technologies that facilitate learning, such as the use of digital blackboards, adapted software (Seale et al. 2015); disability support offices (Riddell, Tinklin, and Wilson 2004); or personal support, referring to the students' own personal strategies implemented to deal with their difficulties (Prowse 2009; Moriña 2015).

Other studies have focused (Table 2), although to a lesser extent, on exploring the transition processes from secondary education to the university (Eckes and Ochoa 2005; Gill 2007; Garrison-Wade 2012; Patrick and Wessel 2013). These works have described both the difficulties encountered with and ideas for improvement of the transition of students with disabilities. These studies concluded that, for people with disabilities, the transition processes to the university are fragile and can easily be compromised. The transition to post-secondary education is a period when more vulnerabilities are revealed, which can lead to students dropping out of the university. This stage is a difficult one for many students, but it may be especially challenging for those with disabilities because of academic and social adjustment issues (Jacklin et al. 2007; Fuller et al. 2009; Fordyce et al. 2013; Hong 2015; Lovet et al. 2015; Wessel et al. 2015). The transition process influences the beginning of the students' experience within higher education and sets a tone for involvement which often continues until graduation. The main source of difficulty in the transition lies in the fact that the student

**Table 2.** Students' voice (transition processes).

| Article citations | Target populations | Key research findings |
| --- | --- | --- |
| Fordyce et al. (2013) | 30 students who are deaf or hard of hearing | Need to improve the transition processes |
| Fuller et al. (2009) | 35 students with disabilities | Barriers: untrained faculty and negative attitudes |
| Garrison-Wade (2012) | 59 students with disabilities 6 disability resource coordinators | Barriers: negative attitudes Facilitators: self-determination; planning efforts; post-secondary supports (networking and mentoring) |
| Getzel and Thoma (2008) | 34 students with disabilities | Transition (a) problem solving, (b) understanding one's disability, (c) goal-setting, and (d) self-management as critical skills that students need to be effective self-advocates to secure needed supports and services. |
| Hong (2015) | 16 students with disabilities | Barriers: faculty perception, fit of advisors; peer image and social pressure; college stressors; quality of support services |
| Lombardi, Murray, and Kowitt (2016) | 200 students with disabilities | Certain relationship types can make meaningful differences in positively affecting college experiences of students with disabilities, and illustrate the importance of considering types of relationships and quality of social support in future research on social networks |
| Patrick and Wessel (2013) | 12 students with disabilities | Faculty mentor was crucial in their transition; Faculty, staff, and administrators should recognise the importance of providing individualised support to students with disabilities; difficult academic transition to college |
| Wessel et al. (2015) | 10 students who used a wheelchair 4 parents | Students were able to self-advocate well. Students in wheelchairs need to learn how to be vocal about their needs, the process of becoming a self-advocate; Essential support from the disability office during the first year, the most difficult moment |

must often adapt to new organisational, educational and social contexts (Thomas 2008). When they arrive at the university, the needs of students with disabilities are similar to those they had in high school, except now they have to be more self-directed in managing their own lives (Getzel and Thoma 2008; Hong 2015). In addition, many students do not know which support services are available or what legal rights they have.

A successful transition during the first year seems to be critical to the student's ultimate retention and success (Goodman and Pascarella 2006). Tinto (1988) found that the first six weeks are particularly crucial because it is the period in which students are most susceptible and sensitive to feelings of marginalisation. Wessel et al. (2009) also found that the dropout rate was highest for students with disabilities during the first weeks of the semester. The main source of difficulty in transition lies in the fact that the student must often adapt to new organisational, educational and social contexts (Thomas 2008). Kochhar-Bryant and colleagues (Kochhar-Bryant, Bassett, and Webb 2009) refer to the transition from secondary to post-secondary settings as a *transition cliff* for people with disabilities when many may feel disconnected from the university community (Getzel and Thoma 2008; Hong 2015).

Studies show that many universities have begun to implement some form of intervention to increase retention during the first year of university (Upcraft, Gardner, and Barefoot 2005). There also seem to be some key factors that help in the transition processes, including self-awareness, self-determination and support, self-management, adequate preparation for university and assistance technology (Garrison-Wade 2012). Also, networking and relationships with their fellow students (Jacklin et al. 2007; Crosling, Thomas, and Headney 2008; Lombardi, Murray, and Kowitt 2016) and mentoring (by students of the last courses or by faculty members) were critical for achieving experiences of success in the university (Patrick and Wessel 2013). Getzel (2008) stated that students with disabilities benefit from faculty that have increased awareness and knowledge of the characteristics and needs of students with disabilities, and from faculty that insert concepts of universal design into their instruction. Communication with tutors and other staff members is also a key issue for a successful transition process (Beck and Davidson 2001). Other aspects such as peer support, academic support and academic accommodations are also considered as protective factors (Hartley 2010).

A third theme analysed in other investigations refers to hidden disabilities (see Table 3), with regard to whether or not to disclose a disability. In these studies, 'invisible' disabilities

**Table 3.** Students' voice (hidden disabilities).

| Article citations | Target populations | key research findings |
|---|---|---|
| Hadjikakou and Hartas (2008) | 15 students with disabilities | Dilemma about disclosing or not disclosing the disability, staff not well trained in disabilities, no teaching adaptations |
| | Deans and faculty members | University: reactive responses |
| Lourens and Swartz (2016) | 23 students with visual disability | The politics of visibility and invisibility are central to the experience of disability; fear of being stigmatised |
| Martin (2010) | 54 students with disabilities | Not disclosing the disability because prior experience caused harm; need for training of the staff |
| Mullins and Preyde (2013) | 10 students with invisible disabilities | Social barriers related to negative social attitudes; other people questioned the validity of their invisible disabilities; effects of stigma; decisions not disclose their disability |

refer to disabilities that have no physical manifestation and cannot be readily identified by others (Mullins and Preyde 2013). According to Gibson (2012), people with invisible disabilities think that having this type of disability has affected them negatively in their university studies. In this author's study (Moriña 2015), the university students felt that the academic staff and the other students questioned the validity of their disabilities because they were not visible. In many cases, they even had to present additional documents to demonstrate their disability. This was emotionally very difficult for them and made them feel less legitimate. Many university students indicated that they preferred not to disclose their disability and did so only in their closest relationships or when it was necessary, for example, when they needed some kind of adaptation or, as Prowse (2009) states, to obtain economic support, as in the case of free college tuition.

Students' perceptions about hidden disabilities is closely related to the concept of 'normality' and they may choose non-disclosure if they desire to be considered and treated with 'normality' (Riddell, Tinklin, and Wilson 2004; Claiborne et al. 2010; Hong 2015). They may also choose not to share their disability if they feel that disclosure would place them at a disadvantage or they the fear being stigmatised or labelled (Martin 2010; Lourens and Swartz 2016); or simply because they think they have no special needs or disability (Hadjikakou and Hartas 2008). In general, these students, with either a visible or an invisible disability, may not want to be identified with a disability (Barnes 2007). As some studies explain, requesting some type of aid does not imply that they do not want to be treated like any other peer (Riddell, Tinklin, and Wilson 2004).

### Research on faculty's response to students with disabilities

Regarding investigations of the faculty (Table 4), the three topics that usually appear are: attitudes of the faculty members towards students with disabilities; faculty training in disability issues and inclusive education; and putting into practice universal design for learning strategies.

Some studies on attitudes deserve special mention, such as that of Lombardi, Vukovic, and Sala-Bars (2015), in which they measured and compared the attitudes of faculty members in Spain, Canada and the United States. In this work, it was concluded that the academic staff showed a positive attitude towards disabilities and, although they valued the strategies of inclusive education in theory, they did not implement them in practice. Similar results were reached in the investigations of Cook, Rumrill, and Tankersley (2009) and Zhang et al. (2010). Interestingly, these results do not coincide with the opinions of the students with disabilities (discussed earlier) who identified the attitudes of the faculty members towards them as the most significant barrier in their careers (Collins 2000; Hong and Himmel 2009; Coriale, Larson, and Robertson 2012).

The second issue related to the faculty is the need for training and sensitisation towards disabilities. Several studies have focused on training university professors in the field of disability (Debrand and Salzberg 2005; Hockings, Brett, and Terentjevs 2012; Lovet et al. 2015; Moriña, Cortés-Vega, and Molina 2015). Training the faculty to (more appropriately or effectilvey) respond to the needs of the students with disabilities is critical for higher education (Lovet et al. 2015). Some universities have already taken on this challenge and have designed awareness training programmes and prepared their academic staff for this undertaking. Worthy of mention, for example, are the Teachability (2002) proposal in Scotland

**Table 4.** Faculty.

| Article citations | Target populations | Key research findings |
| --- | --- | --- |
| Black, Weinberg, and Brodwin (2014) | 73 faculty members | Faculty incorporate guidelines for universal design in their instruction to help create a more inclusive educational environment for students with disabilities; faculty require training in the principles of universal design |
| Cook, Rumrill, and Tankersley (2009) | 307 faculty members | Issues related to law, Universal Design for Instruction, and disability characteristics were important but were not being addressed satisfactorily |
|  |  | Issues related to willingness to provide accommodations were neither highly important nor being addressed satisfactorily |
| Coriale, Larson, and Robertson (2012) | 1 student with cerebral palsy 1 assistant | The presence of an assistant influences interpersonal dynamics between students and faculty negative attitudes of the faculty members |
| Davies, Schelly, and Spooner (2013) | 63 faculty | Instructors who received training reported a positive change in their use of universal design learning strategies |
| Debrand and Salzberg (2005) | 420 members of the Association on Higher Education and disability (USA) | A critical factor for the success of the students is the faculty. |
|  |  | Positive effects of training the teaching staff in disabilities |
| Hitch, Macfarlane, and Nihill (2015) | 38 Australian universities 42 staff and Deans | A minority of Australian universities refer to inclusive teaching or UDL in their policies and procedures |
| Hong and Himmel (2009) | 116 faculty members | Attitudes of the faculty members towards students with disabilities as the most significant barrier in their careers |
| Lombardi and Murray (2011) | 112 faculty members | Disability-related training may positively affect faculty attitudes towards disabilities and inclusive instruction |
| Lombardi, Vukovic, and Sala-Bars (2015) | 1195 faculty members | The majority of faculty receive little to no training in effective teaching practices that will benefit diverse learners, including students with disabilities |
|  |  | Universal Design for Instruction for inclusion |
| Lovet et al. (2015) | 5 faculty members | Barriers: transition from high school to college, being unaware that the student has a disability, insufficient disability support staff, inadequate training |
| Moriña, Cortés-Vega, and Molina (2015) | 44 student with disabilities | Faculty not informed about or trained in disability |
| Zhang et al. (2010) | 206 faculty members | Need for training |
|  |  | Improving the faculty's personal beliefs may be essential for students with disabilities |

(University of Strathclyde), the materials designed by Healey and colleagues (Healey et al. 2001) in England (University of Gloucestershire) and Debrand and Salzberg (2005) proposal in the United States (Utah State University). In some of the studies, it is concluded that the attitude of the faculty members improved after they had been trained and had more experience in how to respond to the needs of the students with disabilities (Lombardi and Murray 2011; Murray, Lombardi, and Wren 2011; Hong 2015).

A last issue referring to the teaching faculty is linked to universal design for learning, training in this aspect and its practical implementation in university classrooms. Universal design for learning is an approach to teaching that is characterised by the proactive design and use of inclusive strategies that benefit *all* the students. That is, the range of possible learning needs of the students is anticipated, designing curricula with everyone in mind, for example, providing information in various formats at the same time (e.g. printed and online books). University students with disabilities have reported that they benefit from the academic staff who apply the principles of the universal design for learning (McGuire and Scott 2006; Hitch, Macfarlane, and Nihill 2015).

The findings show that if the faculty members used the universal design, then the changes to be introduced in the syllabuses for students with disabilities (e.g. adaptations of the materials, methodologies or assessments), including the most common ones – extended exam time and note-taking services – would not be necessary (Lombardi, Murray, and Gerdes 2011). In addition, it is argued that the universal design for learning benefits all students, with or without disabilities (i.e. handing out the PowerPoint notes, which have been designed using accessibility criteria, offering detailed assessment criteria through headings or providing a virtual environment of the subject with online resources so students can access the electronic material whenever they need it). However, faculty are not usually trained and do not incorporate universal design for learning into their instruction (Davies, Schelly, and Spooner 2013; Black, Weinberg, and Brodwin 2014; Hitch, Macfarlane, and Nihill 2015).

## Higher education as an opportunity: context that contributes to social and educational inclusion

Although some students with disabilities have had to deal with difficult university trajectories, the university also represents opportunities for empowerment, social and occupational inclusion (Fuller, Bradley, and Healey 2004; Wehman 2006; Cook, Rumrill, and Tankersley 2009; Shaw 2009; Johnson and Nord 2011; Papay and Griffin 2013).

Some university students with disabilities even argue that going to the university should be strongly encouraged for people with disabilities, as it is a way to improve their quality of life and to expand their occupational prospects (Moriña 2015). This experience can increase their opportunities to get and keep a job, to obtain higher revenues and achieve an independent life. Moriña (2015) and Weldon and Riddell (2007), found that students with disabilities value higher education as a positive experience because it provided them with a normalised context which they wished to continue. In some cases, the university experience is seen as an opportunity that strengthens them personally in the face of the difficulties derived from their disability, which they encounter every day in their lives. In the case of disabilities that are due to external events, the importance granted to the university is even greater, because, as they state, the fact of studying university courses motivates and encourages them and also serves as an escape to overcome the difficulties associated with their disability (Moriña 2015).

A university education is a powerful tool for these university students to reinvent themselves and revalidate an identity that may have been impaired in other educational stages (Prowse 2009). It could even be stated that many university students with disabilities are resilient people, as they have had to face adverse situations and overcome barriers (Zakour and Gillespie 2013).

However, not only students with disabilities benefit from the experience in higher education, but also the teaching and learning processes are enriched by having diverse students in the classrooms. In this sense, the presence of students with disabilities helps build a better university.

## Conclusions: policies, strategies, processes and actions to develop an inclusive education

We conclude by exploring some policies, strategies, processes and actions that can contribute to ensuring the success of all the students. We believe that a series of transformations, both at the institutional level and in the classroom practices, could be considered in higher education to move towards a more inclusive university.

First, university spaces should be fully accessible, with no physical barriers of any type. In this context, it is crucial that spaces be based on the universal design principle so that environments are accessible to all users (Powell 2013).

Second, universities should consider the especially sensitive transition of students with disabilities during their first year and even the first weeks of attendance. The university should be proactive action in transition planning to avoid early leaving and to foster academic success for students with disabilities (Fordyce et al. 2013). Strategies might include special orientation sessions, tutorials (e.g. assigning a student in a higher year or an instructor as a counsellor) or having reference persons or groups related to the disability among the faculty

Finally, higher education should support training the faculty, not only in the discipline they teach and investigate, but also in how to teach. Instructional and methodological strategies to address the needs of students with disabilities should be mandatory for all personnel. Faculty members should be sensitised, informed and trained in how to carry out inclusive pedagogy and universal designs for learning (Pliner and Johnson 2004; Spratt and Florian 2015).

In conclusion, it is not enough for the university to guarantee access to students with disabilities. Its policies and practices must be revised to ensure that education is inclusive – guaranteeing that *all* the students can participate fully and that *all* can benefit from a process of quality teaching and learning.

## Disclosure statement

No potential conflict of interest was reported by the author.

## Funding

This work was supported by Ministry of Economy and Competitiveness of Spain [grant number EDU2013-46303-R].

## References

Ainscow, M. 1998. "Exploring Links between Special Needs and School Improvement." *Support for Learning* 13 (2): 70–75.

Ainscow, M. 2015. *Towards Self-Improving School Systems: Lessons from a City Challenge*. London: Routledge.

Armstrong, F., and L. Barton. 1999. "Is There Anyone There Concerned with Human Rights? Cross-Cultural Connections, Disability and the Struggle for Change in England." In *Disability, Human Rights and Education: Cross Cultural Perspectives*, edited by F. Armstrong and L. Barton, 210–229. Milton Keynes: Open University Press.

Barnes, C. 2007. "Disability, Higher Education and the Inclusive Society." *British Journal of Sociology of Education* 28 (1): 135–145.

Beck, H. P., and W. D. Davidson. 2001. "Establishing an Early Warning System: Predicting Low Grades in College Students from Survey of Academic Orientations Scores." *Research in Higher Education* 42 (6): 709–723.

Black, R. D., L. A. Weinberg, and M. G. Brodwin. 2014. "Universal Design for Instruction and Learning: A Pilot Study of Faculty Instructional Methods and Attitudes Related to Students with Disabilities in Higher Education." *Exceptionality Education International* 24: 48–64.

Claiborne, L., S. Cornforth, A. Gibson, and A. Smith. 2010. "Supporting Students with Impairments in Higher Education: Social Inclusion or Cold Comfort?" *International Journal of Inclusive Education* 15 (5): 513–527.

Collins, K. D. 2000. "Coordination of Rehabilitation Services in Higher Education for Students with Psychiatric Disabilities." *Journal of Applied Rehabilitation Counseling* 31: 36–39.

Cook, L., P. D. Rumrill, and M. Tankersley. 2009. "Priorities and Understanding of Faculty Members regarding College Students with Disabilities." *International Journal of Teaching and Learning in Higher Education* 21 (1): 84–96.

Coriale, L., G. Larson, and J. Robertson. 2012. "Exploring the Educational Experience of a Social Work Student with a Disability: A Narrative." *Social Work Education* 31 (4): 422–434.

Crosling, G., L. Thomas, and M. Headney, eds. 2008. *Improving Student Retention in Higher Education*. New York: Routledge Falmer.

Davies, P. L., C. L. Schelly, and C. L. Spooner. 2013. "Measuring the Effectiveness of Universal Design for Learning Intervention in Postsecondary Education." *Journal of Postsecondary Education and Disability* 26 (3): 5–37.

Debrand, C. C., and C. H. Salzberg. 2005. "A Validated Curriculum to Provide Training to Faculty Regarding Students with Disabilities in Higher Education." *Journal of Postsecondary Education and Disability* 18: 49–62.

Doughty, H., and J. Allan. 2008. "Social Capital and the Evaluation of Inclusiveness in Scottish Further Education Colleges." *Journal of Further and Higher Education* 32 (3): 275–284.

Eckes, S. E., and T. A. Ochoa. 2005. "Student with Disabilities: Transitioning from High School to Higher Education." *American Secondary Education* 33 (3): 6–20.

European Agency for Development in Special Needs Education. 2012. *Profile of Inclusive Teachers*. Odense: European Agency for Development in Special Needs Education.

European Commission. 2010. *European Disability Strategy 2010–2020: A Renewed Commitment to a Barrier-Free Europe*. http://eur-lex.europa.eu/LexUriServ/LexUriServ.do?uri=COM:2010:0636:FIN:en:PDF

Fordyce, M., S. Riddell, R. O'Neill, and E. Weedon. 2013. *Post-School Transitions of People Who Are Deaf or Hard of Hearing*. Final report. Edinburgh: University of Edinburgh. http://www.docs.hss.ed.ac.uk/education/creid/Reports/30i_NDCS_PostSchTransit_InterimRpt.pdf

Forlin, C. 2013. "Changing Paradigms and Future Directions for Implementing Inclusive Education in Developing Countries." *Asian Journal of Inclusive Education* 1 (2): 19–31.

Fuller, M., and A., Bradley, and M. Healey. 2004. "Incorporating Disabled Students within an Inclusive Higher Education Environment." *Disability and Society* 19 (5): 455–468.

Fuller, M., J. Georgeson, M. Healey, A. Hurst, K. Kelly, S. Riddell, H. Roberts, and E. Weedon. 2009. *Improving Disabled Students' Learning*. London: Routledge.

Gairín, J., and C. I. Suárez. 2014. "Clarificar E Identificar a Los Grupos Vulnerables." [Clarifying and Identifying Vulnerable Groups]. In *Colectivos Vulnerables En La Universidad. Reflexiones Y Propuestas Para La Intervención* [Vulnerable Collectives in the University. Reflections and Proposals for Intervention], edited by J. Gairín, 35–61. Madrid: Wolters Kluwer España, S.A.

Garrison-Wade, D. F. 2012. "Listening to Their Voices: Factors That Inhibit or Enhance Postsecondary Outcomes for Students with Disabilities." *International Journal of Special Education* 27 (2): 113–125.

Getzel, E. 2008. "Addressing the Persistence and Retention of Students with Disabilities in Higher Education: Incorporating Key Strategies and Supports on Campus." *Exceptionality* 16 (4): 207–219.

Getzel, E. E., and C. A. Thoma. 2008. "Experiences of College Students with Disabilities and the Importance of Self-Determination in Higher Education Settings." *Career Development and Transition for Exceptional Individuals* 31: 77–84.

Gibson, S. 2012. "Narrative Accounts of University Education: Socio-Cultural Perspectives of Students with Disabilities." *Disability and Society* 27 (3): 353–369.

Gibson, S. 2015. "When Rights Are Not Enough: What is? Moving towards New Pedagogy for Inclusive Education within UK Universities." *International Journal of Inclusive Education* 19 (8): 875–886.

Gill, L. A. 2007. "Bridging the Transition Gap from High School to College: Preparing Students with Disabilities for a Successful Postsecondary Experience." *Teaching Exceptional Children* 40 (2): 12–15.

Goodman, K., and E. Pascarella. 2006. "First-Year Seminars Increase Persistence and Retention: A Summary of the Evidence from How College Affects Students." *Peer Review* 8 (3): 26–28.

Hadjikakou, K., and D. Hartas. 2008. "Higher Education Provision for Students with Disabilities in Cyprus." *Higher Education* 55: 103–119.

Hartley, M. T. 2010. "Increasing Resilience: Strategies for Reducing Dropout Rates for College Students with Psychiatric Disabilities." *American Journal of Psychiatric Rehabilitation* 13 (4): 295–315.

Healey, M., A. Jenkins, J. Leach, and C. Roberts. 2001. *Issues in Providing Learning Support for Disabled Students Undertaking Fieldwork and Related Activities.* Gloucestershire: Geography Discipline Network. http://www2.glos.ac.uk/gdn/disabil/overview/overview.pdf

Hitch, D., S. Macfarlane, and C. Nihill. 2015. "Inclusive Pedagogy in Australian Universities: A Review of Current Policies and Professional Development Activities." *The International Journal of the First Year in Higher Education* 6 (1): 135–145.

Hockings, C., Paul Brett, and M. Terentjevs. 2012. "Making a Difference – Inclusive Learning and Teaching in Higher Education through Open Educational Resources." *Distance Education* 33 (2): 237–252.

Hong, B. S. S. 2015. "Qualitative Analysis of the Barriers College Students with Disabilities Experiences in Higher Education." *Journal of College Student Development* 56 (3): 209–226.

Hong, B. S., and J. Himmel. 2009. "Faculty Attitudes and Perceptions toward College Students with Disabilities." *College Quarterly* 12 (3): 6–20.

Hopkins, L. 2011. "The Path of Least Resistance: A Voice-Relational Analysis of Disabled Students' Experiences of Discrimination in English Universities." *International Journal of Inclusive Education* 15: 711–727.

Jacklin, A., C. Robinson, L. O'Meara, and A. Harris. 2007. *Improving the Experiences of Disabled Students in Higher Education*. York: Higher Education Academy.

Johnson, D. R., and D. Nord. 2011. "Students with Disabilities in Higher Education: Participating in America's Future." *Impact* 23 (3): 2–3.

Kochhar-Bryant, C., D. S. Bassett, and K. W. Webb. 2009. *Transition to Postsecondary Education for Students with Disabilities*. Thousand Oaks, CA: Corwin Press.

Leyser, Y., L. Greenberger, V. Sharoni, and G. Vogel. 2011. "Students with Disabilities in Teacher Education: Changes in Faculty Attitudes toward Accommodations over Ten Years." *International Journal of Special Education* 26 (1): 162–174.

Liasidou, A. 2014. "Critical Disability Studies and Socially Just Change in Higher Education." *British Journal of Special Education* 41: 120–135.

Lombardi, A. R., and C. Murray. 2011. "Measuring University Faculty Attitudes toward Disability: Willingness to Accommodate and Adopt Universal Design Principles." *Journal of Vocational Rehabilitation* 34: 43–56.

Lombardi, A. R., C. Murray, and H. Gerdes. 2011. "College Faculty and Inclusive Instruction: Selfreported Attitudes and Actions Pertaining to Universal Design." *Journal of Diversity in Higher Education* 4 (4): 250–261.

Lombardi, A., C. Murray, and J. Kowitt. 2016. "Social Support and Academic Success for College Students with Disabilities: Do Relationship Types Matter?" *Journal of Vocational Rehabilitation* 44: 1–13.

Lombardi, A., B. Vukovic, and I. Sala-Bars. 2015. "International Comparisons of Inclusive Instruction among College Faculty in Spain, Canada, and the United States." *Journal of Postsecondary Education and Disability* 28 (4): 447–460.

Lourens, H., and L. Swartz. 2016. "'It's Better If Someone Can See Me for Who I Am': Stories of (in)Visibility for Students with a Visual Impairment within South African Universities." *Disability and Society* 31 (2): 210–222.

Lovet, T. S., N. Kresier, E. Camargo, M. Grubbs, E. J. Kin, P. L. Burge, and S. M. Culver. 2015. "STEM Faculty Experiences with Students with Disabilities at a Land Grant Institution." *Journal of Education and Training Studies* 3 (1): 27–38.

Madriaga, M., K. Hanson, C. Heaton, H. Kay, S. Newitt, and A. Walker. 2010. "Confronting Similar Challenges? Disabled and Non-Disabled Students' Learning and Assessment Experiences." *Studies in Higher Education* 35 (6): 647–658.

Martin, J. M. 2010. "Stigma and Student Mental Health in Higher Education." *Higher Education Research and Development* 29 (3): 259–274.

Matthews, N. 2009. "Teaching the 'Invisible' Disabled Students in the Classroom: Disclosure, Inclusion and the Social Model of Disability." *Teaching in Higher Education* 14 (3): 229–239.

McGuire, J. M., and S. S. Scott. 2006. "An Approach for Inclusive College Teaching: Universal Design for Instruction." *Learning Disabilities: A Multidisciplinary Journal* 14: 21–32.

Messiou, K., M. Ainscow, G. Echeita, S. Goldrick, Max, Hope, I. Paes, M. Sandoval, C. Simon, and T. Vitorino. 2016. "Learning from Differences: A Strategy for Teacher Development in Respect to Student Diversity." *School Effectiveness and School Improvement* 27 (1): 45–61.

Moriña, A. 2015. "We Aren't Heroes, We're Survivors: Higher Education as an Opportunity for Students with Disabilities to Reinvent an Identity". *Journal of Further and Higher Education,* 1–12.

Moriña, A., M. D. Cortés-Vega, and V. Molina. 2015. "Faculty Training: An Unavoidable Requirement for Approaching More Inclusive University Classrooms." *Teaching in Higher Education* 20 (8): 795–806.

Moriña, A., R. López, and V. Molina. 2015. "Students with Disabilities in Higher Education: A Biographical-Narrative Approach to the Role of Lecturers." *Higher Education Research and Development* 34: 147–159.

Mullins, L., and M. Preyde. 2013. "The Lived Experience of Students with an Invisible Disability at a Canadian University." *Disability and Society* 28 (2): 147–160.

Murray, C., A. Lombardi, and C. T. Wren. 2011. "The Effects of Disability-Focused Training on the Attitudes and Perceptions of University Staff." *Remedial and Special Education* 32: 290–300.

Oliver, M. 1990. *The Politics of Disablement*. Basingstoke: Macmillan.

Papay, C., and Megan Griffin. 2013. "Developing Inclusive College Opportunities for Students with Intellectual and Developmental Disabilities." *Research and Practice for Persons with Severe Disabilities* 38 (2): 110–116.

Patrick, S., and R. D. Wessel. 2013. "Faculty Mentorship and Transition Experiences of Students with Disabilities." *Journal of Postsecondary Education and Disability* 26 (2): 105–118.

Pliner, S. M., and J. R. Johnson. 2004. "Historical, Theoretical, and Foundational Principles of Universal Instructional Design in Higher Education." *Equity and Excellence in Education* 37: 105–113.

Powell, J. J. W. 2013. "From Ableism to Accessibility in the Universal Design University." *Review of Disability Studies: An International Journal* 8 (4): 33–45.

Prowse, S. 2009. "Institutional Construction of Disabled Students." *Journal of Higher Education Policy and Management* 31: 89–96.

Pumfrey, P. D. 2008. "Moving towards Inclusion? The First-Degree Results of Students with and without Disabilities in Higher Education in the UK: 1998–2005." *European Journal of Special Needs Education* 23 (1): 31–46.

Quinn, J. 2013. Drop-out and Completion in Higher Education in Europe Among Students from Under-Represented Groups. European Commission by the Network of Experts on Social Aspects of Education and Training NESET, European Union.

Reindal, S. M. 2016. "Discussing Inclusive Education: An Inquiry into Different Interpretations and a Search for Ethical Aspects of Inclusion Using the Capabilities Approach." *European Journal of Special Needs Education* 31 (1): 1–12.

Riddell, S., T. Tinklin, and A. Wilson. 2004. "Disabled Students in Higher Education: A Reflection on Research Strategies and Findings." In *Disability Policy and Practice: Applying the Social Model*, edited by C. Barnes and G. Mercer, 81–98. Leeds: The Disability Press.

Sapon-Shevin, M. 2003. "Inclusion: A Matter of Social Justice." *Teaching All Students* 61 (2): 25–28.

Seale, J., J. Georgeson, C. Mamas, and J. Swain. 2015. "Not the Right Kind of 'Digital Capital'? An Examination of the Complex Relationship between Disabled Students, Their Technologies and Higher Education Institutions." *Computers and Education* 82: 118–128.

Shaw, J. 2009. "The Diversity Paradox: Does Student Diversity Enhance or Challenge Excellence?" *Journal of Further and Higher Education* 33 (4): 321–331.

Shevlin, M., M. Kenny, and E. Mcneela. 2004. "Participation in Higher Education for Students with Disabilities: An Irish Perspective." *Disability and Society* 19: 15–30.

Skinner, M. E. 2004. "College Students with Learning Disabilities Speak Out: What It Takes to Be Successful in Postsecondary Education." *Journal of Postsecondary Education and Disability* 17 (2): 91–104.

Spratt, J., and L. Florian. 2015. "Inclusive Pedagogy: From Learning to Action. Supporting Each Individual in the Context of 'Everybody'." *Teaching and Teacher Education* 49: 89–96.

Strnadová, I., V. Hájková, and L. Květoňová. 2015. "Voices of University Students with Disabilities: Inclusive Education on the Tertiary Level – A Reality or a Distant Dream?" *International Journal of Inclusive Education* 19 (10): 1080–1095.

Teachability. 2002. *Teachability Project: Creating an Accessible Curriculum for Students with Disabilities*. Glasgow: University of Strathclyde.

Thomas, L. 2008. "Learning and Teaching Strategies to Promote Students Retention and Success." In *Improving Student Retention in Higher Education*, edited by G. Crosling, L. Thomas, and M. Headney, 69–81. New York: Routledge Falmer.

Thomas, L. 2016. "Developing Inclusive Learning to Improve the Engagement, Belonging, Retention, and Success of Students from Diverse Groups." In *Widening Higher Education Participation*, edited by M. Shah, A. Bennett, and E. Southgate, 135–159. Oxford: Elsevier.

Tinto, V. 1988. "Stages of Student Departure: Reflections on the Longitudinal Character of Student Learning." *The Journal of Higher Education* 59 (4): 438–455.

(UN) United Nations . 2006. *Convention on the Rights of Persons with Disabilities and Optional Protocol*: UN, Paris. http://www.un.org/disabilities/convention/conventionfull.shtml

Upcraft, M. L., J. N. Gardner, and B. O. Barefoot, eds. 2005. *Challenging and Supporting the First-Year Student: A Handbook for Improving the First Year of College*. San Francisco, CA: Jossey-Bass.

Weedon, E., and S. Riddell. 2016. "Higher Education in Europe: Widening Participation". In *Widening Higher Education Participation,* edited by M. Shah, A. Bennett, and E. Southgate, 49–61. Oxford: Elsevier.

Wehman, P. 2006. *Life beyond the Classroom: Transition Strategies for Young People with Disabilities*. 4th ed. Baltimore, MD: Paul Brookes.

Weldon, E., and S. Riddell. 2007. *Transition into and Out of Higher Education: The Experiences of 'Disabled' Students*. Edinburgh: Scotland University of Edinburgh. http://arts.gtc.org.uk(gtcni/handle/2428/49096

Wessel, R., D. Jones, C. Blanch, and L. Markle. 2015. "Pre-Enrollment Considerations of Undergraduate Wheelchair Users and Their Post-Enrollment Transitions." *Journal of Postsecondary Education and Disability* 28 (1): 57–71.

Wessel, R. D., J. A. Jones, J. Markle, and C. Westfall. 2009. "Retention and Graduation of Students with Disabilities: Facilitating Student Success." *Journal of Postsecondary Education and Disability* 21 (3): 116–125.

Wilson, K. L., K. A. Murphy, A. G. Pearson, B. M. Wallace, V. G. S. Reher, and N. Buys. 2016. "Understanding the Early Transition Needs of Diverse Commencing University Students in a Health Faculty: Informing Effective Intervention Practices." *Studies in Higher Education* 41 (6): 1023–1040.

Zakour, M. J., and D. F. Gillespie. 2013. *Community Disaster Vulnerability*. New York: Springer.

Zhang, D., L. Landmark, A. Reber, H. HsienYuan Hsu, O. Kwok, and M. Benz. 2010. "University Faculty Knowledge, Beliefs, and Practices in Providing Reasonable Accommodations to Students with Disabilities." *Remedial and Special Education* 31 (4): 276–286.

# Academic self-efficacy, sense of coherence, hope and tiredness among college students with learning disabilities

Shiri Ben-Naim, Roni Laslo-Roth, Michal Einav, Hadar Biran and Malka Margalit

**ABSTRACT**

Some resilient students with LD succeed 'against the odds' and reach college. The goals of the study are to explore their resources and barriers during their studies. The relationships between academic self-efficacy (ASE) and personal resources (sense of coherence (SOC) and hope) among college students with learning disabilities (LD) will be examined. The sample consisted of 438 college students divided into two subgroups: 149 students with LD and 289 Non-LD students. Results indicated that college students with LD reported lower levels of ASE, as well as lower levels of hope subscales and SOC. Persistent challenges of early learning distress experienced by those students during school periods continue to be prevalent during their college years. The ASE was predicted by the personal resources, and the risk factor (tiredness lost its significance). The importance of personal resources (SOC and hope subscales) was further emphasised by the mediation model (PROCESS). They mediated the relationships between LD and ASE. These outcomes call for empowering interventional programmes in order to promote hopeful thinking and personal coherence.

## Introduction

Colleges present students with enhanced academic demands and new social environment. For the resilient students with LD, who were able to overcome the academic challenges and participate in higher education studies, this is an exciting, fearful and anxiety-provoking period. The objectives of the current study are to explore resources and barriers during this period in order to further support their resilience. Indeed, during the transitional period from adolescents to adulthood, all youngsters experience many changes in their executive functioning that affect their social, emotional and cognitive processes (Luna 2009). For students with learning disabilities (LD), the transition to college may present additional burden and risk factors since it revives early stresses and past frustrations from their elementary and high school struggles (Feldman et al. 2016). Their academic self-efficacy (ASE) often predicts their adjustment to the new environment and success. It should be acknowledged that students with disabilities share some difficulties with non-disabled students, but they often encounter many more barriers in their learning (Madriaga et al. 2010). The goals of the current study are to examine the relationships between academic self-efficacy and personal resources among college students with LD.

Students with LD are identified by their academic challenges and disabilities in attention, inhibition and self-monitoring (Berninger, Swanson, and Griffin 2015; Horowitz-Kraus 2014; Shaywitz and Shaywitz 2008). They are noted for their personal histories of school-related frustrations, as well as anxiety and internalising symptomatology in anticipation of possible academic failure (Klassen, Tze, and Hannok 2013; Nelson and Harwood 2011). They often face significant academic challenges and social distress during their academic years, including the especially challenging high school periods (Idan and Margalit 2014). For this group of students, transition to college offers the possibility of new opportunities, yet, at the same time, poses new academic and social challenges. For example, in Vickerman and Blundell's study (2010), students reported that learning remained a critical and challenging issue, the proposed accommodation was not satisfactory and the academic staff were not meeting the students' needs and expectations for support and help. In this study, a special focus of concern was also related to the students' limited consideration of future expectations, reflecting their painful immersion in the current struggling. In an additional study, the existing gaps between the students' expectations for assistance and the supportive staff perceptions were also a major source of disappointment and distress. Especially upsetting was the finding that the voices of students with disabilities were sometimes intelligible to the staff (Claiborne et al. 2011).

However, regardless of the distress and barriers, research has suggested that some resilient students with LD succeed 'against the odds' (Maurice 2002). Ryan (2007) proposed the self-determination theory that has focused attention on the social-contextual conditions as a source for promoting self-motivation. In his study, he emphasised the importance of goals' identification and persistent training. This approach emphasised the significance of the three fundamental psychological needs that may be considered as the basis for understanding resilience, self-motivation and the ability for making and maintaining change: the *need for autonomy*, the *need for competence* and the *need for relatedness*.

In an attempt to further clarify the source of resiliency, Hobfoll (2011) proposed that coping with stressors in life is conceptualised in the context of resource loss, gain and maintenance. Conservation of resources (COR) theory is a stress and motivational theory, proposing that resources influence individuals' abilities to control and impact their environments successfully and thus are linked to resiliency (Hobfoll et al. 2003). Personal resources are functional in achieving goals and stimulating personal growth (Xanthopoulou et al. 2009). Psychological stress occurs in one of the three following conditions: (1) when resources are threatened; (2) when resources are lost; and (3) when individuals invest resources and do not obtain the expected level of return (Hobfoll 2001). In our study, we hypothesised that specific personal resources such as the sense of coherence (SOC) and hope will mediate the effects that LD have on ASE. The selection of these concepts is based on their common use in resource literature, and especially in past research demonstrating their relationships with academic achievement (Phan 2012; Rand, Martin, and Shea 2011). We also hypothesised that the deficiency of resources demonstrated by feelings of tiredness and fatigue, as an expression of academic burnout, will also mediate these relationships.

The following section provides description of the concept of ASE, followed by descriptions of the two different resources – SOC and hope – and a short review of the literature regarding their importance in education and LD. A review of tiredness and academic burnout, as a threat to one's resources, and its ramifications will conclude the review.

## *Academic self-efficacy*

Self-efficacy has been defined as a belief in one's ability to organise and perform courses of action (Bandura 1997, 2015). Bandura postulated that individuals with high self-efficacy often approach threatening situations as challenges, set high goals and sustain effort in the face of failures or setbacks. These tendencies, in turn, enhance personal accomplishments and decrease vulnerability to lowered well-being. In their meta-analysis, de Ridder et al. (2012) demonstrated that self-efficacy contributed to academic achievement beyond the intervening roles of contextual conditions. ASE refers to specific personal beliefs about one's ability to organise, regulate and execute actions to attain desired levels of academic performance (Zimmerman, Bandura, and Martinez-Pons 1992). Students with high ASE are confident in their capacity to meet academic requirements, to plan and organise their learning, to avoid distractions and to persist in their efforts (Bandura 1997).

Within educational settings, self-efficacy and ASE were identified as notable predictors of students' achievement (e.g. Caprara et al. 2011; Cheng and Chiou 2010; Feldman and Kubota 2015; Høigaard et al. 2015; Usher and Pajares 2008; Zimmerman 2000). Research has also shown that students with LD often report lower ASE, and ASE has been shown to relate to their actual achievements (Idan and Margalit 2014). However, personal resources may mediate the impact of these lower levels of ASE and school frustrations. In the next sections, in line with the COR model (Hobfoll 2011), we shall focus on two personal resources: SOC and hope.

## *Sense of coherence*

SOC construct was developed by Antonovsky (1987), referring to the understanding of why people manage to stay healthy despite stressful life events. SOC refers to a stable generalised orientation in relation to perceiving and controlling the environment for meaningful and appropriate action (Lindblad et al. 2016). SOC reflects the extent in which an individual is likely to construe a stressor as comprehensible and worth overcoming, as well as the individual's appraisal that he or she will manage to overcome such stressors. Therefore, SOC is a measure of an individual's coping resistance when facing stress (Antonovsky 1993). Research has suggested that students with high SOC often believe that they are in control of their lives. When they face a stressful situation, they embrace a wide repertoire of coping strategies, and select the most appropriate strategy to cope with the stressor. Life experiences structure the SOC during the developmental periods, reflecting interactions between individuals and their contextual demands. Thus, it is not surprising that the persistent challenges faced by students with LD are expressed in their lower SOC. Several studies examined the SOC of children, adolescents and young adults with LD, and reported consistently of a lower SOC than their peers without LD (Al-Yagon 2012; Sharabi, Sade and Margalit forthcoming).

In a longitudinal study, investigating a different, yet related neurodevelopmental disorder, adolescents were assessed for ADHD symptoms at the age of 16 and at the age of 21. While symptoms' severity at the age of 16 predicted symptoms' severity at the age of 21, this effect was stronger for adolescents who reported lower SOC at the age of 16. Additionally, higher SOC at the age of 16 was associated with lower ADHD severity, thus acting as a protecting factor from symptom severity (Edbom et al. 2010). Considering the SOC construct as an index of personal resource, it is not surprising that the developmental frustrations and academic struggles of those with LD are often expressed by lower levels of SOC.

While SOC reflects the developmental outcomes of past experiences, hope conceptualisation provides the individuals' anticipations for the future.

## *Hope*

As defined within Snyder's Hope Theory, hope is a cognitive construct involving individuals' expectations of successful goal attainment (Snyder 2002). Hope reflects individuals' perceptions of their ability to (1) identify and conceptualise meaningful goals, (2) develop specific strategies to reach these goals (pathways thinking) and (3) initiate and sustain the motivation and personal energy for using these strategies (agency thinking) (Hellman, Pittman, and Munoz 2013). Hopeful individuals often construct detailed strategies for attaining their goals, as well as energise themselves in pursuing the pathways to do so. Furthermore, they do not ignore the possibility of obstacles and devise alternative pathways when they encounter barriers while pursuing their goals (Du and King 2013).

Within educational settings, research reported that hope predicts students' achievement (e.g. Feldman, Rand, and Kahle-Wrobleski 2009). In a six-year longitudinal study, college students' hope scores predicted their overall grade point averages even after controlling for variance related to entrance scores (Snyder et al. 2002).

Individuals with LD from different age groups often report lower hope scores than their non-LD peers (Sharabi and Margalit 2014). Past experiences of failed goal pursuits often are associated with lower hope (Idan and Margalit 2014). Many students with LD who are attending colleges and universities have experienced such frustrated goal pursuits in their past academic and social environments (Connor 2012).

The complex relationships between those concepts are demonstrated in a study that followed students entering their first year in college. Students' LD status directly predicted lower ASE at the beginning of the year. Yet, after a month in college, LD status predicted ASE only indirectly, mediated by hope at the beginning of the year and by hope after a month, thus indicating that students who develop higher levels of hopeful thinking may adjust better to academic life (Feldman et al. 2016). Yet, one of the key threats to successful academic functioning is the experience of chronic tiredness or fatigue that will be described next.

## *Tiredness as an expression of academic burnout*

We all feel tired from time to time. In fact, at any given time, 1 in every 5 people feel unusually tired and 1 in 10 have prolonged fatigue. Women tend to feel tired more than men (Newnham 2005). Tiredness has been defined by Merriam-Webster dictionary (http://www.merriam-webster.com/dictionary/tired) as feeling drained of strength and energy, fatigued often to the point of exhaustion, resulting in the difficulty in initiating or sustaining voluntary activities. This experience often corresponds with reduced academic performance (Mizuno et al. 2011). Ongoing research related to the mechanisms underlying fatigue recognises its complex, dynamic and interactive nature (Tanaka et al. 2015). For instance, research demonstrated that school performance was negatively related with daytime tiredness (Kronholm et al. 2015), and the study of college students further demonstrated that fatigue and self-reported tiredness were related to the experience of stress, and had significant negative effects on participants' learning and cognitive performance (Palmer 2013). Additionally, feeling tired while facing academic demands may be considered as a sign of distress such as academic burnout.

Burnout is defined as a psychological syndrome in response to a chronic stressor that is manifested in emotional exhaustion and reduced personal accomplishments (Maslach 1998). Although burnout was originally studied in the work context (Ventura, Salanova, and Llorens 2015), research demonstrated that burnout is a prevalent phenomenon in educational settings as well. Students may experience academic burnout reflected by feelings of fatigue, tiredness and emotional exhaustion in response to study demands, and reduced efficacy in the learning chores (Rahmati 2015; Shin et al. 2011).

In line with the COR model, individuals tend to develop stress when they invest resources and do not obtain the expected level of return (Hobfoll 2001). Thus, learning disability may be considered as a source of stress in educational settings that can lead to enhanced tiredness and academic burnout. The connection between burnout and self-efficacy is demonstrated in Leiter's (1992) statement that burnout is 'a crisis in self-efficacy'. Indeed, research that compared academic burnout in university students with high and low levels of self-efficacy demonstrated negative relationships between self-efficacy and academic burnout (Rahmati 2015).

## *The present study*

The present study aimed at examining the relationships between students' LD, their ASE and the role of personal resources in mediating those relationships. The current study extends the existing knowledge and understanding about the struggles of college students, by examining the relationships across the complex resource and risk factors among students with and without disabilities. It has a theoretical importance with clear educational implications. Considering the documented impact LD has on ASE, the complex relationships of personal resources such as SOC and hope have with those concepts and the impact of tiredness as a risk factor, we hypothesised that students with LD will demonstrate lower ASE compared to their non-LD counterparts, and that SOC, hope and tiredness will mediate this effect.

## **Method**

### *Participants*

The sample consisted of 438 students from colleges in the centre of Israel. An announcement was presented in colleges' Facebook page, students' personal Facebook accounts and social networks, providing a link to students who agree to participate. The students were divided into two subgroups, in line with their self-identification as students with Specific LD (according to the DSM5 definition, Al-Yagon et al. 2013) who got accommodations for specific LD from the Dean of students in their colleges. The second group consisted of students who were not diagnosed and did not get any testing accommodation: 149 students with LD with mean age of 25.91, SD = 4.85 (107 females, mean age = 25.08, SD = 4.02 and 42 males; mean age 28.02, SD = 6.07. $t(148) = 3.45, p < 0.01$), and 289 non-LD students with mean age of 24.63, SD = 4.20 (215 females, mean age 24.49, SD = 4.72; 74 males, mean age 25.05, SD = 1.96. No significant differences were found between the age groups). The comparisons of groups' ages using two-way ANOVAs (group LD/non-LD X gender females/males) revealed a main effect for groups $F(1434) = 12.98, P < 0.01$, partial $\eta^2 = 0.029$, a main effect for gender $F(1434) = 12.58, P < 0.01$, partial $\eta^2 = 0.028$, and significant interactions $F(1434) = 5.76, P < 0.05$, partial $\eta^2 = 0.013$. Students with LD were older than the non-LD group, and females were significantly younger than males only in the group with LD. No significant differences were found between LD/non-LD groups in gender proportions (using $X^2$).

### *Students with LD*

They were self-identified by two questions: 'have you ever been assessed and found with LD' and 'do you get testing accommodations by the Dean of students' office in your college. No information was obtained regarding ADHD or the severity of the LD. Usually in Israel, students at the college levels were previously diagnosed (often in high schools) as students with LD as their primary area of disability condition, using Israeli Ministry of Education criteria consistent with the Law of Special Education and Ministry of Education regulations. These criteria included the presence of a Verbal and/or Performance IQ score in the average range or above and an evidence of a processing deficit in one or more cognitive or linguistic domains.

Students with LD had been identified, via psycho-educational evaluation, as demonstrating LD in reading, writing and/or mathematics. Most difficulties in reading and writing at the college stage were reflected in a slower reading and writing pace relative to their peers as well as attention difficulties. Students with special difficulties other than LD were not included in the sample.

## *Measures*

### *Academic self-efficacy (ASE)*

The Hebrew adaptation of the *Academic Self-Efficacy Scale* (Zimmerman, Bandura, and Martinez-Pons 1992) consists of 11 statements describing the students' confidence about how they can cope with different academic tasks in order to succeed in their studies and self-regulate their learning activities (e.g. 'I can remember what has been studied in class and the textbook'). The measure uses a seven-point Likert scale with endpoints of 1 (*not sure at all*) and 7 (*completely confident*). A Cronbach's alpha of 0.87 was obtained for the measure with participants in earlier studies (Lackaye and Margalit 2008). In the present study, Cronbach's alpha was 0.93.

### *Hope*

A Hebrew adaptation (Lackaye and Margalit 2006) of the State Hope Scale (SHS) (Snyder 2002) was used to assess levels of hopeful thinking. The SHS consists of three items that tap pathways (e.g. 'There are lots of ways around any problem that I am facing now') and three items for agency thinking (e.g. 'At the present time, I am energetically pursuing my goals').

Respondents rate the degree to which each statement applies to them at the present moment on a 1 (*definitely false*) to 8 (*definitely true*) scale. Cronbach's alpha for the entire questionnaire in the current study was 0.95, for the agency subscale Cronbach's alpha was 0.87 and for the pathways subscale was 0.93.

## Sense of coherence scale – SOC (Antonovsky 1987)

The short version of the self-report scale was used to rate students' sense of confidence in themselves; in their world; their 'comprehensibility' – feelings that they understood their environment; their 'manageability' of their environment and feelings of control; and their sense of meaningfulness and involvement in a variety of areas. The scale consisted of 13 items which was rated on a seven-point Likert-type scale, ranging from 1 to 7. For example, statements such as 'Doing the things you do every day is ....' were rated from descriptors such as 'a source of pain and boredom' (1) to 'a source of deep pleasure and satisfaction' (7). Higher scores reflected a greater extent of the descriptor. Cronbach's alpha for internal consistency in the current study was 0.82.

## Tiredness measure

Students with LD often complained about their distress due to chronic tiredness and fatigue, interfering with the effectiveness of their learning. Due to the interest in students' exhaustion and fatigue, reflecting academic burnout, a single question was presented on a seven-point Likert-type scale, ranging from 1 to 7: In your daily activities and tasks do you often feel 1 – *not tired* to 7 – *very tired*. Mean score: 4.17, SD = 1.55.

## Data analytic procedure

The preliminary analysis consisted of a MANOVA to examine the differences between students with and without LD and Pearson correlations in order to examine associations among the research measures. A hierarchical regression was performed to examine predictors of the students' ASE.

Based on theorised methods in which SOC and hope may mediate the relations between LD status and academic self-efficacy, as well as with tiredness and burnout, a mediation model was examined, using Preacher and Hayes's (2008) bootstrapping method with 5000 resamples with replacement. Bootstrapping was used instead of the Sobel testing or the Baron and Kenny (1986) mediation technique since bootstrapping provides a more reliable estimate of indirect effects, does not assume normality and evaluates total, direct and indirect effects (Preacher and Hayes 2008). Bootstrapping also has higher power and better type I error control than other mediation analyses. It tests the intervening variables' indirect effect as a whole model and does not require the interpretation of each path. Instead, significance was determined by examining the 95% confidence interval produced by bootstrapping mediation analyses. In order for the mediation model to attain significance, the confidence interval must not include zero. This approach has two advantages over alternative methods of testing mediation. First, multiple mediating variables can be assessed simultaneously. Second, bootstrapping methods were used to generate confidence intervals (CI) for estimates of the products of a and b model coefficients for the indirect or mediated effects.

# Results

## Preliminary analyses

First, in order to control type I error, we performed an omnibus MANOVA with LD status (LD vs. non-LD) and gender (male/female) serving as independent variables and paths, agency, SOC and ASE as dependent variables. The MANOVA yielded a main effect for LD, $F(4431) = 19.85$, $p = 0.00$, partial $\eta^2 = 0.156$, a main effect for gender $F(4431) = 3.58$, $p = 0.01$, partial $\eta^2 = 0.032$. The interaction was not significant. Means, SDs and F scores of the univariate analysis are presented in Tables 1 and 2. As expected, students with LD reported lower scores on the two measures of hope: paths and agency, and lower SOC and lower ASE. The $t$-test comparisons of the tiredness level revealed, as expected, that students with LD reported a higher level of fatigue (LD, $M = 4.37$, $SD = 1.51$, Non-LD = 4.07, $SD = 1.56$, $t (436) = -1.90$, $p = 0.029$, 1-tailed).

In order to explore the associations among research measures, we performed Pearson correlations. Inter-correlations among measures are presented in Table 3.

## Predictors of students' well-being: academic self-efficacy

In order to examine if the LD status, gender, level of tiredness, agency, paths and SOC predict ASE, a multiple hierarchical regression was performed with ASE serving as the criterion variable. Table 4 presents B, SE, B and β values for this multiple hierarchical regression analysis. At step one, in order to control the demographic variables, LD status, age and gender were entered into the model, explaining 17.5% of the variance. At this stage, LD and gender were significant predictors. At step two, the tiredness level was added to the model as a significant predictor, adding 3.6% to the prediction, and reaching $R^2 = 0.211$. At the third step, the two hope subscales (paths and agency) were entered, adding 26.7% to the variance prediction. At this step, the level of tiredness remained a significant variable, together with the two hope measures, LD and gender. In the fourth step, when the SOC was entered as a personality strength measure, it added 2.3% to the prediction of the variance, reaching $R^2 = 0.501$.

At this fourth step, LD (negative relations), gender, paths, agency and SOC (positive relations) were significant predictors. However, the contribution of the tiredness level lost its significance in this step. The results of the regression analysis indicated that LD, gender and personal resources (hope and SOC) were significant predictors of the ASE. The introduction of the SOC reduced the prediction of the tiredness. In order to further examine the specific role of the predictors, a mediation analysis was performed to identify the mediating variables between LD and ASE.

## Mediation analyses

In order to further examine if the relations between LD and ASE could be accounted for by the personal resources: agency, paths, and SOC, as well as by the level of tiredness, we performed a mediation analysis. The mediation analyses were tested using the bootstrapping method, with bias-corrected confidence estimates (MacKinnon, Lockwood, and Williams 2004; Preacher and Hayes 2004). In the present study, 95% confidence interval of the indirect effects was obtained with 5000 bootstrap resamples (Preacher and Hayes 2004).

**Table 1.** Means, standard deviations and F scores for ANOVAs between students with and without learning disabilities.

| Variable | LD | Non-LD | F(1,434) | Partial $\eta^2$ |
|---|---|---|---|---|
| Path |  |  |  |  |
| M | 5.73 | 6.89 | 61.02** | 0.123 |
| SD | 1.60 | 1.25 |  |  |
| Agency |  |  |  |  |
| M | 5.50 | 6.57 | 60.27** | 0.122 |
| SD | 1.41 | 1.14 |  |  |
| SOC |  |  |  |  |
| M | 4.44 | 4.86 | 25.02** | 0.055 |
| SD | 0.76 | 0.77 |  |  |
| ASE |  |  |  |  |
| M | 4.85 | 5.76 | 57.97** | 0.188 |
| SD | 1.32 | 0.89 |  |  |

Note. ASE = Academic Self-Efficacy; LD = Students with learning disabilities; Non-LD = Students without learning disabilities; and SOC = Sense of Coherence.
**$p<0.01$.

**Table 2.** Means, standard deviations and F scores for ANOVAs between male and female students.

| Variable | Male | Female | F(1,434) | Partial $\eta^2$ |
|---|---|---|---|---|
| Path |  |  |  |  |
| M | 6.16 | 6.62 | 9.07** | 0.020 |
| SD | 1.55 | 1.44 |  |  |
| Agency |  |  |  |  |
| M | 5.89 | 6.31 | 8.45** | 0.019 |
| SD | 1.33 | 1.32 |  |  |
| SOC |  |  |  |  |
| M | 4.60 | 4.76 | 3.41 | 0.008 |
| SD | 0.78 | 0.79 |  |  |
| ASE |  |  |  |  |
| M | 5.11 | 5.57 | 12.96** | 0.029 |
| SD | 1.16 | 1.12 |  |  |

Note. ASE = Academic Self-Efficacy; LD = Students with learning disabilities; Non-LD: Students without learning disabilities; and SOC = Sense of Coherence.
**$p<0.01$.

We found a significant mediation effect of personal resources (agency, paths and SOC) with respect to the relation between LD and ASE (indirect effect = −0.6211, SE = 0.09, 95% CI = [LLCI = −0.8029, ULCI = −0.4644]. It was found that LD (as opposed to non-LD) was negatively related to Agency (B = −1.07, se = 0.13, t = −8.56, p = 0.00, 95% CI = [LLCI = −1.3139, ULCI = −0.8233].) and to Paths (B = −1.16, se = 0.14, t = −8.32, p = 0.00, 95% CI = [LLCI = −1.4327, ULCI = −0.8850]). It was also found that LD was negatively associated with SOC (B = −0.42, se = 0.08, t = −5.45, p = 0.00, 95% CI = [LLCI = −0.5737, ULCI = −0.2695]). Lastly, results indicated that the personal resource mediators (agency, paths and SOC) were associated with ASE (see Figure 1 and Table 5). In this model, the tiredness measure was not a significant mediator. Thus, we found a significant mediation effect of agency, paths and SOC with respect to the relation between LD and the ASE level. Beta coefficients for all of the paths in this model appear in Figure 1.

**Table 3.** Pearson correlations among variables.

| Variable | 1 | 2 | 3 | 4 | 5 |
|---|---|---|---|---|---|
| 1. Path | – | | | | |
| 2. Agency | 0.90** | – | | | |
| 3. SOC | 0.36** | 0.40** | – | | |
| 4. ASE | 0.65** | 0.64** | 0.44** | – | |
| 5. Tiredness | −0.14** | −0.15** | −0.38** | −0.20** | – |

Note. ASE = Academic Self-Efficacy; SOC = Sense of Coherence.
**$p < 0.01$.

**Table 4.** Hierarchical Regression Analysis for predicting Academic Self-Efficacy.

| Step | B | SE B | β |
|---|---|---|---|
| **Step 1** | | | |
| LD | −0.88 | 0.11 | −0.36** |
| Age | −0.02 | 0.01 | −0.08 |
| Gender | 0.40 | 0.11 | 0.15** |
| **Step 2** | | | |
| LD | −0.83 | 0.10 | −0.34** |
| Age | −0.02 | 0.01 | −0.09* |
| Gender | 0.43 | 0.11 | 0.17** |
| Tiredness | −0.14 | 0.03 | −0.19** |
| **Step 3** | | | |
| LD | −0.35 | 0.09 | −0.14** |
| Age | 0.01 | 0.01 | 0.03 |
| Gender | 0.26 | 0.09 | 0.10** |
| Tiredness | −0.08 | 0.03 | −0.11** |
| Paths | 0.27 | 0.06 | 0.34** |
| Agency | 0.22 | 0.07 | 0.26** |
| **Step 4** | | | |
| LD | −0.30 | 0.09 | −0.12** |
| Age | 0.00 | 0.01 | 0.02 |
| Gender | 0.22 | 0.09 | 0.09* |
| Tiredness | −0.04 | 0.03 | −0.05 |
| Paths | 0.27 | 0.06 | 0.35** |
| Agency | 0.17 | 0.07 | 0.20* |
| SOC | 0.26 | 0.06 | 0.18** |

Note. LD = learning disabilities; SOC = Sense of Coherence.
*$p < 0.05$; **$p < 0.01$.

## Discussion

This study examined the unique contribution of personal resources (i.e. SOC, hope subscales: agency and paths) and tiredness as a risk factor to ASE – among college students with and without LD. Preliminary analysis focused attention on the relations between LD and the following measures: ASE, hope subscales, SOC and tiredness. The study addressed college students with LD, expanding earlier studies that assessed children and adolescents with LD (Sharabi and Margalit 2014). Similar to younger groups of children and adolescents, results indicated that college students with LD also reported lower levels of ASE, as well as lower levels of agency, paths and SOC. Hence, it seems that the persistent early learning challenges experienced by those students during elementary and high school periods continue to be prevalent during their college years. This finding is of particular significance considering that among students with LD, those youngsters who are able to continue their studies into colleges and universities are among the successful and resilient ones. Therefore, it is rather

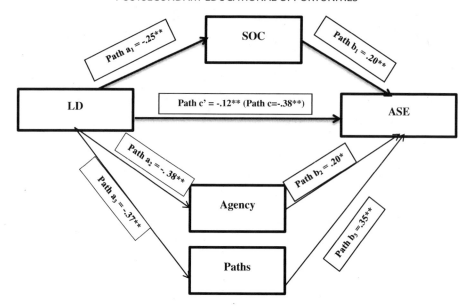

**Figure 1.** Direct and indirect effects of LD on ASE through SOC, agency and paths (beta scores).
Note. ASE = Academic Self-Efficacy; LD = learning disabilities; and SOC = Sense of Coherence. $*p < 0.05$; $**p < 0.01$.

**Table 5.** Indirect and Direct Effects of LD on ASE.

|  | B | SE | LLCI | ULCI |
|---|---|---|---|---|
| Agency | −0.1842 | 0.0817 | −0.3674 | −0.0374 |
| Paths | −0.3127 | 0.0892 | −0.5039 | −0.1571 |
| SOC | −.01243 | 0.0326 | −0.2011 | −0.0710 |
| Direct effect |  |  |  |  |
| LD | −0.2898 | 0.9010 | −0.4669 | −0.1127 |

Note. ASE = Academic Self-Efficacy; LD = learning disabilities; and SOC = Sense of Coherence.

disappointing and even challenging that regardless of their documented academic success, their ongoing struggles continue to be reflected in reduced personal strength expressed by lower SOC, reduced future expectations reflected in their diminished agency and pathways scores and elevated feelings of tiredness and fatigue, reflecting academic burnout. The results of the study demonstrated the critical role of past experiences in shaping and structuring the perceptions of the present contextual conditions and demands in the college. Maybe the reality that in order to achieve success in college these students have to invest more effort and more time than their peers further affects their SOC and self-efficacy. Perhaps also the decreased personal resources reflect the joint impact of several additional risk factors such as: the expected increased academic demands in college, combined together with the need for establishing new social relations, while at that period, youngsters have to face more autonomy and responsibility for the studies. They may be afraid to disappoint their families and themselves.

However, it should also be emphasised that many students with LD were able to continue demonstrating resiliency in their college studies. In order to further clarify the sources of their resilience, the study examined the factors that predict their ASE.

## ASE predictors

As was previously noted, higher levels of ASE predict successful performance in college studies (Feldman and Kubota 2015). Since ASE is highly correlated with academic achievements (Di Giunta et al. 2013), the beliefs students hold about their capacities to regulate their learning are important predictors of success at educational settings.

The predictive role of two related risk factors was examined in this study: LD and tiredness. It has been earlier documented that LD predicts lower ASE (McIlroy et al. 2015). Tiredness was also studied in relation to ASE and academic functioning (Palmer 2013), yet surprisingly, to our best knowledge, tiredness as an expression of academic burnout was not studied among college students with LD. Since students who face prolonged and chronic academic difficulties may experience burnout, it may be considered as a risk factor that further burdens their efforts to stay involved in their studies. Surprisingly, hope beliefs by themselves, as an expression of future expectations, did not mediate the risk of fatigue and academic burnout. Yet, the joint mediating roles of SOC together with hope have been emphasised, as will be further explained.

SOC reflects students' beliefs that they can comprehend the demands of the situation (including academic ones), that they can manage challenging and demanding tasks and that their activities are meaningful and significant to their lives. Thus, students with high SOC will be able to focus their effort, even when they feel tired and academically burned out, in order to achieve academic success. Therefore, SOC reflects personality strengths and predicts resiliency, regardless of academic challenges and frustrations.

The mediation model also focused attention on hope as referring to future expectations and beliefs. The current study examined two subscales of hope, indicating not only to the ability to define meaningful goals, but also to the capacity to develop effective paths in order to reach those goals, to cope with barriers and to design alternative pathways.

Results also indicated that within the joint effect of SOC and hope, feelings of academic burnout and exhaustion lose their impact. Yet, it should be noted that hope alone does not mediate fatigue, and regardless the mediation of personal resources, the impact of LD remained significant (although reduced).

## Limitations, implications and future directions

This study has several limitations. First, it is based on correlational research. Longitudinal studies and controlled experimental research may further clarify the dynamic processes and outcomes across academic studies. In addition, the sample was self-identified as students with LD, and no information was available regarding the severity of the LD or comorbidity with ADHD. An additional limitation is the self-reported questionnaires, which may emphasise subjective experiences. Specifically, the topic of tiredness was only briefly assessed, and deserves a more thorough and detailed examination. Future studies may include additional approaches such as in-depth interviews and different groups of college students. In addition, a day-to-day diary report may clarify periodical fluctuations, with implications for fatigue management strategies.

In addition, this study focused on students mostly from humanistic departments, behavioural studies and business administration departments in several colleges in Israel. Comparisons among students from different departments and cultural contexts could lead to a comprehensive understanding of the dynamic relations between LD, personal resource risk factors and ASE.

## *Educational implications*

At a time when universities and colleges emphasise the need for testing accommodations for students with LD, the current study chose to focus on the emotional meaning of their day-to-day struggles and its implications. This resilient group of students was able to overcome academic barriers during high school years, and start their academic studies in colleges. Indeed, they are already survivors, but their struggles are not over. As the current study's results suggest, their beliefs about their abilities to succeed reflect their histories, personal strengths and future hopes. These results carry several important educational implications for higher education institutions. First, it focuses attention on students' future expectations, meaningful goals and hopes. Therefore, it may be vital that disability support centres develop programmes that will meet the needs for empowering personality strength through focusing on envisions of future goals. They also have to sensitise awareness of fatigue expressions as demonstrated dangers of academic burnout. Enhancing the awareness of the academic staff to these students' needs may promote their options for success, and enable them to actualise their SOC. The results of this study pinpointed attention at the benefits of scaffolding the academic learning environments in such a way as to incrementally provide all students, specifically those with LD, with meaningful learning experiences, which will lead to higher academic expectations and success by accentuating hopeful approaches to the future and resilient self-efficacies.

Second, results indicate that LD students report higher levels of tiredness as compared to their non-LD peers. This result emphasises the debilitating ramifications LD may carry on students: feeling drained of strength and energy when facing academic challenges. Not surprisingly, students who were tired had lower ASE, validating Palmer's (2013) study that found significant negative effects of tiredness on participants' learning and cognitive performance. However, interestingly, the results also indicated that SOC levels reduced the previously noted effect of tiredness on ASE. These results may suggest that those who enjoy a stronger, stable, generalised orientation towards accurately perceiving and controlling their environment may be more inclined to maintain a sense of ASE, despite changing levels of fatigue and burnout. This complex result pattern is in line with Hobfoll's (2011) COR theory proposing that resources such as SOC may mediate individuals' abilities to control and impact their environments successfully, thereby linked to resiliency and successful outcomes. Future studies may shed light on additional resources, both individual and contextual, that may promote resiliency and strengthen one's self-efficacy, academically or otherwise.

Finally, addressing the hope construct, results indicate that both constructs – paths and agency – carry meaningful mediating effects on the relationship between LD and ASE. These results are in line with Snyder's Hope Theory (2002) viewing hope as an integrated, cohesive cognitive construct outlining individuals' overall expectations of successful goal attainment. The hope construct, and its relation to LD on the one hand, and ASE on the other, emphasises the importance that future cognitions have on the ability of individuals to cope with their difficulties and obstacles. The role of future cognitions in predicting coping and quality of adaptation is still not as prevalent as past experiences in this field of psychology and future research is still needed to emphasise its significance. In addition, appreciating the importance of contexts, future studies may develop educational approaches to support the shaping of learning environments as communities of hope and personal empowerment for all students (Shade 2006).

The challenges that students with disabilities continue to face within our colleges and universities call for a special attention. It should be emphasised that the accommodations are only a partial answer to the challenging realities experienced by students with disabilities. It is our obligation to examine in depth the emotional cost of the barriers, staff resistance and obstacles on the way to enhance full inclusion within our institutes of higher education.

In summary, the goal of this study was to explore the emotional consequences LD may carry on students' ASE, recognising its critical corollaries to performance and achievements in the higher academic systems. The study's results indicate that personal resources such as SOC and hope, and to some extent, risk factors such as tiredness, may mediate the otherwise perceived inevitable, detrimental link between LD and ASE. These results carry important implications to those who are burdened by their disabilities and are encouraging the development of prevention and intervention programmes that address this prevalent issue. We are confident that the results of this study will help promote a deeper understanding for the joint impact of the risks and challenges experienced by students with LD in colleges. We hope that higher education institutions will start developing varied types of support to meet the differential needs of all students in inclusive academic environments.

## Disclosure statement

No potential conflict of interest was reported by the authors.

## References

Al-Yagon, M. 2012. "Subtypes of Attachment Security in School-age Children with Learning Disabilities." *Learning Disability Quarterly* 35 (3): 170–183. doi:10.1177/0731948712436398.

Al-Yagon, M., C. Cornoldi, W. Cavendish, A. J. Fawcett, M. Grünke, L. Y. Hung, and C. Vio. 2013. "The Proposed Changes for *DSM-5* for SLD and ADHD: International Perspectives – Australia, Germany, Greece, India, Israel, Italy, Spain, Taiwan, United Kingdom, and United States." *Journal of Learning Disabilities* 46 (1): 58–72. doi:10.1177/0022219412464353.

Antonovsky, A. 1987. *Unraveling the Mystery of Health*. San Francisco, CA: Jossey-Bass.

Antonovsky, A. 1993. "The Structure and Properties of the Sense of Coherence Scale." *Social Science Medicine* 36: 725–733. doi:10.1016/0277-9536(93)90033-Z.

Bandura, A. 1997. *Self-efficacy: The Exercise of Control*. New York: Freeman.

Bandura, A. 2015. "On Deconstructing Commentaries Regarding Alternative Theories of Self-regulation." *Journal of Management* 41 (4): 1025–1044. doi:10.1177/0149206315572826.

Baron, R. M., and D. A. Kenny. 1986. "The Moderator-mediator Variable Distinction in Social Psychological Research: Conceptual, Strategic, and Statistical Considerations." *Journal of Personality and Social Psychology* 51 (6): 1173–1182. doi:10.1037/0022-3514.51.6.1173.

Berninger, V. W., H. L. Swanson, and W. Griffin. 2015. "Understanding Developmental and Learning Disabilities within Functional-systems Frameworks: Building on the Contributions of J. P. Das". In *Cognition, Intelligence, and Achievement: A Tribute to J. P. Das*, edited by T. C. Papadopoulos, R. K. Parrila, and J. R. Kirby, 397–418. San Diego, CA: Elsevier Academic Press.

Caprara, G. V., M. Vecchione, G. Alessandri, M. Gerbino, and C. Barbaranelli. 2011. "The contribution of Personality Traits and Self-efficacy Beliefs to Academic Achievement: A Longitudinal Study." *British Journal of Educational Psychology* 81: 78–96. doi:10.1016/j.paid.2003.11.003.

Cheng, P., and W. Chiou. 2010. "Achievement, Attributions, Self-efficacy, and Goal Setting by Accounting Undergraduates." *Psychological Reports* 106: 54–64. doi:10.2466/pr0.106.1.54-64.

Claiborne, L. B., S. Cornforth, A. Gibson, and A. Smith. 2011. "Supporting Students with Impairments in Higher Education: Social Inclusion or Cold Comfort?" *International Journal of Inclusive Education* 15 (5): 513–527. doi:10.1080/13603110903131747.

Connor, D. J. 2012. "Actively Navigating the Transition Into College: Narratives of Students with Learning Disabilities." *International Journal of Qualitative Studies in Education* 25: 1005–1036. doi:10.1080/09518398.2011.590158.

Di Giunta, L., G. Alessandri, M. Gerbino, P. L. Kanacri, A. Zuffiano, and G. V. Caprara. 2013. "The Determinants of Scholastic Achievement: The Contribution of Personality Traits, Self-esteem, and Academic Self-efficacy." *Learning and Individual Differences* 27: 102–108. doi:10.1016/j.lindif.2012.07.010.

Du, H., and R. B. King. 2013. "Placing Hope in Self and Others: Exploring the Relationships among Self Construal, Locus of Hope, and Adjustment." *Personality and Individual Differences* 54 (3): 332–337. doi:10.1016/j.paid.2012.09.015.

Edbom, T., K. Malmberg, P. Lichtenstein, M. Granlund, and J.-O. Larsson. 2010. "High Sense of Coherence in Adolescence is a Protective Factor in the Longitudinal Development of ADHD Symptoms." *Scandinavian Journal of Caring Sciences* 24: 541–547. doi:10.1111/j.1471-6712.2009.00746.x.

Feldman, D. B., O. B. Davidson, S. Ben-Naim, E. Maza, and M. Margalit. 2016. "Hope as a Mediator of Loneliness and Academic Self-efficacy Among Students With and Without Learning Disabilities During the Transition to College." *Learning Disabilities, Research & Practice* 31: 63–74. doi:10.1111/ldrp.12094.

Feldman, D. B., and M. Kubota. 2015. "Hope, Self-efficacy, Optimism, and Academic Achievement: Distinguishing Constructs and Levels of Specificity in Predicting College Grade-point Average." *Learning and Individual Differences* 37: 210–216. doi:10.1016/j.lindif.2014.11.022.

Feldman, D. B., K. L. Rand, and K. Kahle-Wrobleski. 2009. "Hope and Goal Attainment: Testing a Basic Prediction of Hope Theory." *Journal of Social and Clinical Psychology* 28: 479–497. doi:10.1521/jscp.2009.28.4.479.

Hellman, C., M. Pittman, and R. Munoz. 2013. "The First Twenty Years of the Will and the Ways: An Examination of Score Reliability Distribution on Snyder's Dispositional Hope Scale." *Journal of Happiness Studies* 14 (3): 723–729. doi:10.1007/s10902-012-9351-5.

Hobfoll, S. E. 2001. "The Influence of Culture, Community, and the Nested-self in the Stress Process: Advancing Conservation of Resources Theory." *Applied Psychology* 50 (3): 337–421. doi:10.1111/1464-0597.00062.

Hobfoll, S. E. 2011. "Conservation of Resource Caravans and Engaged Settings." *Journal of Occupational and Organizational Psychology* 84 (1): 116–122. doi:10.1111/j.2044-8325.2010.02016.x.

Hobfoll, S. E., R. J. Johnson, N. Ennis, and A. P. Jackson. 2003. "Resource Loss, Resource Gain, and Emotional Outcomes Among Inner City Women." *Journal of Personality and Social Psychology* 84 (3): 632–643. doi:10.1037/0022-3514.84.3.632.

Høigaard, R., V. B. Kovač, N. C. Øverby, and T. Haugen. 2015. "Academic Self-efficacy Mediates the Effects of School Psychological Climate on Academic Achievement." *School Psychology Quarterly* 30: 64–74. doi:10.1037/spq0000056.

Horowitz-Kraus, T. 2014. "Pinpointing the Deficit in Executive Functions in Adolescents With Dyslexia Performing the Wisconsin Card Sorting Test: An ERP Study." *Journal of Learning Disabilities* 47: 208–223. doi:10.1177/0022219412453084.

Idan, O., and M. Margalit. 2014. "Socioemotional Self-perceptions, Family Climate, and Hopeful Thinking Among Students With Learning Disabilities and Typically Achieving Students From the Same Classes." *Journal of Learning Disabilities* 47: 136–152. doi:10.1177/0022219412439608.

Klassen, R., V. Tze, and W. Hannok. 2013. "Internalizing Problems of Adults With Learning Disabilities: A Meta-analysis." *Journal of Learning Disabilities* 46: 317–327. doi:10.1177/0022219411422260.

Kronholm, E., R. Puusniekka, J. Jokela, J. Villberg, A. S. Urrila, T. Paunio, and J. Tynjälä. 2015. "Trends in Self-reported Sleep Problems, Tiredness and Related School Performance Among Finnish Adolescents from 1984 to 2011." *Journal of Sleep Research* 24 (1): 3–10. doi:10.1111/jsr.12258.

Lackaye, T., and M. Margalit. 2006. "Comparisons of Achievement, Effort, and Self-perceptions Among Students With Learning Disabilities and Their Peers From Different Achievement Groups." *Journal of Learning Disabilities* 39 (5): 432–446. doi:10.1177/00222194060390050501.

Lackaye, T., and M. Margalit. 2008. "Self-efficacy, Loneliness, Effort and Hope: Developmental Differences in the Experiences of Students with Learning Disabilities and their nonLD Peers at Two Age Groups." *Learning Disabilities: A Contemporary Journal* 6 (2): 1–20.

Leiter, M. P. 1992. "Burn-out as a Crisis in Self-efficacy: Conceptual and Practical Implications". *Work & Stress* 6 (2): 107–115; doi: 10.1080/02678379208260345.

Lindblad, C., K. Sandelin, L. M. Petersson, C. Rohani, and A. Langius Eklöf. 2016. "Stability of the 13-Item Sense of Coherence (SOC) Scale: A Longitudinal Prospective Study in Women Treated for Breast Cancer." *Quality of Life Research* 25 (3): 753–760. doi:10.1007/s11136-015-1114-4.

Luna, B. 2009. "Developmental Changes in Cognitive Control Through Adolescence." *Advances in Child Development and Behavior* 37: 233–278.

MacKinnon, D. P., C. M. Lockwood, and J. Williams. 2004. "Confidence Limits for the Indirect Effect: Distribution of the Product and Resampling Methods." *Multivariate Behavioral Research* 39 (1): 99–128. doi:10.1207/s15327906mbr3901_4.

Madriaga, M., K. Hanson, C. Heaton, H. Kay, S. Newitt, and A. Walker. 2010. "Confronting Similar Challenges? Disabled and Non-disabled Students' Learning and Assessment Experiences." *Studies in Higher Education* 35 (6): 647–658. doi:10.1080/03075070903222633.

Maslach, C. 1998. "A Multidimensional Theory of Burnout". In *Theories of Organizational Stress*, edited by C. L. Cooper, 68–85. Oxford, UK: Oxford University Press.

Maurice, M. 2002. "Resilience Elements in Students with Learning Disabilities." *Journal of Clinical Psychology* 58: 291–298. doi:10.1002/jclp.10018.

McIlroy, D., K. Poole, Ö. F. Ursavas, and A. Moriarty. 2015. "Distal and Proximal Associates of Academic Performance at Secondary Level: A Mediation Model of Personality and Self-Efficacy." *Learning and Individual Differences* 38: 1–9. doi:10.1016/j.lindif.2015.01.004.

Mizuno, K., M. Tanaka, S. Fukuda, K. Imai-Matsumura, and Y. Watanabe. 2011. "Relationship Between Cognitive Functions and Prevalence of Fatigue in Elementary and Junior High School Students." *Brain Development* 33: 470–479. doi:10.1016/j.braindev.2010.08.012.

Nelson, J. M., and H. Harwood. 2011. "Learning Disabilities and Anxiety: A Meta-Analysis." *Journal of Learning Disabilities* 44: 3–17. doi:10.1177/0022219409359939.

Newnham, D. 2005. "Tiredness". *The Times Educational Supplement* 4637:F11–F14. http://www.lexisnexis.com/hottopics/lnacademic/?verb=sr&csi=235865&sr=HEADLINE(Tiredness)%2BAND%2BDATE%2BIS%2B2005.

Palmer, L. K. 2013. "The Relationship Between Stress, Fatigue, and Cognitive Functioning." *College Student Journal* 47 (2): 312–325.

Phan, H. P. 2012. "Relations Between Informational Sources, Self-efficacy and Academic Achievement: A Developmental Approach." *Educational Psychology* 32 (1): 81–105. doi:10.1080/01443410.2011.625612.

Preacher, K., and A. Hayes. 2004. "SPSS and SAS Procedures for Estimating Indirect Effects in Simple Mediation Models." *Behavior Research Methods, Instruments, & Computers* 36 (4): 717–731. doi:10.3758/BF03206553.

Preacher, K., and A. Hayes. 2008. "Asymptotic and Resampling Strategies for Assessing and Comparing Indirect Effects in Multiple Mediator Models." *Behavior Research Methods* 40 (3): 879–891. doi:10.3758/BRM.40.3.879.

Rahmati, Z. 2015. "The Study of Academic Burnout in Students with High and Low Level of Self-efficacy". *Procedia-Social and Behavioral Sciences* 171: 49–55. doi:10.1016/j.sbspro.2015.01.087

Rand, K. L., A. D. Martin, and A. M. Shea. 2011. "Hope, But Not Optimism, Predicts Academic Performance of Law Students Beyond Previous Academic Achievement." *Journal of Research in Personality* 45 (6): 683–686. doi:10.1016/j.jrp.2011.08.004.

de Ridder, D. T. D., G. Lensvelt-Mulders, C. Finkenauer, F. M. Stok, and R. F. Baumeister. 2012. "Taking Stock of Self-control: A Meta-analysis of How Trait Self-control Relates to a Wide Range of Behaviors." *Personality and Social Psychology Review* 16 (1): 76–99. doi:10.1177/1088868311418749.

Ryan, R. M. 2007. "Motivation for Physical Activity Research on Persistence, Performance, and Enjoyment in Sport, Exercise, and Everyday Life From a Self-determination Theory Viewpoint." *Journal of Sport & Exercise Psychology* 29: S2–S2.

Shade, P. 2006. "Educating Hopes." *Studies in Philosophy and Education* 25 (3): 191–225. doi:10.1007/s11217-005-1251-2.

Sharabi, A., and M. Margalit. 2014. "Predictors of Positive Mood and Negative Mood Among Children with Learning Disabilities and their Peers." *International Journal for Research in Learning Disabilities* 2: 18–41.

Sharabi, A., S. Sade, and M. Margalit. Forthcoming. "Virtual Connections, Personal Resources, Loneliness and Academic Self-Efficacy among College Students with and without LD". *European Journal of Special Needs Education*. doi: 10.1080/08856257.2016.1141542.

Shaywitz, S. E., and B. A. Shaywitz. 2008. "Paying Attention to Reading: The Neurobiology of Reading and Dyslexia." *Development and Psychopathology* 20: 1329–1349. doi:10.1017/S0954579408000631.

Shin, H. J., B. Y. Kim, M. Y. Lee, H. K. Noh, K. H. Kim, and S. M. Lee. 2011. "A Short-term Longitudinal Study of Mental Health and Academic Burnout Among Middle School Students". *The Korean Journal of School Psychology* 8 (2): 133–152. doi: 10.16983/kjsp.2011.8.2.133

Snyder, C. R. 2002. "Hope Theory: Rainbows in the Mind." *Psychological Inquiry* 13 (4): 249–275. doi:10.1207/S15327965PLI1304_01.

Snyder, C. R., H. Shorey, J. Cheavens, K. M. Pulvers, V. H. Adams, and C. Wiklund. 2002. "Hope and Academic Success in College." *Journal of Educational Psychology* 94: 820–826. doi:10.1037//0022-0663.94.4.820.

Tanaka, M., S. Tajima, K. Mizuno, A. Ishii, Y. Konishi, T. Miike, and Y. Watanabe. 2015. "Frontier Studies on Fatigue, Autonomic Nerve Dysfunction, and Sleep-rhythm Disorder." *The Journal of Physiological Sciences* 65 (6): 483–498. doi:10.1007/s12576-015-0399-y.

Usher, E. L., and F. Pajares. 2008. "Self-efficacy for Self-regulated Learning: A Validation Study." *Educational and Psychological Measurement* 68 (3): 443–463. doi:10.1177/0013164407308475.

Ventura, M., M. Salanova and S. Llorens. 2015. "Professional Self-efficacy as a Predictor of Burnout and Engagement: The Role of Challenge and Hindrance Demands". *The Journal of Psychology* 149 (3): 277–302. doi: 10.1080/00223980.2013.876380

Vickerman, P., and M. Blundell. 2010. "Hearing the Voices of Disabled Students in Higher Education." *Disability & Society* 25 (1): 21–32. doi:10.1080/09687590903363290.

Xanthopoulou, D., A. B. Bakker, E. Demerouti, and W. B. Schaufeli. 2009. "Reciprocal Relationships Between Job Resources, Personal Resources, and Work Engagement." *Journal of Vocational Behavior* 74 (3): 235–244. doi:10.1016/j.jvb.2008.11.003.

Zimmerman, B. 2000. "Self-efficacy: An Essential Motive to Learn." *Contemporary Educational Psychology* 25: 82–91. doi:10.1006/ceps.

Zimmerman, B. J., A. Bandura, and M. Martinez-Pons. 1992. "Self-motivation for Academic Attainment: The Role of Self-efficacy Beliefs and Personal Goal Setting." *American Educational Research Journal* 29: 663–676. doi:10.3102/00028312029003663.

# Functioning and participation problems of students with ADHD in higher education: which reasonable accommodations are effective?

Dorien Jansen, Katja Petry, Eva Ceulemans, Saskia van der Oord, Ilse Noens and Dieter Baeyens

**ABSTRACT**

Students with ADHD struggle in higher education as a result of various functioning and participation problems. However, there are remaining gaps in the literature. First, it remains unclear how often and during which teaching and evaluation methods problems arise. Second, we do not yet know which reasonable accommodations are most effective to deal with the functioning. And third, we do not know which accommodations are most effective to address participation problems of students with ADHD in higher education. This study addresses these three gaps in literature. In total, 86 students with ADHD, 42 student counsellors and 86 students without a disability participated in a survey-based study. The results show that students with ADHD most frequently experience problems with sustaining and focusing attention and it is demonstrated that most problems arise during classical teaching or evaluation methods. Finally, the perception of the effectiveness of reasonable accommodations is strongly dependent on which problems students experience in higher education. These findings suggest that it is important to consider both personal and environmental characteristics when selecting and implementing reasonable accommodations.

## Background

Thomas, a 22-year-old university student, was diagnosed with ADHD at the age of 19. Currently, he is enrolled in the third year of a bachelor programme. As a child, Thomas experienced difficulty with focusing his attention. The teacher often reprimanded him because he was daydreaming or looking out the window. His parents also noticed that he was very active and had a lot of energy. Thomas always participated in a lot of sports activities. When he was around his friends, parents or teachers, he was very impulsive and interrupted them a lot. Thomas was also described as a boy who was very impatient and hated waiting for something or somebody. During adolescence, Thomas learned how to cope better with his difficulties from childhood and in middle school, he was described as a very creative and intelligent teenager. He graduated with average grades and continued his studies at a university. At university, his difficulties staying focused, planning and organising, and impulsive behaviour became more impairing. Now, his high levels of energy have decreased but Thomas ruminates a lot. He feels worried that he will miss deadlines or forget important information and has difficulty relaxing. Because of these problems, Thomas encounters a lot of difficulties at university. He, for example, has problems studying for exams and keeping his attention focused on the professor or his books, or misses deadlines due to his problems with planning and organising.

Thomas is a typical student with Attention Deficit/Hyperactivity Disorder (ADHD) in higher education. ADHD is described in the Diagnostic and Statistical Manual of mental disorders (DSM-5; APA, 2013) as a neurodevelopmental disorder which is characterised by a relatively stable pattern of impairing symptoms of inattention, hyperactivity and/or impulsivity. Thomas is not the only student with ADHD in higher education. Research already shows that there is an increase in the number of students with disabilities in general, and students with ADHD in particular, who are enrolling in higher education (DuPaul et al. 2009). According to the 2014 annual report of the University of Leuven (Belgium), the number of students with a disability enrolling in higher education increased by 6% in comparison to the year before (University of Leuven 2014). This trend was noticeable in the last 10 years within the University. One of the largest groups of students with a disability enrolling in higher education is students with a psychiatric disorder, including students with ADHD (University of Leuven 2014). Overall, it is presumed that approximately 2–8% of all students in higher education experience symptoms associated with ADHD (DuPaul et al. 2009).

Despite the increasing number of students with ADHD enrolling in higher education, their chances of graduation remain low. The literature suggests that students with ADHD are more likely to repeat classes, obtain lower grade point averages and are more likely to drop out of higher education without a degree in comparison to students without a disability (Advokat, Lane, and Luo 2011; Antshel et al. 2011; DuPaul et al. 2009). These indicators of performance in higher education may result from various problems such as attention and executive functioning problems that students with ADHD experience in higher education. In this study, the term 'functioning and participation problems' is used to refer to the broad diversity of ADHD-related problems. Previous research has already mapped the functioning and participation problems of students with ADHD in higher education (Weyandt and DuPaul 2008). More recently, the reciprocal relationship between these problems and between personal and environmental characteristics has been stressed in a literature review: Emmers et al. (2016) used the International Classification of Functioning, Disability and Health (ICF; WHO 2001) to determine various functioning and participation problems (See Figure 1) that have an impact on the academic functioning of students with ADHD in higher education. This ICF framework has a broad scope on the functioning of individuals and includes both personal as well as environmental characteristics.

First, it is shown that students with ADHD can encounter problems with executive functions such as organising and planning, time management, working memory, cognitive flexibility and inhibition (Barkley and Murphy 2011; Reaser et al. 2007). Second, students with ADHD have problems with sustained and focused attention, with completing tasks and experience frequent daydreaming, hyperactivity and impulsivity (Weyandt and DuPaul 2008).

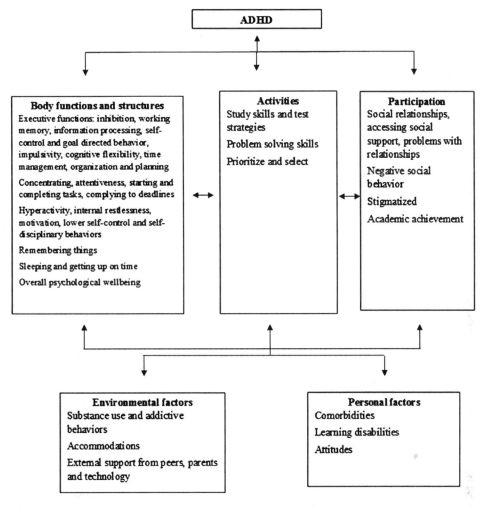

Figure 1. Functioning and participation of students with ADHD in higher education according to the ICF framework (Emmers et al., 2016).

Finally, students with ADHD can face other problems, such as problems with selecting main ideas and prioritising, social functioning and motor coordination (Reaser et al. 2007; Weyandt et al. 2013). Research on these various functioning and participation problems is, to a large extent, fragmented. Because of this, knowledge regarding the frequency and the relative impact of these experienced functioning and participation problems on academic success, measured in one sample, is unavailable. Baverstock and Finlay (2003) also mention that general practitioners or student counsellors have little knowledge regarding ADHD and the support for students with ADHD in higher education. This study aims to fill the gaps in the literature.

Second, previous studies have mainly focused on the personal characteristics (i.e. the functioning and participation problems) of students with ADHD in higher education. However, it remains unclear how often and under which environmental circumstances these problems occur in higher education (see Figure 1; Kettler 2012). Research on learning disabilities already reveals that external or environmental characteristics can cause difficulties for students with a disability in higher education (Denhart 2008). Environmental characteristics of an institution of higher education can be situated on different levels, for example: the policy of the institution, the pedagogic competences of the lecturers and also the methods used to educate students. All European institutions of higher education use the European Credit Transfer System (ECTS) to describe the various, standardised methods lecturers can use in their colleges. Because of their direct impact on the learning environment of students and because of their comparability between (European) institutions of higher education, these teaching and evaluation methods will be examined. Other environmental characteristics such as institutional policy and the number of students attending a course can influence the academic functioning of students with ADHD but have a more indirect link to the individual students with ADHD.

As a first step towards an improvement in academic functioning, both the personal (e.g. functioning and participation problems) and environmental (e.g. teaching and evaluation methods) characteristics need to be investigated. Based on this information, support can be tailored to the needs of the students with ADHD in higher education. In the setting of higher education, reasonable accommodations are often selected as adjusted measures of support for these students with ADHD (Kettler 2012). Additionally, Reaser and colleagues (2007) suggested that it is important that reasonable accommodations or adjustments respond to the experienced functioning and participation problems that students with ADHD experience in higher education. Reasonable accommodations are defined by Harrison and colleagues (Harrison et al. 2013, 6) as

> changes to practices in schools that hold a student to the same standard as students without disabilities, but provide more benefit to students with a disability (i.e. differential boost) to mediate the impact of the disability on access to the general education curriculum.

It is assumed that well-adjusted and effective reasonable accommodations are needed to enhance the academic achievement and to provide equal participation for students with ADHD in higher education and also to improve the outcomes of these students in further life (Kettler 2012). Institutions of higher education have been obligated to offer these reasonable accommodations to students with ADHD after ratifying, for instance, the UN Convention on the Rights of Persons with Disabilities (2006) or the Americans with Disabilities Act (ADA 1990).

Despite this obligation, research on the effectiveness of reasonable accommodations is scarce. The few studies that do examine the effectiveness of reasonable accommodations use a methodological design that cannot generate ADHD-specific conclusions as the participating students with ADHD are often included in a broader group of students with emotional or behavioural problems (Harrison et al. 2013). Also, the existing literature often focuses on students with ADHD in primary or secondary education (Hart et al. 2011; Pariseau et al. 2010). In view of the developmental trajectory of ADHD symptoms, it is unclear whether these results can be transferred to students with ADHD in higher education. Additional research including only students with ADHD in higher education is needed in order to guide student counsellors and educators towards implementing effective reasonable accommodations adjusted to the target group (Harrison et al. 2013).

Therefore, three research issues were addressed in this study. First, we examined how frequent the different functioning and participation problems described in the review by Emmers et al. (2016) occurred for students with ADHD in higher education and whether these problems are ADHD specific. Three groups of informants were recruited for this investigation: students with ADHD to the data of students without a disability and student counsellors. Second, we researched during which teaching and evaluation methods these functioning and participation problems emerged. Finally, we investigated which reasonable accommodations were perceived to be most effective in dealing with the functioning and participation problems of students with ADHD in higher education. The last two research questions were answered based on the reports of the participating students with ADHD.

## Method

### Participants

Students with ADHD, students without a disability and student counsellors were recruited to participate in this study. Student counsellors are professional coaches in higher education who emotionally and practically support students with a disability in general and with ADHD in particular. For instance, these counsellors help students with ADHD with planning and they select and implement reasonable accommodations. Students with ADHD were included as a target group to gain insight in their own experience regarding the three research questions. Students without a disability were recruited to examine whether the functioning and participation problems are ADHD specific, while student counsellors were included to provide a general perception on the functioning and participation problems of the average student with ADHD in higher education. The insights of student counsellors and the answers of the students without a disability were compared to the data of the students with ADHD at the group level (i.e. research question 1).

Students with ADHD could participate in the survey research when (1) they were enrolled in an institution for higher education in Flanders, (2) they were diagnosed with ADHD by a psychiatrist (and his/her multidisciplinary team) and (3) they used reasonable accommodations in higher education. In order to receive reasonable accommodations, students had to follow a formal procedure which includes providing proof of their particular condition(s). Students handed in a diagnostic report to the student counsellor, who would then validate whether this report was provided by a psychiatrist (and his/her multidisciplinary team) and if it showed that the student met the criteria for ADHD described in the fifth edition of the Diagnostic and Statistical Manual of Mental Disorders (DSM-5; APA 2013).

Students without a disability were eligible to participate when (1) they were enrolled in an institution for higher education in Flanders, and (2) they had no known disability. Student counsellors were included in the survey when (1) they were working as a student counsellor in an institution for higher education in Flanders, and (2) they were supporting students with ADHD as part of their counselling assignment.

In total, 86 students with ADHD, 42 student counsellors and 250 students without a disability participated in this study. From these 250 students without a disability, 86 were matched to the 86 students with ADHD based on three characteristics. First, the two groups of students were matched on gender and the number of years they were enrolled in higher education. In total, 51 students with ADHD and 51 without a disability were female (59.3%). The students with ADHD and the students without a disability were enrolled in higher education for approximately 3 years (ADHD: $M = 3.31$, $SD = 1.91$; without a disability: $M = 3.26$, $SD = 1.72$; $t(170) = .21$, $p > .05$). Second, the aim was to match the students with ADHD and students without a disability based on their enrolment in a professional or academic educational programme. However, the groups differed significantly with respect to this characteristic ($\chi^2(1) = 31.86$, $p < .01$), indicating that significantly more students with ADHD in our sample were enrolled in an academic educational programme ($n = 43$, 50.0%) than students without a disability ($n = 9$, 10.5%) and matching was not possible. Therefore, it was decided to match the two samples based on their enrolment in an educational programme group (i.e. (1) Humanities and Social Sciences, (2) Science, Engineering and Technology and (3) Biomedical Sciences). At group level, most of the students were enrolled in the groups Humanities and Social Sciences (ADHD: $n = 59$, 68.6%; without a disability: $n = 58$, 67.4%) and Science, Engineering and Technology (ADHD: $n = 24$, 27.9%; without a disability: $n = 18$, 20.9%; $\chi^2(2) = 4.64$, $p > .05$).

When comparing the students in the two groups, no significant differences were found in the number of years that the students were enrolled in their current institution of higher education (ADHD: $M = 2.66$, $SD = 1.79$; without a disability: $M = 2.27$, $SD = 1.11$; $\chi^2(7) = 8.39$, $p > .05$) and regarding the year of the educational programme they were attending ($\chi^2(12) = 19.51$, $p > .05$). On average, the participating students were enrolled in the second or third year of the bachelor's programme. In line with expectations, no gender differences were found with regard to characteristics related to the enrolment in higher education (e.g. the number of females and males enrolled in a professional or academic educational programme or the number of years students were enrolled in higher education), except for the enrolment in different programme groups (University of Leuven 2014). Confirming previous data (University of Leuven 2014), female students were enrolled significantly more in the group of Humanities and Social Sciences (ADHD: $n = 42$; without a disability: $n = 42$) than male students (ADHD: $n = 16$; without a disability: $n = 16$; $\chi^2(2) = 13.29$, $p = .001$).

The student counsellors were mainly female ($n = 35$; 83.3%). They had between 1 and 22 years of experience as a student counsellor in higher education ($M = 10.74$, $SD = 7.51$). One student counsellor (2.4%) worked at a university, while the other 41 student counsellors were employed in six different university colleges (96.6%).

## *Procedure*

Students with ADHD, students without a disability and student counsellors were recruited in seven different institutions of higher education in Flanders. The student counsellors received an email with an information letter explaining the design and goals of the study and an invitation to participate. Additionally, the student counsellors were asked to send this information letter to students with ADHD, who were registered as a student with a disability, and to students without a disability in their institution of higher education. Students without a disability were also recruited via social media and during lectures. If students with ADHD, students without a disability or student counsellors were interested in participating, they were asked to contact the researcher. All participants received, read and signed an informed consent if they agreed to join the study. The study was approved by the ethical committee of the department of Applied Psychology, Thomas More University College.

## *Measures*

A survey was constructed to examine the three research questions. This survey was administered online using Qualtrics software and took about 40 minutes to complete for students with ADHD. Because students without a disability and student counsellors only had to answer the questions related to the first research question, the survey took about 20 minutes to complete for these two groups of informants. The three components of the survey examined the functioning and participation problems of students with ADHD, the teaching and evaluation methods during which they experienced these problems and the effectiveness of reasonable accommodations.

## *Functioning and participation problems*
Seventeen different functioning and participation problems, found in a recent literature review, were included in a survey (Emmers et al. 2016). The frequency of occurrence of these 17 different functioning and participation problems was examined. Students with ADHD, as well as students without a disability were asked whether or not they experienced each specific problem in higher education (e.g. 'I experience impairing problems with sustaining and focusing my attention'). Students could answer each question with yes or no. Additionally, student counsellors were asked the extent to which the average student with ADHD experienced each functioning and participation problem in higher education (e.g. 'Students with ADHD experience impairing problems with sustaining and focusing their attention') on a scale from 1 (totally not present) to 10 (always present). If the answer of the student counsellor was equal to or larger than 5, the answer counted as a 'Yes'-answer in order to calculate frequencies. A panel of five academic and professional ADHD experts was invited by the authors to verify the transparency of each question for students with ADHD in higher education.

## *Teaching and evaluation methods*
When students with ADHD reported a specific problem in higher education (i.e. when they had given a 'Yes'-answer), they were asked during which teaching and evaluation methods this problem emerged (e.g. 'During which types of teaching and evaluation methods do you experience this problem with sustaining and focusing attention?'). The students were given 14 different teaching and evaluation methods for each experienced problem, which were described in the ECTS, for example: a lecture or a closed book exam. An overview of these methods can be found in the results section (Table 3). The description of each of these methods was listed in Supplemental file 1. For each functioning and participation problem, the students had to tick off during which types of methods they experienced a specific problem. It was possible to tick off multiple methods.

## *Effective reasonable accommodations*
For each experienced functioning and participation problem, a number of reasonable accommodations used by students with ADHD were predetermined through a literature search (Harrison et al. 2013). Afterwards, an expert panel was invited to appoint the reasonable accommodations to specific functioning and participation problems, taking the specific objective of each reasonable accommodation into account. For example, the functioning and participation problem 'planning and organising' was linked to the following reasonable accommodations: extended examination duration (i.e. to compensate the difficulty with planning during an exam) or visual time indication (i.e. to help students with time management). This list of reasonable accommodations, combined with specific functioning and participation problems, was presented to students with ADHD. First, students had to indicate

if they were offered a particular reasonable accommodation to deal with a specific problem (e.g. 'Was extended examination duration offered to you to deal with your impairing problem with planning and organising?'). Second, all students with ADHD had to rate the experienced (when they used the accommodation) or expected effectiveness (when they did not use it) on a five-point Likert scale (1: very ineffective to 5: very effective). Finally, if students with ADHD used reasonable accommodations that were not listed in the survey, they could add these accommodations and rate their experienced effectiveness. However, only two students with ADHD added a reasonable accommodation and rated the experienced effectiveness. As a rule of thumb, a cut-off score of 3 out of 5 for perceived effectiveness of a reasonable accommodation was used. Reasonable accommodations that scored less than 3 out of 5 were not considered to be effective and are not listed in the results. Additionally, at least 10% or more of students with ADHD had to rate the perceived effectiveness in order to be included in this study.

## Analyses

### Descriptive statistics

Frequencies were used to analyse the functioning and participation problems (i.e. research question 1), while frequencies, ranges, means and standard deviations were adopted to analyse the perceived effectiveness of reasonable accommodations (i.e. research question 3). Finally, chi square statistics were used to compare data from students with ADHD with the data of the student counsellors and students without a disability with respect to the first research question.

### Two-mode partitioning

Two-mode partitioning was used to gain insight into the probability with which the functioning and participation problems of students with ADHD emerged during the teaching and evaluation methods (i.e. research question 2). Specifically, since both the functioning and participation problems and the teaching and evaluation methods contained a large number of items, the number of items was reduced by simultaneously clustering both variables using two-mode partitioning. In this approach, two functioning and participation problems are assigned to the same cluster, if they show up as equally likely during the teaching and evaluation methods. Similarly, two methods are classified in the same cluster, if they elicit different functioning and participation problems to a similar extent (Schepers and Hofmans 2009). In this study, the number of clusters in the solution had not previously been determined. Therefore, we looked at different models and selected one based on interpretability on the one hand, and goodness-of-fit vs. the complexity balance on the other hand (i.e. using the CHull procedure; Schepers, Ceulemans, and Van Mechelen 2008). Next, the two-mode partitioning yields a so-called core matrix which reflects the strength of the relationship between each cluster of problems and each cluster of methods. In the literature, no rule of thumb had been described to interpret these core values. Here, we decided to interpret these values in terms of a probability. This means that, if the core value is .50, then students with ADHD have a 50% chance of experiencing this specific cluster of functioning and participation problem during the specific cluster of teaching and evaluation methods.

# Results

## Functioning and participation problems

The results regarding the frequency of experienced functioning and participation problems can be found in Table 1.

The results showed that the most frequently experienced functioning and participation problems by students with ADHD in higher education were problems with sustaining and focusing attention, frequent daydreaming, difficulty completing tasks and difficulty planning and organising. When comparing the answers of the student counsellors to the results of the students with ADHD, two significant differences were found. The frequency of difficulty sitting still ($\chi^2(1) = 4.96, p < .05$) and impulsivity problems ($\chi^2(1) = 4.04, p < .05$) was rated higher by student counsellors than by students with ADHD themselves. However, students with ADHD and student counsellors were consistent in reporting the frequency of occurrence of all other functioning and participation problems. Furthermore, students without a disability experienced all functioning and participation problems significantly less frequently than students with ADHD except for losing things ($\chi^2(1) = 3.30, p > .05$) and having few or no friends ($\chi^2(1) = .012, p > .05$), indicating that these two functioning and participation problems occurred to the same extent in both groups of students.

Table 1. Functioning and participation problems of students with and without ADHD according to the students and student counsellors.

|  | Students with ADHD N | Students with ADHD % | Students without ADHD N | Students without ADHD % | Student counsellors N | Student counsellors % |
|---|---|---|---|---|---|---|
| Sustained and focused attention problems | 69 | 95.8 | 46 | 53.5 | 40 | 95.2 |
| Daydreaming | 51 | 79.7 | 45 | 53.6 | 27 | 75.0 |
| Difficulty completing tasks | 47 | 71.2 | 33 | 38.8 | 29 | 80.6 |
| Difficulty planning and organising | 41 | 70.7 | 37 | 44.6 | 27 | 79.4 |
| Internal restlessness | 40 | 63.5 | 22 | 26.2 | 20 | 55.6 |
| Impulsive behaviour[a] | 35 | 55.6 | 22 | 26.2 | 27 | 75.0 |
| Making careless mistakes | 31 | 55.4 | 20 | 23.8 | 18 | 56.3 |
| Difficulty prioritising | 30 | 52.6 | 19 | 22.9 | 19 | 57.6 |
| Forgetful | 29 | 51.8 | 24 | 28.6 | 15 | 50.0 |
| Working memory problems | 25 | 43.1 | 12 | 14.5 | 17 | 50.0 |
| Difficulty following instructions | 19 | 33.9 | 3 | 3.6 | 15 | 48.4 |
| Losing things[b] | 19 | 33.9 | 17 | 20.2 | 11 | 36.7 |
| Difficulty with cognitive flexibility | 18 | 30.5 | 3 | 3.6 | 16 | 45.7 |
| Difficulty with coordination | 20 | 31.7 | 2 | 2.4 | 12 | 34.3 |
| Not listening when being spoken to | 20 | 30.3 | 10 | 11.8 | 12 | 33.3 |
| Difficulty sitting still[a] | 19 | 30.2 | 6 | 7.1 | 19 | 52.8 |
| Few or no friends[b] | 3 | 5.4 | 4 | 4.9 | 3 | 10.0 |

[a]Significant difference between students with ADHD and student counsellors ($p < .05$). [b]Non-significant difference between students with and without ADHD ($p > .05$).

## Functioning and participation problems during teaching and evaluation methods

The two-mode partitioning yielded a model with four clusters of functioning and participation problems (Table 2) and five clusters of teaching and evaluation methods (Table 3). This model accounted for 82.99% of the variance in how often particular problems showed up during specific methods.

The core values that displayed the strength of the relationship between each cluster of functioning and participation problems with each cluster of teaching and evaluation methods are shown in Table 4. According to the results, the chances of experiencing attention problems (probability = .82), regulation problems (probability = .70), social problems (probability = .67) and inefficient study skills (probability = .58) were highest during classical teaching methods. Additionally, students with ADHD also had a high chance of experiencing

**Table 2.** Clusters of functioning and participation problems.

| Cluster 1 | Cluster 2 | Cluster 3 | Cluster 4 |
|---|---|---|---|
| Attention problems | Inefficient study skills | Regulation problems | Social problems |
| Problems sustaining and focusing attention | Difficulty with completing tasks | Impulsive behaviour | Few or no friends |
| Daydreaming | Difficulty planning and organising | Losing things | |
| Internal restlessness | Difficulty following instructions | Difficulty sitting still | |
| Difficulty prioritising | Making careless mistakes | Problems with cognitive flexibility | |
| Forgetfulness | | Not listening when being spoken to | |
| Working memory problems | | Difficulty with motor coordination | |

**Table 3.** Clusters of ECTS teaching and evaluation methods.

| Cluster 1 | Cluster 2 | Cluster 3 | Cluster 4 | Cluster 5 |
|---|---|---|---|---|
| Classical teaching methods | Activating teaching methods | Classical evaluation methods | Alternative evaluation methods | Thesis |
| Lecture | Excursion | Writing a paper | Oral exam | Bachelor or master thesis |
| Practical | Internship | Closed book exam | Practical exam | |
| | Self- or peer evaluation | Open book exam | Portfolio | |
| | Process evaluation | Multiple-choice exam | | |

**Table 4.** Core values of the two-mode partitioning.

| | Classical teaching methods | Activating teaching methods | Classical evaluation methods | Alternative evaluation methods | Bachelor or master thesis |
|---|---|---|---|---|---|
| Attentional problems | 0.82 | 0.31 | 0.69 | 0.49 | 0.49 |
| Inefficient study skills | 0.58 | 0.21 | 0.65 | 0.48 | 0.45 |
| Regulation problems | 0.70 | 0.23 | 0.40 | 0.34 | 0.25 |
| Social problems | 0.67 | 0.00 | 0.08 | 0.00 | 0.67 |

attention problems and inefficient study skills during classical evaluation methods (probability = .69 and .65) while there was a high chance of encountering social problems when writing a thesis (probability = .67). The chances of experiencing attention problems, regulation problems and inefficient study skills were lowest during the activating teaching methods (probabilities, respectively, .31, .23, and .21). Other results can be found in Table 4.

### *Effective reasonable accommodations*

The perceived effective reasonable accommodations for each functioning and participation problem are listed in Table 5. Five functioning and participation problems, namely: losing things (cluster 1), not listening when being spoken to (cluster 1), daydreaming (cluster 3), internal restlessness (cluster 3) and having less or no friends (cluster 4), were not included in the table since no effective reasonable accommodations were found to deal with these problems.

Within the cluster 'attention problems', effective reasonable accommodation was identified by students with ADHD for four functioning and participation problems (see Table 5). For three out of four functioning and participation problems, the reasonable accommodation of extended examination duration was reported as the most effective. Besides this effectiveness, ADHD students with attentional problems also reported this accommodation as most used ($n$ = 92.8%). For students who described themselves as being forgetful, only one effective reasonable accommodation, namely: alternative exam format (i.e. changing a written exam into an oral exam), was defined. However, only a small group of students reporting forgetfulness (20%) used this accommodation, meaning that this result cannot be generalised for all students with ADHD.

Within the cluster 'inefficient study skills', effective reasonable accommodations were mentioned for all four functioning and participation problems (see Table 5). Extended examination duration was perceived to be effective in dealing with all four functioning and participation problems. Additionally, exam deferral was shown to be most effective for students who experienced problems with planning and organising. Other effective reasonable accommodations were identified for each functioning and participation problem and can be found in Table 5.

The results of the cluster 'regulation problems' showed that for each functioning and participation problem, only one or two effective reasonable accommodations were reported (see Table 5). For example, students with ADHD who experienced impulsive behaviour perceived an alternative exam format as effective.

Finally, students with ADHD, who encountered a specific functioning and participation problem but did not use a specific reasonable accommodation, had to rate the expected effectiveness of each reasonable accommodation. It was shown that the expected effectiveness was typically lower than the experienced effectiveness of students with ADHD who did use the reasonable accommodation. Significant differences are marked in Table 5 using an asterisk (*).

## Discussion

This study examined three research questions, namely: (1) how frequent the different functioning and participation problems occurred for students with ADHD in higher education

**Table 5.** Effective reasonable accommodations for the functioning and participation problems within each cluster.

| Attentional problems | | N used (%) | M (SD) Experienced[a] | Range | M (SD) Perceived[b] |
|---|---|---|---|---|---|
| Sustaining and focusing attention problems | Extended examination duration | 64 (92.8) | 4.44 (1.04) | 1–5 | 3.60 (1.34)** |
| | Designated seat during exam room | 13 (18.8) | 4.15 (1.07) | 2–5 | 2.32 (1.30)*** |
| | Visual time indication | 35 (50.7) | 4.03 (1.07) | 1–5 | 3.68 (1.47) |
| | More time for tasks | 11 (15.9) | 4.00 (1.34) | 1–5 | 3.29 (1.50) |
| | Taking the exam in smaller groups | 19 (27.5) | 3.68 (1.38) | 1–5 | 2.60 (1.51) |
| | Using a computer during lectures | 21 (30.4) | 3.43 (1.29) | 1–5 | 2.31 (1.26)* |
| | Recording the lecture | 19 (20.3) | 3.29 (1.14) | 2–5 | 2.76 (1.49)* |
| Difficulty prioritising | Extended examination duration | 28 (93.3) | 4.57 (.84) | 2–5 | 1.00 (0.00)*** |
| | Oral explanation | 9 (30.0) | 4.33 (.87) | 3–5 | 3.29 (1.45) |
| | Alternative exam format | 7 (23.3) | 3.37 (1.40) | 1–5 | 2.61 (1.53) |
| Forgetful | Alternative exam format | 6 (20.7) | 3.33 (1.37) | 1–5 | 2.86 (1.46) |
| Working memory problems | Extended examination duration | 24 (96.0) | 4.79 (.51) | 3–5 | 3.00 (/)** |
| | Exam deferral | 10 (40.0) | 4.40 (1.27) | 1–5 | 3.60 (1.06)* |
| | Using a computer | 5 (20.0) | 3.40 (1.52) | 1–5 | 2.25 (1.07) |
| *Inefficient study skills* | | | | | |
| Difficulty completing tasks | Extended examination duration | 41 (87.2) | 4.54 (.84) | 1–5 | 2.33 (1.63)*** |
| | Taking the exam in smaller groups | 14 (29.8) | 4.23 (1.09) | 2–5 | 2.35 (1.37)** |
| | Oral explanation | 13 (27.7) | 3.71 (1.20) | 1–5 | 3.18 (1.45) |
| | Using a computer during lectures | 14 (29.8) | 3.64 (1.34) | 1–5 | 2.39 (1.30)** |
| Planning and organising | Exam deferral | 12 (29.3) | 4.58 (.67) | 3–5 | 3.79 (1.37) |
| | Extended examination duration | 40 (97.6) | 4.50 (.91) | 1–5 | 1.00 (0.00)*** |
| | Visual time indication | 25 (61.0) | 4.16 (.99) | 2–5 | 3.13 (1.63)* |
| | Support from student counsellor | 17 (41.5) | 3.88 (1.11) | 1–5 | 3.67 (1.27) |
| Difficulty following instructions | Extended examination duration | 18 (94.7) | 4.22 (1.11) | 2–5 | 3.00 (/) |
| | Oral explanation | 5 (26.3) | 3.40 (1.34) | 1–5 | 3.00 (1.62) |
| Making careless mistakes | Extended examination duration | 31 (100.0) | 4.29 (1.10) | 3–5 | / |
| | Oral explanation | 9 (29.0) | 4.22 (.83) | 3–5 | 3.18 (1.53) |
| | Alternative examination format | 6 (19.4) | 3.83 (.98) | | 2.80 (1.44) |
| *Regulation problems* | | | | | |
| Impulsive behaviour | Alternative examination format | 6 (17.1) | 4.17 (1.17) | 2–5 | 2.59 (0.27) |
| Difficulty sitting still | Taking the exam in smaller groups | 6 (31.6) | 4.50 (0.22) | 4–5 | 3.00 (0.39) |
| Difficulty with cognitive flexibility | Using a computer during lectures | 8 (44.4) | 3.63 (1.77) | 1–5 | 2.60 (1.51) |
| Difficulty with motor coordination | Using a computer during lectures | 8 (40.0) | 3.00 (1.60) | 1–5 | 2.50 (1.17) |
| | Using a computer during exams | 4 (20.0) | 3.00 (1.41) | 1–4 | 2.44 (1.41) |

[a]Perceived effectiveness rated by students with ADHD who used the reasonable accommodation to deal with the specific functioning and participation problem. [b]Expected effectiveness rated by students with ADHD who did not use the reasonable accommodation but did experience the specific functioning and participation problem. *Significant difference between the experienced and perceived effectiveness of an accommodation ($p < .05$); **Significant difference between the experienced and perceived effectiveness of an accommodation ($p < .01$); ***Significant difference between the experienced and perceived effectiveness of an accommodation ($p < .001$).

and if these problems are ADHD specific, (2) during which teaching and evaluation methods these problems emerged and (3) which reasonable accommodations were perceived to be most effective in dealing with the functioning and participation problems of students with ADHD in higher education. In order to examine the first research question, students with ADHD, student counsellors and students without a disability participated in a survey research. The recruitment of three groups of informants allowed us to compare the answers of students with ADHD with the perception of student counsellors and to the occurrence of the functioning and participation problems in a general sample of students without a disability. The other two research questions were answered by students with ADHD only. Students with ADHD were diagnosed by a psychiatrist (and his/her multidisciplinary team). This meets the Belgian and several international guidelines which stipulate that the psychiatrist coordinates the diagnostic research in cooperation with a multidisciplinary team consisting of a psychologist, a physical therapist and a speech therapist, amongst others (National Institute for Health and Clinical Excellence 2008; Superior Health Council 2013). This multidisciplinary team, supervised by a psychiatrist, is primarily needed because of the high chances of comorbid disorders for individuals with ADHD (OCD, learning disabilities; Gilbert 2005; Weyandt and DuPaul 2006).

With respect to the first research question, it was concluded that, on a group level, students with ADHD primarily experienced problems with sustaining and focusing attention, frequent daydreaming, completing tasks and planning and organising. These findings are consistent with literature regarding this topic (DuPaul et al. 2009).

Furthermore, two significant differences were found between the reports of students with ADHD and student counsellors. Student counsellors rated the occurrence of difficulty sitting still and impulsive behaviour significantly more frequently than students with ADHD. On the one hand, this may indicate that student counsellors have little knowledge about the developmental perspective of ADHD symptoms, namely that impulsivity and hyperactivity decrease and attention problems remain stable with increasing age (Rao 2004). On the other hand, it is possible that students with ADHD lack self-insight and self-knowledge and tend to underreport the severity of their impairment (Kooij et al. 2008).

Moreover, no differences between students with ADHD and without a disability were found for social problems (i.e. having few or no friends) and for losing things. This result could mean that students with ADHD are equal to students without a disability with regard to experiencing these problems in higher education and these problems are not ADHD specific. However, it is also possible that the students with ADHD underreported the severity of their problems. Another explanation could be that by the time these students enrol in higher education, they have learned how to cope with these difficulties through intervention programmes (for example, by interacting appropriately, by making lists and/or putting everything in the same place). Unfortunately, no information regarding previous treatment was obtained during this study. With respect to the other functioning and participation problems, it became clear that students with ADHD do experience these problems significantly more frequently than students without a disability.

To answer the second research question, the functioning and participation problems were clustered in four groups. These clusters are in line with the literature, where attentional problems are always discussed as one large group of impairing symptoms of ADHD, as well as symptoms of hyperactivity and impulsivity (regulation problems) and study skills (APA 2013; Weyandt and DuPaul 2008). The fourth group, namely: social problems, was separated in a cluster, probably because of the low frequency of occurrence in comparison to other problems. Second, the teaching and evaluation methods were clustered into five groups. Consistent with the literature (Struyven, Dochy, and Janssens 2008), classical and activating teaching methods were separated. It became clear that the probability of experiencing problems was highest during classical teaching and evaluation methods, except for the low chance of experiencing social problems during classical evaluation methods. These classical teaching and evaluation methods are implemented very frequently in higher education, hereby increasing the chances for students with ADHD to encounter problems. At the same time, it was shown that the probability of experiencing problems during alternative evaluation methods and during activating teaching methods was lower. This is in line with previous literature regarding students with ADHD in primary and secondary education, suggesting that the performance of these students increases when they can participate actively (Farrell 2008).

Lastly, the students with ADHD rated the effectiveness of reasonable accommodations. It was concluded that the implementation of reasonable accommodations is important as each student with ADHD rated at least one reasonable accommodation as effective and thus helpful in dealing with their specific functioning and participation problems. In line with previous research, extended examination duration was most used by the students with ADHD in this study (Kettler 2012). In addition, this reasonable accommodation was also perceived as the most effective to deal with the majority of functioning and participation problems. As indicated by the wide range of the effectiveness scores, not all students experiencing a specific problem perceived the same reasonable accommodations as effective. This should be taken into account when offering reasonable accommodations to students with ADHD. As expected, the results also indicate that not all functioning and participation problems could be neutralised using reasonable accommodations.

When finally looking at the expected effectiveness scores of students with ADHD, it was found that students with ADHD, who did not use a specific reasonable accommodation, assumed that it would not be helpful for them. Research has already suggested that students have a hard time imagining if and which accommodations would be helpful because they receive inadequate or insufficient information regarding these accommodations (Magnus and Tøssebro 2014). In addition, the perceived effectiveness of accommodations is influenced by the perception and attitude of the student counsellors and the faculty or institution of higher education (Hong and Himmel 2009). Furthermore, research already suggested that students with ADHD refuse reasonable accommodations because they are afraid of being stigmatised by peers or want to succeed on their own (Denhart 2008). Alternatively, it is also possible that reasonable accommodations were well adjusted to the personal characteristics of the students with ADHD and the environmental characteristics of the institution of higher education and thus were not expected be effective for these specific students with ADHD.

## *Limitations*

We recognise that this study has its limitations. First, using a two-mode partitioning results in a reduction of data and also in a loss of detail. However, this statistical analysis was used to make the data more manageable and to provide a general insight into when these functioning and participation problems occur in higher education. It does not imply that the details were not important and that student counsellors do not have to take individual differences between students with ADHD into account.

Second, only teaching and evaluation methods were selected to represent environmental characteristics that could impact the functioning and participation of students with ADHD in higher education. No higher level variables were included in this study (e.g. participation rate in higher education, social inclusion and/or policy of the institution). However, this does not imply that these variables are not important. Future research should also focus on other environmental and personal characteristics, for example: level of participation and academic integration.

Third, reasonable accommodations were listed in the results section if 10% or more of students with ADHD rated the experienced effectiveness (and thus used the reasonable accommodation) in order to avoid a too low a sample size. This means that some reasonable accommodations were removed from the results because only one or two students used the reasonable accommodation, regardless of whether the accommodation was perceived as effective or not. As stated previously, the effectiveness of reasonable accommodations is highly individual. Therefore, it is important for student counsellors to also take into account other, not listed, reasonable accommodations.

Finally, students with ADHD were asked for their subjective opinion on whether or not the used reasonable accommodation was effective. Future research is needed to examine whether reasonable accommodations also have an objective positive effect on the test scores of students with ADHD in higher education, as is suggested by Miller, Lewandowski, and Antshel (2015). Additionally, in order to gain insight into the effectiveness of reasonable accommodations, researchers should focus on why students with ADHD reported that some reasonable accommodations were effective while others were not used and were presumed to be not helpful for them. This way, reasonable accommodations could be selected more carefully and students with ADHD could have equal chances in higher education as students without disabilities

## *Implications for practice*

The results of this study have many practical implications. It was shown that students with ADHD can experience various functioning and participation problems and that these problems vary between students with ADHD. During a first counselling session between the student with ADHD and their student counsellor, the individual problems of the student should be identified. This first counselling session is critical because students with a disability can feel misunderstood (Denhart 2008). Student counsellors should be aware of this issue when talking to students with a disability and avoid presumptions by asking lots of questions and checking their interpretations during the entire session. In addition, it is important that student counsellors also acknowledge the strengths of students with ADHD and integrate these strengths in the support they offer these students in higher education. Second, it is important to make an inventory of the teaching and evaluation methods of the educational programme of the student with ADHD.

Based on these two parameters, student counsellors can propose reasonable accommodations that can be effective for the individual student with ADHD. Reasonable accommodations that can be offered within a specific institution should be listed during an open dialogue between student counsellors, policy-makers, representatives of students and the director of the institution. The proposed reasonable accommodations should then be discussed with the student with ADHD in order to choose the accommodations that were perceived to be effective to deal with specific functioning and participation problems, as was shown in this study. Student counsellors should be aware of the fact that external factors, such as the perception of other students and the fear of being misunderstood, could be the reason why students with ADHD are reluctant to use reasonable accommodations (Denhart 2008). The effectiveness of reasonable accommodations should be emphasised by student counsellors in order to increase the chances of success for students with ADHD. Alternatively, research suggests that coaching or peer-based support can be useful when students with ADHD are reluctant to use reasonable accommodations because they want to be able to succeed on their own. These coaching sessions enhance the competences, executive functioning and general self-efficacy of students with ADHD in higher education (Parker and Boutelle 2009; Zwart and Kallemeyn 2001).

Because of the large range of effectiveness scores, and in line with previous research, it should always be kept in mind that the effectiveness of reasonable accommodations cannot be generalised to all students with a specific disability and that reasonable accommodations should be selected based on the individual needs of the student (Sireci, Scarpati, and Li 2005) Therefore, student mentors should be open to evaluate and reconsider the implemented reasonable accommodations if the individual student with ADHD reports that the accommodations are not working for them.

Additionally, student counsellors could promote the use of the principles of Universal Design for Learning (UDL) to teachers and professors (CAST 2008). The use of these principles could help students with ADHD as well as students without a disability, by providing equal opportunities to learn. UDL states that teachers and professors could adapt to the diversity within the group of students using multiple means of representation, expression and engagement (CAST 2008). For example, by adding visual cues in the lecture or giving a short break, students with ADHD could stay more focused and learn more during the lecture.

Finally, additional support, within or outside the educational context, should be considered if reasonable accommodations are not sufficient. Examples of additional support are psycho-education, psychopharmacological treatment or psychosocial interventions such as planning and organisation training (Boyer et al. 2014).

In summary, this study has presented and supported the hypothesis that students with ADHD frequently face various functioning and participation problems in higher education. It was also shown that the occurrence of a problem is often dependent on the teaching and evaluation methods used. Finally, results have indicated that reasonable accommodations should be selected based on both personal and environmental characteristics and that the effectiveness of reasonable accommodations is dependent on various factors, namely: the experienced functioning and participation problems, the personal preferences of a student with ADHD and environmental characteristics of the institution. The latter conclusion is important for student counsellors to take into account when implementing reasonable accommodations and to guide future research that investigates the effectiveness of reasonable accommodations on an objective performance rating (e.g. test scores). We hope that with this information in hand, student counsellors, faculty and administrators will be better equipped to help students with ADHD, like Thomas, participate and succeed in higher education.

## Acknowledgements

This article was performed as part of a research project on reasonable accommodations in higher education, supported by the Education Development Fund of University of Leuven Association.

## Disclosure statement

No potential conflict of interest was reported by the authors.

## Funding

This work was supported by the Education Development Fund of University of Leuven Association.

## References

Advokat, C., S. M. Lane, and C. Luo. 2011. "College Students with and without ADHD: Comparison of Self-report of Medication Usage, Study Habits, and Academic Achievement." *Journal of Attention Disorders* 15: 656–666. doi:10.1177/1087054710371168.
ADA (Americans with Disabilities Act). 1990. *Public Law 101-336. 42 U.S.C. 12111, 12112*.
Antshel, Kevin, Teresa Hargrave, Mihai Simonescu, Prashant Kaul, Kaitlin Hendricks, and Stephen Faraone. 2011. "Advances in Understanding and Treating ADHD." *BMC Medicine* 9 (72): 1–12. doi:10.1186/1741-7015-9-72.
APA (American Psychiatric Association). 2013. *Diagnostic and Statistical Manual of Mental Disorders*. 5th ed. Arlington, VA: American Psychiatric Publishing.
Barkley, Russell A., and Kevin R. Murphy. 2011. "The Nature of Executive Function (EF) Deficits in Daily Life Activities in Adults with ADHD and Their Relationship to Performance on EF Tests." *Journal of Psychopathology and Behavioral Assessment* 33: 137–158. doi:10.1007/s10862-011-9217-x.
Baverstock, A. C., and F. Finlay. 2003. "Who Manages the Care of Students with Attention Deficit Hyperactivity Disorder (ADHD) in Higher Education?" *Child: Care, Health and Development* 29 (3): 163–166. doi:10.1046/j.1365-2214.2003.00327.x.

Boyer, B. E., H. M. Geurts, P. J. Prins, and S. Van der Oord. 2014. "Two Novel CBTs for Adolescents with ADHD: The Value of Planning Skills." *European Child and Adolescent Psychiatry* 24 (9): 1075–1090. doi:10.1007/s00787-014-0661-5.

CAST. 2008. *Universal Design for Learning Guidelines Version 1.0.* Wakefield, MA: CAST.

Denhart, H. 2008. "Deconstructing Barriers: Perceptions of Students Labeled with Learning Disabilities in Higher Education." *Journal of Learning Disabilities* 41 (6): 483–497. doi:10.1177/0022219408321151.

DuPaul, G. J., L. L. Weyandt, S. M. O'Dell, and M. Varejao. 2009. "College Students with ADHD: Current Status and Future Directions." *Journal of Attention Disorders* 13 (3): 234–250. doi:10.1177/1087054709340650.

Emmers, E., D. Jansen, K. Petry, S. van der Oord, and D. Baeyens. 2016. "Functioning and Participation of Students with ADHD in Higher Education according to the ICF-framework, a Systematic Literature Review." *Journal of Further and Higher Education.* Advanced online publication. doi:10.1080/0309877X.2015.1117600.

Farrell, M. 2008. *Educating Special Children. an Introduction to Provision for Pupils with Disabilities and Disorders.* New York: Routledge.

Gilbert, P. 2005. "Attention-deficit/Hyperactivity Disorder in Community College Students: A Seldom Considered Factor in Academic Success." *Journal of Social Work in Disability and Rehabilitation* 4 (1-2): 57–75. doi:10.1300/j198v04n01_04.

Harrison, Judith R., Nora Bunford, Steven W. Evans, and Julie S. Owens. 2013. "Educational Accommodations for Students with Behavioral Challenges: A Systematic Review of the Literature." *Review of Educational Research* 83 (4): 551–597. doi:10.3102/0034654313497517.

Hart, Katie, Greta Massetti, Gregory Fabiano, Meaghan Pariseau, and William Pelham. 2011. "Impact of Group Size on Classroom On-task Behavior and Work Productivity in Children with ADHD." *Journal of Emotional and Behavioral Disorders* 19 (1): 55–64. doi:10.1177/1063426609353762.

Hong, Barbara S. S., and Joy Himmel. 2009. "Faculty Attitudes and Perceptions toward College Students with Disabilities." *College Quarterly*, 12 (3): 1–15. http://collegequarterly.ca/2009-vol12-num03-summer/hong-himmel.html.

Kettler, Ryan J. 2012. "Testing Accommodations: Theory and Research to Inform Practice." *International Journal of Disability, Development and Education* 59 (1): 53–66. doi:10.1080/1034912X.2012.654952.

Kooij, J. J. S., A. M. Boonstra, S. H. N. Swinkels, E. M. Bekker, I. de Noord, and J. K. Buitelaar. 2008. "Reliability, Validity, and Utility of Instruments for Self-Report and Informant Report concerning Symptoms of ADHD in Adult Patients." *Journal of Attention Disorders* 11 (4): 445–458. doi:10.1177/1087054707299367.

Magnus, Eva, and Jan Tøssebro. 2014. "Negotiating Individual Accommodation in Higher Education." *Scandinavian Journal of Disability Research* 16 (4): 316–332. doi:10.1080/15017419.2012.761156.

Miller, Laura A., Lawrence J. Lewandowski, and Kevin M. Antshel. 2015. "Effects of Extended Time for College Students with and without ADHD." *Journal of Attention Disorders* 19 (8): 678–686. doi:10.1177/1087054713483308.

National Institute for Health and Clinical Excellence. 2008. *Annual Report and Accounts.* London: NICE.

Pariseau, Meaghan, Gregory Fabiano, Greta Massetti, Katie Hart, and William Pelham. 2010. "Extended Time on Academic Assignments: Does Increased Time Lead to Improved Performance for Children with Attention-Deficit/Hyperactivity Disorder?" *School Psychology Quarterly* 25 (4): 236–248. doi:10.1037/a0022045.

Parker, David R., and Karen Boutelle. 2009. "Executive Function Coaching for College Students with Learning Disabilities and ADHD: A New Approach for Fostering Self-determination." *Learning Disabilities Research and Practice* 24 (4): 204–215. doi:10.1111/j.1540-5826.2009.00294.x.

Rao, Shaila. 2004. "Faculty Attitudes and Students with Disabilities in Higher Education: A Literature Review." *College Student Journal* 38 (2): 191–198. doi:10.5539/ies.v6n12p74.

Reaser, Abigail, Frances Prevatt, Yaacov Petscher, and Briley Proctor. 2007. "The Learning and Study Strategies of College Students with ADHD." *Psychology in the Schools* 44 (6): 627–638. doi:10.1002/pits.20252.

Schepers, J., E. Ceulemans, and I. Van Mechelen. 2008. "Selecting among Multi-mode Partitioning Models of Different Complexities: A Comparison of Four Model Selection Criteria." *Journal of Classification* 25: 67–85. doi:10.1007/s00357-008-9005-9.

Schepers, J., and J. Hofmans. 2009. "TwoMP: A MATLAB Graphical User Interface for Two-mode Partitioning." *Behavior Research Methods* 41 (2): 507–514. doi:10.3758/BRM.41.2.507.

Sireci, S. G., S. E. Scarpati, and S. Li. 2005. "Test Accommodations for Students with Disabilities: An Analysis of the Interaction Hypothesis." *Review of Educational Research* 75 (4): 457–490. doi:10.3102/00346543075004457.

Struyven, Katrien, Filip Dochy, and Steven Janssens. 2008. "Students' Likes and Dislikes regarding Student-activating and Lecture-based Educational Settings: Consequences for Students' Perceptions of the Learning Environment, Student Learning and Performance." *European Journal of Psychology of Education* 23 (3): 295–317. doi:10.1007/BF03173001.

Superior Health Council. 2013. *Good Clinical Practice in the Recognition, Diagnosis and Treatment of ADHD*. Brussels: Superior Health Council.

United Nations. December 13, 2006. *Convention on the Rights of Persons with Disabilities*. [Dutch version]. http://www.ond.vlaanderen.be/leerzorg/VN/verdrag.pdf.

University of Leuven. 2014. *Annual Report 2013–2014*. Belgium: University of Leuven.

Weyandt, L. L., and G. J. DuPaul. 2006. "ADHD in College Students." *Journal of Attention Disorders* 10 (1): 9–19. doi:10.1177/1087054705286061.

Weyandt, L. L., and G. J. DuPaul. 2008. "ADHD in College Students: Developmental Findings." *Developmental Disabilities Research Reviews* 14 (4): 311–319. doi:10.1002/ddrr.38.

Weyandt, L. L., G. J. DuPaul, G. Verdi, J. S. Rossi, A. J. Scentosky, B. S. Vilardo, S. M. O'Dell, and K. S. Carson. 2013. "The Performance of College Students with and without ADHD: Neuropsychological, Academic, and Psychological Functioning." *Journal of Psychological Behavioural Assessment* 35 (4): 421–435. doi: 10.1007/s10862-013-9351-8.

WHO (World Health Organization). 2001. *International Classification of Functioning, Disability and Health (ICF)*. Geneva: WHO.

Zwart, L. M., L. M. Kallemeyn. 2001. "Peer-based Coaching for College Students with ADHD and Learning Disabilities." *Journal of Postsecondary Education and Disability* 15 (1): 1–15. http://eric.ed.gov/?id=EJ653965.

**Supplemental file 1.** Explanation of the 14 different teaching and evaluation methods.

| | Teaching methods |
|---|---|
| **Lecture** | A lecture is a teaching method in which the teacher offers instruction to the entire group of students that enrolled for the course. Lectures can be interactive to a greater or lesser extent; the teacher remains the most important actor. |
| **Practical** | A practical is a teaching method with a consistently high level of interaction between teacher and student, with the teacher acting like a guide/coach. The guidance of the teacher during the contact hours can consist of: <br> • supervision by the teacher and/or teaching staff during exercises; <br> • assistance with individual assignments; <br> • discussions between students, the teacher, and/or the teaching staff; <br> • discussions of assignments given in advance or other input by the students. <br><br> Practicals are usually offered for smaller groups of students. The entire group can be divided into series to this end. |
| **Excursion** | An excursion is a teaching method in which students (on the basis of information structured in advance) are confronted in the field with one or more concrete applications or phenomena; the students discuss the observations and findings with the teacher/teaching staff. |
| **Internship** | An internship is a supervised practical training for students, so they can develop professional competences in confrontation with practice on the job. |
| **Self- or peer- evaluation** | Teaching staff need not be the only ones evaluating students; the students themselves may also have a role in the evaluation process. Students can evaluate themselves on the basis of criteria defined in advance (self-assessment). They may also evaluate students in a particular group or (some of) their fellow group members (peer-assessment). |
| **Process evaluation** | A process evaluation refers to the systematic gathering of information about the learning process curve. The final result of the learning process is not the only focus here; instead, the emphasis is especially on the way in which the student realized and strove to attain the objectives. |
| | Evaluation methods |
| **Writing a paper** | A paper is a written product that is the result of a particular task in which students demonstrate that they are engaging with a field of study content-wise, that they can approach and solve a problem like experts, and that they have acquired certain competences (e.g. consulting and processing literature). As an evaluation method, a paper is similar to a take-home exam. A paper, however, encompasses a broader task than the take-home exam. The student also works on it for a longer time period. A project is a variant of the paper, smaller in scope, and it can take different forms (short assignment, exercise, etc.) |
| **Closed book exam** | A written exam is an evaluation method in which the student is given questions that s/he is to answer (sometimes electronically). The answers are used to assess the extent to which the student masters the course objectives. There is no direct contact between the student and the examiner. Both open and close-ended questions can be used in written exams. Specifically, during a closed book exam, the students cannot use any textbooks or notes. These exams are usually used to assess knowledge and insight. |
| **Open book exam** | A written exam is an evaluation method in which the student is given questions that s/he is to answer (sometimes electronically). The answers are used to assess the extent to which the student masters the course objectives. There is no direct contact between the student and the examiner. Both open and close-ended questions can be used in written exams. Specifically, during an open book exam, students may use their textbook or notes. These exams are usually used to assess insight. |
| **Multiple-choice exam** | During a multiple-choice exam, the student chooses the correct answer from a number of possible answer alternatives. These questions may be used to assess both knowledge and insight. |
| **Oral exam** | An oral exam is an evaluation method that assesses to what extent the student masters the outlined objectives through a conversation between the examiner and the student. Oral exams predominantly work with open-ended questions. |
| **Practical exam** | A practical exam is a concluding (final) exam that assesses to what extent the student has acquired a competence decisive for or characteristic of the profession. This often happens in an authentic practice setting (sometimes in the workplace). |
| **Portfolio** | A portfolio is a collection of documents/assignments that serve as evidence for the learning process and for a student's performance in a particular area. The student him/herself puts together the portfolio on the basis of his/her personal document selection. |
| **Bachelor's or master's thesis** | A bachelor's paper is an assignment with which a bachelor's degree can be completed. A master's paper is an assignment with which a master's degree can be completed. The result reflects the student's overall critical-reflective attitude or his/her research attitude. |

European Communities. (2009). *ECTS Users' Guide*. Luxembourg: Office for Official publications of the European Communities.

# Making the transition to post-secondary education: opportunities and challenges experienced by students with ASD in the Republic of Ireland

Sheena Bell, Cristina Devecchi, Conor Mc Guckin and Michael Shevlin

**ABSTRACT**
Internationally there are increasing numbers of young people on the ASD spectrum attending higher education. Early transition planning is essential and students with ASD often require support to articulate their post-school educational goals and actively participate in transition planning meetings. Services within higher education are primarily designed to provide academic supports however, non-academic supports may be an even more crucial factor in enabling successful transitions for young people on the ASD spectrum who often experience heightened anxiety within an unfamiliar environment. Within this paper, the results of a small-scale exploratory study of the transition experiences of six young people on the ASD spectrum to post-secondary education will be shared. There was limited evidence that transition planning had been initiated as a formal process for the six students. Accessing support in higher education proved to be a complex process for some students who required sustained input from parents to ensure that they would utilise the supports available. Encouraging the development of self-determination skills, a key predictor of success in higher education, needs to begin in secondary school. It is anticipated insights from this study can contribute to the development of an embedded infrastructure to support effective transitions for students with ASD to post-secondary education.

## Introduction

International and national policy initiatives have begun to focus on enabling people from traditionally marginalised groups to fully participate within society (DES 2001; OECD 2011). These initiatives are often designed to address inherent inequities such as economic and social disadvantage that are apparent within society. In particular, the historically poor educational outcomes for students with special educational needs (SEN) and/or disabilities have been highlighted (Lewis, Robertson, and Parsons 2005; Watson and Nolan 2011). Parallel systems of special and mainstream education combined with a heavy emphasis on student assessments often resulted in negative labelling for the children and young people identified as having SEN (Hart, Grigal, and Weir 2010; McCoy, Banks, and Shevlin 2012). It has proved difficult to challenge these embedded approaches to the education of children classified as having SEN and many traditional features of special education have re-emerged and in some cases been strengthened. Thus, in spite of progressive policies and attempted school reforms, students with SEN are often relegated to being just another group that require special treatment apart from their peers (McCoy, Banks, and Shevlin 2012). This pattern has been replicated in the Republic of Ireland where there has been a concerted struggle by parents and advocates to ensure that children and young people identified on the autistic spectrum disorder (ASD) spectrum have access to and can progress through *all* levels of the education system. This paper shares the results of a small-scale study exploring the experiences of six young people on the ASD spectrum transitioning from secondary education. The findings are discussed in relation to the supports available to, and challenges experienced by, these young people during their transition to post-secondary education. This research is preliminary in nature given the limited experience within the Republic of Ireland in facilitating transition to post-secondary education for this cohort of students.

## Background

Over the last 20 years, there has been a concerted effort by Irish legislators and policy-makers to address issues of inequality affecting people with disabilities and/or SEN within Irish society (Griffin and Shevlin 2011). Regulations facilitating access, transfer, and progression for all learners were provided in the Qualifications Act (1999) and it was anticipated that learners with disabilities and/or SEN would benefit from this initiative. Implementing these regulations within existing structures at the post-secondary education level has proved challenging. Implementation has required a number of measures including the adaptation of existing programmes and the design of flexible delivery systems combined with reasonable accommodations aimed 'to promote equality and combat discrimination' (NQAI 2003, 6). Under these regulations, universities were required to develop policies to support the access, transfer, and progression of students from socioeconomically disadvantaged backgrounds, those with disabilities and/or SEN and those from traditionally marginalised communities (DES 2001).

Since the publication of the *Action Group on Access to Third Level* report (DES 2001) some progress has been made to address inequities in relation to access to higher education (18 years +) educational opportunities However, this progress has been uneven across marginalised groups and young people who often continue to experience significant barriers (AHEAD 2016). National targets for participation of specific groups of students were established (HEA 2010) and steps were taken to support reaching these targets. The provision of the Fund for Students with Disabilities has had a significant impact on the capacity of higher education institutions to respond to the support needs of individuals experiencing disabilities and/or SEN (HEA 2015). The Fund for Students with Disabilities provides for a range of supports including assistive technology, sign language interpreters, note takers and extra tuition. It also facilitated the appointment of Disability Officers in the majority of higher education institutions. These Disability Officers have responsibility for establishing support services for students with disabilities and/or SEN within their institutions.

Access initiatives such as Disability Access Route to Education (DARE) were established by higher education institutions to provide reasonable accommodations in relation to admission to higher education for students with disabilities and/or SEN. Students who qualified for DARE could gain access to their chosen area of study with a reduced entry score in the Leaving Certificate examination (a terminal national examination for secondary education that determines entry to courses in higher education). The most recent participation figures (AHEAD 2016) indicate that a total of 10,773 students with disabilities and/or SEN comprise approximately 5.1% of total student population within higher education. The last decade has witnessed a steady increase in the participation rates of students with disabilities and/or SEN in higher education though it seems that relatively smaller numbers are undertaking postgraduate study (AHEAD 2016). While students with disabilities were more likely to be studying subjects within Arts and Humanities, students with ASD were marginally more likely to be studying in Science and Computing. On completion of secondary education, students can enrol in further education courses which are designed to cater to students who do not wish to enter or are not deemed eligible to enter higher education. Current figures for students with disabilities studying in further education are not readily available, although Trant (2011) reported that approximately 600 students accessed support from The Fund for Students with Disabilities in the academic year 2009–2010.

## Access, transfer and progression

International data indicate that young people with disabilities and/or SEN were less likely to participate in higher education than their contemporaries without disabilities (OECD 2011). Irish data confirm the international trend and indicates that people with disabilities were much less likely to participate in higher education compared to their non-disabled peers (Watson and Nolan 2011). While several factors might explain the limited participation of individuals with disabilities in higher education, it is clear that secondary schools play a critical role in enabling young people with disabilities and/or SEN to access appropriate pathways to higher education (OECD 2011). The OECD international review, *Inclusion of students with disabilities in tertiary education and employment* (2011), examined access and transfer pathways for students with disabilities and/or SEN. The review indicated that there are major obstacles for students with disabilities, including the failure of many schools to begin transition planning early in secondary school (OECD 2011).

Internationally, there are increasing numbers of young people on the ASD spectrum attending higher education and this has become the focus of research designed to understand the transition process needed to support the success of this group of young people. Wei et al. (2016) reported that within the USA there is lower enrolment in higher education among this cohort compared to their peers without disabilities, a finding also evident internationally (Madriaga et al. 2008).

Several critical factors were identified as essential to successful transition planning for students with disabilities and/or SEN: (i) early transition planning allowing for informed choices based on accessible information and enabling full participation of students and parents/carers in the planning process (Griffin et al. 2014; Lewis, Robertson, and Parsons 2005); (ii) addressing financial, transport and accommodation issues (Marriott 2008); and (iii) social and academic issues arising from transition to higher education (Palmer, O'Kane, and Owens 2009).

## Transition planning

Hendricks and Wehman (2009) point out that students with ASD comprise a heterogeneous group so individually tailored support programmes are required. Early transition planning (10–13 years) is considered essential with more intensive transition planning taking place when students are in the 14–16-year age range. School professionals and parents need to expand their expectations for these young people and not base their expectations on perceived student limitations. Transition planning needs to have an explicit focus on enabling these young people to improve their interpersonal skills so they can function in a variety of life environments (Hendricks and Wehman 2009).

There appears to be a significant gap between young students with disabilities and their parents and school professionals regarding expectations for post-secondary educational opportunities. Strong self-determination skills appear to be a critical factor in enabling young people within this cohort to make successful transitions to higher education (Getzel and Thoma 2008). Because self-determination is so important for success, Wei et al. (2016) recommended beginning transition planning early in the secondary years. They further suggest that providing support for setting post-school educational goals and for active participation in transition planning meetings is critical for students with ASD. Griffin et al. (2014) reported that young people on the ASD spectrum were less likely to attend transition meetings compared to their peers who had disabilities and/or difficulties in learning. Even when young people with ASD attended their transition meetings there was a discernible pattern of very limited engagement. Strong parental involvement in the education of the young person was positively correlated to active participation by the young person in the scheduled transition planning meetings. Within the US context where transition planning is mandated, the Individual Education Plan (IEP) becomes very useful. The student's strengths and limitations can be identified and the priorities outlined in the transition planning can form an integral element in the student's IEP (Roberts 2010; Wei et al. 2016).

## Transfer to post-secondary education

VanBergeijk, Klin, and Volkmar (2008) commented that adapting to the complex demands of a higher education setting can present significant difficulties for students with ASD, who may rely on the rote application of social skills which may be inappropriate. Young people with ASD may also face a number of interpersonal challenges and parents can often help college practitioners gain a deeper understanding of barriers experienced by the student in their daily lives (Madriaga et al. 2008).

Student attrition and failure is most common during the first year and increasingly higher education institutions are developing programmes to enable first year students to adapt to the social and academic demands of college life. These programmes aim to ensure that students make 'meaningful connections' to higher education (Palmer, O' Kane, and Owens 2009) through addressing common needs of the student population including developing a sense of belonging, adapting to multiple life roles, availing of integrated support systems and dealing with practical issues such as accommodation and transportation. Palmer, O' Kane, and Owens (2009) conceptualise this initial phase of higher education as 'betwixt spaces' and emphasise that students need to learn to persevere through this critical time and develop binding social ties through meaningful relationships.

Many young people on the ASD spectrum can experience social isolation in their secondary school lives. According to Madriaga et al. (2008) some young people on the ASD spectrum experienced a euphoric reaction to entry to higher education. The authors commented that for these young people a new beginning provided a welcome respite to the social isolation experienced during their lives in secondary school and an opportunity to recast themselves within a different environment. The majority of young people who chose not to disclose reported feeling uncomfortable at the prospect of sharing their disability with their lecturers and their peers (Beardon, Martin, and Woolsey 2009). The choice not to disclose is often influenced by the desire of young people to avoid being labelled according to their disability and have a 'fresh start' in this new academic environment (Getzel and Thoma 2008; Jacklin 2011).

Support services within higher education are primarily designed to provide academic supports and to ensure curricular access for students with disabilities and/or difficulties in learning. However, non-academic supports may be a crucial factor in enabling successful transitions for young people on the ASD spectrum who may experience heightened anxiety within an unfamiliar environment. Higher education supports can consist of explicit instruction in life skills and how to manage a challenging and complex environment. Self-determination skills are also considered crucial in negotiating a pathway through higher education and these skills can be practised and refined within this educational environment. Beardon, Martin, and Woolsey (2009) caution against adopting a deficit model in relation to the inclusion of young people on the ASD spectrum within higher education institutions. Their research very clearly indicates that successful transitions for these young people are highly dependent on the understanding of their unique needs within the higher education environment. Young people within this cohort reported difficulties in social interaction with their peers and with the academic staff. Extensive social demands are evident in higher education from induction to assessment procedures involving group work. Hart, Grigal, and Weir (2010) observed that students with ASD can face particular challenges with non-verbal communication, socialising and adapting to a very stimulating higher education environment. Yet, there appeared to be limited social supports available within higher education to enable these young people to navigate this complex social environment.

While there is an increasing emphasis on facilitating social interaction in college life, less attention has been given to social aspects of the classroom (Zager and Alpern 2010). Gobbo and Shmulsky (2014) observed that students with ASD can experience limited mental flexibility which can cause difficulties with long-term planning, time management and participating successfully in group work. Often, these types of supports involving explicit guidance on life skills are not readily available within higher education (Zager and Alpern 2010) and as a result students with ASD may struggle with social aspects of the classroom environment. Group work, for example, can present particular challenges for students with ASD and these students will probably require explicit guidance on how to negotiate and play a positive role within a group setting (Roberts 2010).

Jacklin and Robinson (2007) observed that support services needed to be flexible enough to provide varied supports that may include: material resources, focused guidance and information, and encouragement from peers encountering similar issues in adapting to college life. Higher education structures must incorporate the interactional and relational aspects of support to facilitate successful adaptations for students on the ASD spectrum. Young people, with ASD, in Beardon, Martin, and Woolsey's (2009) study reported that support to understand the behaviour of their neuro-typical peers would have significantly reduced the social challenges they experienced on a daily basis. Mentoring programmes, for example, have been found to be effective (Beardon, Martin, and Woolsey 2009; Hart, Grigal, and Weir 2010). Also, facilitating informal interaction among students and between staff and students has been reported as beneficial for this student cohort.

Faculty and staff perceived that students with ASD can struggle with the social skills required for classroom and curricular engagement, critical thinking which entails generalising from specific examples, and evident anxiety that can inhibit learning (Gobbo and Shmulsky 2014). In spite of these challenges, they also identified strengths for these students including passionate interests and their acquisition of accurate detailed knowledge. Faculty and staff adapted their teaching to take account of the strengths and difficulties experienced by students with ASD: designing more structured approaches; making course demands very explicit; using very precise questioning and setting clear expectations about required answers; offering opportunities for students to follow their interests; and increasing their sensitivity and awareness of how increased anxiety can be manifested.

Transition from secondary to post-secondary education constitutes a complex process for students with ASD, their families and support services in post-secondary education settings. It is clear that transition planning needs to begin early in secondary school and to ensure a smooth transition process, students with ASD and their families need to be active participants along with school personnel. Individualised transition programmes taking account of student strengths and difficulties can emerge from this carefully designed collaborative process. Transfer to post-secondary education settings can be facilitated through the provision of supports that focus on both academic and social aspects of life in the new setting. Supports need to be viewed as individualised rather than generic, to ensure that students with ASD can fully participate academically and socially in the post-secondary setting.

## Method

### *Purpose of the study and research questions*

The purpose of this study was to explore how six young people with ASD experienced transition at two separate time points: (i) 'pre-transition' when they had the 'aspiration' of making the transition to higher education, and (ii) 'post-transition' when they had (or had not) made the transition to higher education. Our research questions included:

(1) What are the experiences of students with ASD in accessing and progressing to post-secondary education settings?
(2) What resources and supports are available to students with ASD to accommodate them making this progression?

(3) What major issues and barriers arise with regards to access, progression and transition for students with ASD?

## Participants

This study forms a subsection of a broader study examining transition experiences from secondary to post-secondary education settings for students with SEN in the Republic of Ireland. The general sampling process involved the following steps: (i) consulting the database of the funding body which contained a list of those students with SEN who were receiving support in secondary schools in the Republic of Ireland (No pupil identifying information was contained in the data given to the researchers.); (ii) from the database, the research team identified a sample of students with different forms of SEN; (iii) the research team subdivided the database into four approximated geographical areas, including urban and rural, representing north Ireland, south Ireland, east Ireland and west Ireland; (iv) the research team identified possible participants from a range of school types: secondary (traditional academically oriented schools usually with religious management and often single sex); vocational (state run schools often catering for socio-economically disadvantaged areas and mixed gender); community (state run schools, locally organised, multi-denominational and mixed gender).

From the 20 schools who agreed to participate in the pre-transition phase of data collection, 42 students with SEN (including seven with ASD) agreed to participate in the research. A total of 42 student interviews took place (including one parent who was interviewed as a proxy for one student who had severe and profound disability) at the pre-transition phase of the study. One of the students with ASD was unable to participate in the post-transition interviews and the research team decided not to include any data from this student in reporting study findings. Participant demographics for students with ASD is presented below in Table 1. For the purposes of reporting study results, the six students were assigned the following pseudonyms: John, Michael, Frank, Peter, Kieran, Conor. All post-secondary education courses offered in Further Education colleges and Higher Education are assigned a place on the national qualifications framework (levels 5–10).

## Procedures

Students with ASD and their parents were contacted through their school and invited to participate in the research project. In all contact with participants and their parents, it was emphasised that participation was voluntary, and the option to withdraw from the study at

Table 1. Study participants.

| Student | Region; context | School type | Age | Pre-transition choice | Accreditation level |
| --- | --- | --- | --- | --- | --- |
| John | East; urban | Secondary | 18 | Arts PLC | 5 |
| Michael | East; urban | Secondary | 19 | Science HE | 9 |
| Frank | South; urban | Vocational | 18 | Music Technology HE | 8 |
| Peter | East; rural | Community | 18 | Business PLC | 5 |
| Kieran | East; urban | Vocational | 17 | Information Technology | 5 |
| Conor | West; rural | Secondary | 18 | Humanities HE | 8 |

Notes: PLC = Post Leaving Certificate Course (Further Education college); HE = Higher Education (University/Institute of Technology).

any time without providing a reason was available. The research team was conscious of the need to ensure the welfare of research participants; so on receipt of parental written consent, contact was made with the participant by telephone to establish rapport and address any concerns they might have about the research. Parents were also invited to participate in the study though the main emphasis was on ascertaining the experiences of the young people themselves. Two of the parents volunteered to be involved. The research team adopted an 'ethics as a process' (Ramcharan and Cutcliffe 2001) approach, which gave participants the opportunity to negotiate consent to participation at all stages of the research study.

The primary goal of these semi-structured interviews was to gain an understanding of participant experiences regarding the transition process to post-secondary education for students with ASD, and to identify key factors that facilitated or prevented access, transfer, and progression for these students. The pre-transition interviews with the research participants took place in the student's school during the spring term (approximately four months before taking the Leaving Certificate examination that marks the end of secondary education). The research team was anxious to cause the least disruption to the lives of the participants who were in the final stages of preparation for the examination that would determine opportunities available to them in post-secondary education, a time of already heighten stress. Conscious of this and in negotiation with the participants, it was agreed that the maximum amount of time available for the one-to-one semi-structured interview was approximately 30 minutes so that participants could return promptly to their subsequent classes.

All six student interviews at pre-transition phase lasted between 20 and 30 min (not including material addressing the purpose of the research and any clarifications required). The interview protocol was based on an extensive literature review of pertinent issues and included the following core themes: decision-making processes within the school; family involvement in decision-making; supports available within school and local community; levels of awareness of available supports; participant expectations of post-secondary education; participant hopes and fears for future. The two parent interviews focused, in particular, on their involvement in the decision-making process and their perception of supports and barriers to progression to post-secondary education.

Post-transition interviews took place in the participant's post-secondary education setting (four in Further Education colleges; two in Universities). Post-transition interviews were conducted in the autumn term approximately three months after the students commenced their studies in post-secondary education. The semi-structured interviews focused on the transition experiences of the participants: initial transition experience (college and programme inductions and introductions); academic engagement with post-secondary education setting; social engagement with post-secondary education setting; participant sense of belonging in the new setting; their own health and well-being; perceived effectiveness of supports provided; and perceived barriers to participation.

## *Analysis*

All interviews were audio recorded and transcribed verbatim. In the first stage, the initial analytical framework, based on the review of the literature and on peer consultation emergent codes from the field was drawn up. These codes were compiled into themes through a process of lean coding (Creswell 2002). Analysis did not reveal major contradictions in student responses and any inconsistencies in responses that emerged were examined within the findings. During the analytic research phase the research team ensured that data analysis was an ongoing process involving reviewing and comparing initial codes, establishing emergent themes and closely examining data interpretation.

The following key themes emerged at pre-transition: student perspectives about guidance and support received in decision-making processes around choice of post-school options; availability of resources and activities within schools; and student response to engaging in decision-making around post-school options, characterised as student well-being. Students at the pre-transition phase engaged with all of these themes and recounted their experiences in relation to these decision-making processes. At post-transition, these key themes emerged: the nature of the post-school destination was explored; student experience of transition and settling-in; academic and social challenges faced in the new context; how students accessed support and resources; student well-being and future plans.

## Findings

As illustrated in Table 1 above, students had a variety of ambitions with regard to progression to post-secondary education. Three of the students (Conor, Michael, Frank) aimed to attend higher education while the remaining three (John, Peter, Kieran) wished to participate in a Post Leaving Certificate Course (PLC) in a local Further Education college. (PLCs have been designed to provide more practical programmes that build on secondary education and some programmes can lead to third-level education). The post-transition destinations for these students is shown in Table 2 below.

Two students (Michael, Conor) achieved their ambition to access their chosen course in higher education, another (Frank) is pursuing a PLC course with the aim of accessing higher education through this pathway, while two others (Kieran, Peter) managed to achieve their chosen PLC programme. John did not manage to access his chosen PLC course though he had achieved a place on another PLC programme.

### Pre-transition phase

#### School support and knowledge of transition pathways

All six participants reported very positive relationships with support staff in their respective secondary schools. Career guidance professionals, in particular, were appreciated for their support and guidance in making career choices. Students reported being directed to websites giving details of courses and institutions. In the following example, this guidance clearly

**Table 2.** Post-transition destinations.

| Student | Pre-transition choice | Achieved | Current placement |
|---|---|---|---|
| John | Arts PLC | No | PLC |
| Michael | Science HE | Yes | HE |
| Frank | Music Technology HE | No | PLC |
| Peter | Business PLC | Yes | PLC |
| Kieran | Information Technology PLC | Yes | PLC |
| Conor | Humanities HE | Yes | HE |

Notes: PLC = Post Leaving Certificate Course (Further Education college); HE = Higher Education (University/Institute of Technology).

related to career progression as well as simply courses, or a choice of college: 'She helped us by checking them up on the computer. Seeing which one's the best one to go for and what subjects you would like and how much points do we need'(Peter). One student described making full use of the personal service provided by the school careers counsellor, accessing support over a number of years: 'Basically I was up and down to Miss [name of teacher] over the years with appointments, trying to figure out what I wanted to do in life' (Kieran).

However, despite these examples of personal support, there was also evidence that some career guidance personnel lacked the specific knowledge needed to support the transition pathways for students with ASD:

> The school didn't even know about until my Dad said it (a community organization that offered transition support for students with ASD). So they then looked into and Miss [name of teacher], I'm on and off talking to her in the corridor and she said that's fantastic. If she'd known about it she would have told me straight away. (Kieran)

There was limited evidence that transition planning had been initiated as a formal process within the schools attended by the six students. While all students had an IEP there were no specific references to transition planning for post-secondary education and/or work.

Choices made early in the secondary school career of the students can have an impact on post-school destination. In the Irish context, the choice of course and final accreditation in school has a direct impact on accessing courses in further or higher education. For example students following a course for LCA (Leaving Certificate Applied) will not be able to be accepted directly onto a university course without further study. This student summarises the impact of doing an LCA:

> There's no chance of me getting in to [name of college] from doing the Leaving Certificate Applied, so I'll have to do something, I'll just go to the foundation college first and try and work my way up so I can get in. (John)

### *Heightened pressures*

Students with ASD in their final year of school reported facing heightened pressures related to working for high stakes examinations which would give them access to post-compulsory education:

> This year I'm under a huge amount of pressure and the stress will get to me. Like one or two times in the evening I end up going across the road to me local (public house) for about an hour and then go home because it's just the stress. And sometimes I'd up going for hitting a wall or something with stress. (Kieran)

The unpredictability of his future was suddenly of paramount importance to the following student, causing additional stress and he contrasted himself to other students who were not taking the transition period 'too serious'. This feeling of experiencing the world in a different way from peers is a feature of ASD which can lead to feelings of isolation. He continued to explain that he was concerned: 'I think it's finally hit home with me that I had to figure out something to do quickly now … I need to expect what's going to be coming to me. So, for huge anxiety then' (Frank).

Another source of stress can be feelings of apprehension as students anticipate leaving behind support through important personal relationships built up with key professionals over the years. The same student described how he would miss:

… the teachers and everyone now, because I've had a long time to form a bond with them. I can go into a room, I can talk with them all about personal matters and things like that, stuff 1st years can't do. It'll be strange moving to college and not having that any more now, I'll be trapped in myself again. (Conor)

In the pre-transition interview one student was already considering how much direct support he would need and trying to address a difficult dilemma:

On one hand I would prefer going through the same support, but on the other hand I would like to work by myself, because I feel like I can do this by myself, I don't want people overlooking my ability by looking at this. (Frank)

However, there were acknowledgements that this transition period was an important part of maturing and moving onto adult life. The following student had a resigned and possibly realistic approach to moving on: 'I'll probably miss the fun times we had, but I don't really care because you have to move on' (Michael).

## Support for accommodation/transport issues

For certain students, an offer of accommodation, either official or unofficial, was definitely a positive incentive to choose a particular institution. For example, this student was attracted by the possibility of sharing a living space with a social contact: 'Because I've a friend up there and he said I could stay with him if I got in' (Kieran).

The opportunity to continue a previous relationship that the student was comfortable with was clearly a strong influence on his choice. For others, it was a combination of transport and the facilities available. The following student was concerned about the distance of a recommended college from his home territory, where both transport and accommodation would be easier:

They all wanted me to go to [name of college 1] which is a bit of a kip (not very suitable), so I didn't really want to go there. The facilities are kind of good there, but I just wouldn't be interested in going there. [name of college 2, preferred choice] It's kind of close to my house. (John)

## Post-transition phase

As noted earlier two of the six participants made a transition to higher education; the other four participants were enrolled in PLC courses at local Further Education colleges.

## Disclosure of disability and accessing support

In post-compulsory settings, students who had been accustomed to accessing support at school now found themselves in the position of having to take an active role in disclosing their disability in order to access support.

Accessing support in higher education proved to be a complex process for some students with ASD who required sustained input from parents to ensure that they could avail the support available. Michael, who was studying Science in third-level education, was reluctant to initiate accessing support and his parent had to broker an initial personal contact with the support professional: 'Initially it was an absolute nightmare to get him to meet her, to meet, either of them because I think he was deliberately avoiding' [Michael's parent].

His mother explained to the support personnel that her son required explicit guidance in ensuring that a meeting could take place: the support professional told him that 'I will have a red bag on the floor beside me' and so the contact was initiated.' Michael confirmed that the support was available: 'They [The support professionals] contacted us. They just interview you and ask what you need. I get tutors and help with stuff. Study skills and exam skills' (Michael).

In another situation, a parent encouraged her son Conor, who was studying Humanities in third-level education, to seek support and she was proactive in contacting the college support service herself: 'I said, "I'm not interfering". I said, "I just want to, you know, make it known that, or make sure that you knew he was there"' (Conor's parent). However, in this case, the support professional waited until the student himself came forward for help (it is possible that this support service only dealt with students, who were regarded as adults, rather than their parents), which eventually happened. At this point, prompt and timely support was offered, as Conor described:

> I had to approach her.... I just had to explain to her that I have borderline Aspergers. She said she'd do anything to help me out. All I had to do was book an appointment so I booked an appointment – well last week I booked an appointment for tomorrow to help me with the finishing touches on my assignments, for this Thursday and Friday. (Conor)

Finally, in contrast, Frank describes how he had embraced the possibility of leaving his disability label behind by making a conscious decision not to disclose ASD and access support: 'They gave me the choice, whether to tick it and then go into details. I decided to leave that part blank' (Frank). This has enabled him to make a fresh start and develop his own self-confidence: 'It's just good to finally, actually, [have] people having confidence in you, that you can do this yourself' (Frank).

This has had a positive effect on developing self-determination skills and it was clear that he had applied himself and achieved his own targets. In this case, positive feedback in the form of good marks for his work has reinforced his growing self-reliance, as he reported: 'It was a bit hard at first, but seeing that I, seeing my results back and seeing how well I'm actually doing by myself, it's grown confidence in me' (Frank). In a sense, he appeared to have made a transition, not only from school to post-secondary education, but also from dependence to independence.

### *Effectiveness of supports*

The novel demands of higher/further education seems to require a more wide reaching form of support than was perhaps needed in the narrower environment of early school. Kieran highlighted the need for a variety of supporters whilst he was at school, including medical and religious practitioners and demonstrates the complex support needs of some students with ASD:

> It's helped me in a number of ways with Dr [name supplied] has helped me through a lot of personal issues and that. Father [name supplied] has helped me through grieving and Mr [name supplied] has helped me through learning and stuff. Different people ... (Kieran)

Peter required support in social communication as his PLC Business course required interaction with customers as part of a work placement:

> I got a lot of 'very goods', I got four 'very goods' and about ten 'goods' and one 'unsatisfactory' because, one unsatisfactory because I've got a problem with communicating with the customers. (Peter)

Peter felt able to cope with the course intellectually; nevertheless, he experienced difficulties in relation to meeting the expectations for academic writing: 'It's just how to write them and how to write them perfectly and all that's a ... problem and how to lay it out. Some people can be ... can lay out their answers but I can't' (Peter).

All three higher education students recognised that they had the responsibility of managing their schedules and that participation in higher education required significant skills in self-determination: 'Basically it's not like school where you're being bossed around. Here your own thing in your own time basically' [Conor].

In this post-transition phase, the availability of public transport to institutions away from the students' home area was identified as a particular barrier. The location and timing of services did not always match the needs of students, forming an additional challenge for some students.

## Discussion

This study was exploratory in nature and designed to enable policy-makers and practitioners to gain an increased understanding of how students with ASD experienced the transition to the world of post-compulsory education. Despite the study's limited scope a number of important insights have emerged which can enable policy-makers and practitioners provide appropriate support for students with ASD in their transition to post-compulsory education settings. While it is generally recognised that all students can experience difficulties in making this transition (Mc Coy, Smyth, Watson, and Darmody 2014), it is equally evident that students with ASD encounter specific challenges that require nuanced and sensitive responses from policy-makers and practitioners (Getzel and Thoma 2008).

Early transition planning is considered to be advisable for all students (Mc Coy et al. 2014), however, it is essential for students with ASD (Wei et al. 2016). Within this study it was apparent that while very positive relationships had been established with career guidance practitioners, there was limited evidence that focused transition planning was an established component of school provision. In fact, there appeared to be serious gaps in the knowledge of these practitioners that could have serious consequences for the success of the transition process for students with ASD. While transition planning for students with disabilities is mandatory in the USA and usually folded into an IEP, there is no such compulsion for Irish schools and so there is a real risk that this essential element of individual planning can be neglected (Rose, Shevlin, Winter, O'Raw, and Zhao 2012). Furthermore, choices of subject and level of study made early in their secondary career can have a profound impact on post-school career trajectories. Many students with ASD can experience social isolation during their secondary school careers (Madriaga et al. 2008) and it became evident in this study that these students experienced heightened anxiety at the prospect of transition and leaving behind the predictability of trusted school professionals who provided high levels of support.

Disclosure of ASD in order to obtain requisite support has been reported to be problematic for many students (Beardon, Martin, and Woolsey 2009; Getzel and Thoma 2008). This study supported these findings indicating that students with ASD struggled with the whole process of disclosure. Proactive parental involvement was necessary to initiate the process of engagement with the higher education support services, though once this had been addressed, the students reported being more comfortable with accessing support. While technically these students are adults there appears to be a powerful argument for support staff to be willing to engage with parents, particularly in initiating the support process. It appears that the basic social interaction skills required for these types of exchanges may be limited for these students and may require explicit guidance to foster appropriate social interaction skills with support services staff. Developing trusting relationships in a new environment to replace those established in secondary school will require time and patience and this needs to be taken into account by support services staff in designing their support interventions. In this study, one student with ASD may wish to shed the disability label and engage in a 'fresh start' as reported in other studies (Getzel and Thoma 2008; Jacklin 2011). The decision not to disclose has to be respected and the support services staff need to be flexible enough to offer support when the student may encounter difficulties at whatever stage of the academic year.

While there is an awareness of how students with ASD may struggle with aspects of social interaction in higher education (Hart, Grigal, and Weir 2010) less attention has been given to the implicit social demands embedded in curriculum and assessment processes (Zager and Alpern 2010). Though this study was limited to the very early stages of transition into higher/further education, there was emerging evidence that when social interaction is an integral course expectation students with ASD can struggle. Post-secondary education institutions need to be made aware of these possibilities and perhaps incorporate support opportunities into coursework for students with ASD to demonstrate their strengths such as pursuing areas of passionate interest (Gobbo and Shmulsky 2014).

While this study represents a limited snapshot of the transition experiences for students with ASD within the Republic of Ireland, a few insights can be documented. Four of the six students managed to access their first choice course (2 in HE/2 in FE) and another achieved his second choice in higher education. All five students, who achieved their first or second choices, appeared to be content with their choices though it is difficult to know whether the PLC choices were the result of limited ambition or the appropriate level of study for the students concerned. The student who failed to achieve his course choice had limited his choices to a PLC course near home as he was concerned about the prospects of moving away. All students appeared to value the pre-transition support and the availability of school support professionals. At post-transition, students appeared to have settled into their courses despite some initial difficulties in accessing support. Tracking these students through their post-secondary education would yield further valuable insights regarding the quality of the transition process, the appropriateness of the available supports and whether these students become socially integrated within their new educational settings.

## Concluding comments

Students with ASD, like their peers, form a heterogeneous group and require individualised attention and support in order to make successful transitions to post-secondary education within the Republic of Ireland. The importance of early transition planning needs to be made visible and operational through the legislative mandating of IEPs incorporating a transition component. In addition, career guidance professionals require regular updated information about access pathways for students with ASD and opportunities for focused transition planning. Parental support may need to extend into the post-transition phase, in particular with the facilitation of initial contact between the student and the support service. Research studies have indicated that curricular and assessment processes embedded in higher education courses need to be reviewed to ensure that implicit social interaction demands are made explicit and appropriate guidance provided for students with ASD. We, in institutes of higher education, should not underestimate the challenges faced by students with ASD as they leave behind familiar environments and negotiate a pathway through higher and further education. Encouraging the development of self-determination skills, a key predictor of success in post-secondary education, needs to begin in secondary school. It is clear that there is a strong commitment to enabling greater student diversity in post-secondary education in the Republic of Ireland and insights from this study can contribute to the development of an embedded infrastructure to support effective transitions for students with ASD to post-secondary education.

## Disclosure statement

No potential conflict of interest was reported by the authors.

## Funding

This work was supported by the National Council for Special Education, Trim, Co. Meath, Republic of Ireland.

## References

AHEAD (Association for Higher Education Access and Disability) 2016. *Numbers of Students with Disabilities Studying in Higher Education in Ireland*. Dublin: AHEAD Educational Press.

Beardon, Luke, Nicola Martin, and Ian Woolsey. 2009. "What Do Students with Asperger Syndrome or High-functioning Autism Want at University? (In their Own Words)." *Good Autism Practice* 10 (2): 35–43.

Creswell, John W. 2002. *Educational Research: Planning Conducting and Evaluating Quantitative and Qualitative Research*. Upper Saddle River, NJ: Merrill Prentice Hall.

DES (Department of Education and Science) 2001. *Action Group on Access to Third Level Education Report of the Action Group on Access to Third Level Education*. Dublin: Stationery Office.

Getzel, Elizabeth E., and Colleen A. Thoma. 2008. "Experiences of College Students with Disabilities and the Importance of Self-determination in Higher Education Settings." *Career Development and Transition for Exceptional Individuals* 31: 77–84.

Gobbo, Ken, and Solvegi Shmulsky. 2014. "Faculty Experience with College Students with Autism Spectrum Disorders: A Qualitative Study of Challenges and Solutions." *Focus on Autism and Other Developmental Disabilities* 29 (1): 13–22.

Government of Ireland. 1999. *Qualifications (Education and Training) Act*. Dublin: Stationary Office.

Griffin, Sean, and Michael Shevlin. 2011. *Responding to Special Educational Needs: An Irish Perspective*. Dublin: Gill and Macmillan.

Griffin, Megan M., Julie L. Taylor, Richard C. Urbano, and Robert M. Hodapp. 2014. "Involvement in Transition Planning Meetings among High School Students with Autism Spectrum Disorders." *The Journal of Special Education* 47 (4): 256–264.

Hart, Debra, Meg Grigal, and Cate Weir. 2010. "Expanding the Paradigm: Post-secondary Education Options for Individuals with Autistic Spectrum Disorder and Intellectual Disabilities." *Focus on Autism and Other Developmental Disabilities* 25 (3): 134–150.

Hendricks, Dawn R., and Paul Wehman. 2009. "Transition from School to Adulthood for Youth with Autistic Spectrum Disorders." *Focus on Autism and Other Developmental Disabilities* 24 (2): 77–88.

HEA (Higher Education Authority) 2010. *The Fund for Students with Disabilities: Review and Development*. Dublin: Higher Education Authority.

HEA (Higher Education Authority) 2015. *HEA Key Facts and Figures 2014/15*. Dublin: Higher Education Authority.

Jacklin, Angela. 2011. "To be or Not to be 'a disabled student' in Higher Education: The Case of a Postgraduate 'non-declaring' (Disabled) Student." *Journal of Research in Special Educational Needs* 11 (2): 99–106.

Jacklin, Angela, and Carol Robinson. 2007. "What is Meant by 'Support' in Higher Education? Towards a Model of Academic and Welfare Support." *Journal of Research in Special Educational Needs* 7 (2): 114–123.

Lewis, Ann, Chris Robertson, and Sarah Parsons. 2005. *Experiences of Disabled Students and their Families*. Phase 1, Research Report to Disability Rights Commission. Birmingham: University of Birmingham.

Madriaga, Manuel, Dan Goodley, Nick Hodge, and Nicola Martin. 2008. *Enabling Transition into Higher Education for Students with Asperger Syndrome*. York: Higher Education Academy.

Marriott, John. 2008. *Post-16 Education and Disabled Learners: A Guide for Schools, Colleges and for Information, Advice and Guidance Workers*. Leicester: Action on Access.

Mc Coy, Selina, Emer Smyth, Dorothy Watson, and Merike Darmody. 2014. "Leaving School in Ireland: A Longitudinal Study of Post School Transitions." *ESRI Research Series*. Dublin: Economic and Social Research Institute.

McCoy, Selina, Joanne Banks, and Michael Shevlin. 2012. "School Matters: How Context Influences the Identification of Different Types of Special Educational Needs." *Irish Educational Studies* 31 (2): 119–138.

NQAI (National Qualifications Authority of Ireland) 2003. *National Framework of Qualifications: Policies, Actions and Procedures for Access, Transfer and Progression for Learners*. Dublin: National Qualifications Authority of Ireland.

OECD (Organisation for Economic Co-operation and Development) 2011. *Inclusion of Students with Disabilities in Tertiary Education and Employment*. Paris: Organisation for Economic Cooperation and Development.

Palmer, Mark, Pamela O'Kane and Martin Owens. 2009. "Betwixt Spaces: Student Accounts of Turning Point Experiences in the First Year Transition." *Studies in Higher Education* 34 (1): 37–54.

Ramcharan, Paul, and John R. Cutcliffe. 2001. "Judging the Ethics of Qualitative Research: Considering the Ethics as Process Model." *Health & Social Care in the Community* 9 (6): 358–366.

Roberts, Kelly D. 2010. "Topic Areas to Consider When Planning Transition from High School to Postsecondary Education for Students with Autism Spectrum Disorders." *Focus on Autism and Other Developmental Disabilities* 25 (3): 158–162.

Rose, Richard, Michael Shevlin, Eileen Winter, Paul O'Raw, and Yumy Zhao. 2012. "Individual Education Plans in the Republic of Ireland: An Emerging System." *British Journal of Special Education* 39 (3): 110–116.

Trant, Mary-Liz. 2011. "Students with Disabilities in Further Education and Training – A National Perspective." Further Education Conference: Including Students with Disabilities and/or Special Education Needs in Further Education, NAPD (National Association of Principals and Deputy Principals), Dublin, March 23, 2011.

VanBergeijk, Ernst, Ami Klin, and Fred Volkmar. 2008. "Supporting More Able Students on the Autism Spectrum: College and Beyond." *Journal of Autism and Developmental Disorders* 38: 1359–1370.

Watson, Dorothy, and Brian Nolan. 2011. *A Social Portrait of People with Disabilities in Ireland*. Dublin: The Economic and Social Research Institute (ESRI) and the Department of Education and Skills.

Wei, Xin, Mary Wagner, Laura Hudson, Jennifer W. Yu, and Harold Javitz. 2016. "The Effect of Transition Planning Participation and Goal-setting on College Enrollment among Youth with Autism Spectrum Disorders." *Remedial and Special Education* 37 (1): 3–14.

Zager, Dianne, and Carol S. Alpern. 2010. "College-based Inclusion Programming for Transition-age Students with Autism." *Focus on Autism and Other Developmental Disabilities* 25 (3): 151–157.

# Functioning and participation problems of students with ASD in higher education: which reasonable accommodations are effective?

Dorien Jansen, Katja Petry, Eva Ceulemans, Ilse Noens and Dieter Baeyens

**ABSTRACT**

Students with autism spectrum disorder (ASD) experience various functioning and participation problems in higher education, which may cause difficulties such as drop out or low grade point averages. However, it remains unclear how often and during which teaching and evaluation methods the functioning and participation problems occur and which reasonable accommodations are effective in dealing with them. These gaps in the literature are addressed in this survey-based study. In total, 43 students with ASD, 30 student counsellors and 43 students without a disability of institutions of higher education in Flanders (Belgium) participated in the study. The results show that students with ASD most frequently experience problems with verbal and non-verbal communication, are oversensitive to change and have difficulty distinguishing the gist of the syllabus from the details. Furthermore, it is shown that, on average, these problems arise mostly during classical teaching and evaluation methods. Finally, the perceived effectiveness of reasonable accommodations is dependent on the functioning and participation problem experienced by the student with ASD in higher education. In conclusion, both personal and environmental characteristics should be taken into account when selecting and implementing reasonable accommodations for these students.

## Background

Autism spectrum disorder (ASD) is a neurodevelopmental disorder, defined by persistent deficits in social communication and social interaction, and restricted, repetitive patterns of behaviour, interests or activities (APA 2013). Research previously showed that ASD is a persistent disorder, meaning that children who receive an ASD-diagnosis have a large chance of still meeting the criteria for ASD in adulthood (e.g. Billstedt, Carina Gillberg, and Gillberg 2007). However, because of the developmental trajectory of ASD, the two core symptoms of ASD may be experienced differently by children, adolescents and adults (Seltzer et al.

2003). In addition, there is a large heterogeneity of symptoms experienced by individuals with ASD due to the genetic, neurobiological and phenotypic differences between these individuals (Jeste and Geschwind 2014). As a result of the heterogeneity and the evolution of symptoms, problems can differ considerably between individuals with ASD, and may also vary between different stages of life and in different settings (e.g. home, school or leisure time). Therefore, it is important for research to map the symptoms and interpersonal variability of ASD in each stage of life and across different settings.

One of the domains that remained understudied is education for students with ASD in higher education. Nonetheless, this research is warranted because there is an increased number of students with ASD enrolling in higher education (e.g. VanBergeijk, Klin, and Volkmar 2008). Shattuck et al. (2012) already showed that approximately 35% of the individuals with ASD were enrolling in higher education. Additionally, the 2014 annual report of the University of Leuven suggested that the number of students with a psychiatric disability attending higher education was increased by 6% compared to 2013 (University of Leuven 2014). Students with a psychiatric disorder, including students with ASD, are one of the largest groups of students with a disability attending higher education in this university (University of Leuven 2014). Despite the increase in enrolment in higher education, these students with ASD have a larger chance of repeating courses or dropping out of higher education without a degree in comparison to their typically developing peers (e.g. White, Ollendick, and Bray 2011). In order to decrease the academic failure of students with ASD in higher education, institutions are obligated to implement reasonable accommodations (UN Convention 2006). Reasonable accommodations should increase the participation chances of these students. Harrison and colleagues defined reasonable accommodations as

> changes to practices in schools that hold a student to the same standard as students without disabilities but provide more benefit to students with a disability (i.e. differential boost) to mediate the impact of the disability on access to the general education curriculum. (Harrison et al. 2013, 6)

However, there are no regulations or guidelines available regarding which accommodations should be offered and how they should be implemented (Smith 2007). Kettler (2012) previously mentioned that, before selecting and implementing effective reasonable accommodations, both the personal characteristics of the students with a disability, including ASD-specific behaviour, and environmental characteristics of the institutions of higher education should be investigated.

Firstly, the personal characteristics of students with ASD, namely the functioning and participation problems these students experience in higher education, have been investigated only minimally. One recent study by Jansen et al. (forthcoming) mapped the functioning and participation problems of students with ASD using the International Classification of Functioning, Disability and Health (ICF; WHO 2001). This study showed that the functioning and participation problems experienced by students with ASD are present in different domains of functioning (see Figure 1). Firstly, students with ASD may experience problems with executive functioning, such as planning and organising and cognitive flexibility (Berger et al. 2003; Jansen et al., forthcoming; Olu-Lafe, Liederman, and Tager-Flusberg 2014). Secondly, problems with verbal and non-verbal communication and learning strategies were mentioned (Jansen et al., forthcoming; Zürcher et al. 2013). Thirdly, students with ASD can face problems with social relationships and social interaction (Berger et al. 2003; Orsmond et al. 2013). Finally, other sets of problems of students with ASD include stereotypical movements, sensitivity to change and problems with handling stress (Jansen et al., forthcoming).

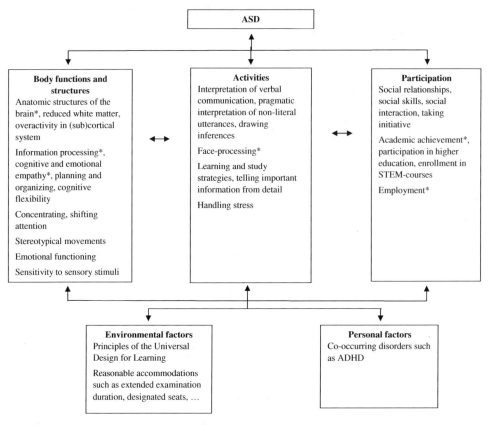

**Figure 1.** Functioning and participation of students with ASD in higher education according to the ICF framework (Jansen, et al., 2016).

By using the ICF framework, Jansen et al. (forthcoming) emphasised the importance of environmental factors when investigating the functioning and participation problems of students with ASD. These environmental factors, for example, addressed through reasonable accommodations, interact with the personal characteristics, such as the experienced functioning and participation problems (Jansen et al., forthcoming; Kettler 2012). In accordance with these results, teaching and evaluation methods may also interact with the effectiveness of reasonable accommodations and have a direct impact on students with ASD in higher education. Other environmental characteristics, such as the availability of classrooms for taking the exams in smaller than usual groups or the number of supervisors available for reading aloud or staying during the extended examination duration, are less important for the individual students with ASD and have a more indirect link to the encountered functioning and participation problems.

As stated before, it is important to gain insight into both the personal characteristics (i.e. functioning and participation problems) of students with ASD and the environmental characteristics (i.e. teaching and evaluation methods) of the institution of higher education. However, it remains unclear how often the functioning and participation problems (Jansen et al., forthcoming) occur and during which teaching and evaluation methods they emerge most. These gaps in literature will be addressed. Knowledge regarding functioning and participation problems offers insight into which reasonable accommodations are most effective for students with ASD in higher education. At this point, it remains unclear how institutions of higher education could support students with ASD in which reasonable accommodations should be offered to these students (Barnhill 2016). By also addressing this issue, this study will add value to existing research (Gelbar, Smith, and Reichow 2014). Previous research that studied the effectiveness of reasonable accommodations mostly included students with ASD in a larger group of students with a disability. Therefore, the results were not ASD specific and could not be generalised for this specific group. Nevertheless, recent qualitative studies with interviews and focus groups did demonstrate that students with ASD experience a need for reasonable accommodations and that these accommodations could have a positive effect on the experienced functioning and participation problems and the academic success of the students (Jansen et al., forthcoming; Van Hees, Moyson, and Roeyers 2015). However, a large-scale empirical study has not yet been conducted.

With this study we wanted to tackle the gaps in the literature with respect to students with ASD in higher education and so the following research questions were examined: (1) How frequently did the identified functioning and participation problems occur for students with ASD in higher education?, (2) During which teaching and evaluation methods did these problems emerge? and (3) Which reasonable accommodations were perceived to be effective in dealing with the experienced functioning and participation problems?

## Method

### *Participants*

Three groups of participants were recruited for this study, namely students with ASD, typically developing controls (TDC) and student counsellors. Students with ASD were included to answer the three research questions based on their own experience. To examine whether the functioning and participation problems identified for students with ASD are in fact specific for included students with ASD (i.e. research question 1), TDC were recruited. Finally, student counsellors were enrolled because of their experience with a variety of students with ASD. Student counsellors are professionals who work in an institution of higher education and support students with a disability in general, and students with ASD in particular with different problems such as planning and organising problems, test anxiety or communication problems. The counsellors were asked to give a general insight into the most common functioning and participation problems of student with ASD in their institution of higher education in order to investigate whether the self-reported specific problems of the students with ASD correspond to the general insight of the student counsellors (i.e. research question 1).

To be eligible to participate in the study, students with ASD had to be (1) enrolled in an institution of higher education in Flanders, Belgium, (2) currently offered reasonable accommodations, and (3) diagnosed with ASD by a psychiatrist or a multidisciplinary team. Student counsellors read the diagnostic report and verified if all criteria described in the fifth edition of the Diagnostic and Statistical Manual of Mental Disorders (DSM-5; APA 2013) were present for the specific student with ASD in higher education before reasonable accommodations were offered. TDC could participate in the survey if they (1) were enrolled in an institution of higher education in Flanders, Belgium, and (2) had no known disability. Finally, student counsellors were eligible to participate when they (1) were working as a student counsellor in an institution of higher education in Flanders, Belgium and (2) were emotionally and practically supporting students with ASD as a part of their job as student counsellor, for example, by organising workshops with respect to stress and anxiety, or by helping students plan their study time.

Based on these inclusion criteria, 43 students with ASD, 30 student counsellors and 250 students without a disability were eligible to participate in this study. Forty-three out of 250 students without a disability were individually matched to the 43 participating students with ASD based on three characteristics, namely gender, the number of years enrolled in higher education and their enrolment in a specific educational programme group (i.e. (1) Humanities and Social Sciences, (2) Science, Engineering, and Technology, and (3) Biomedical Sciences). Firstly, with 16 female students in both groups (37.2%), the participants were predominantly male ($\chi^2(1) = 0.00$, $p > 0.05$). Secondly, all students were enrolled in higher education for about three years (ASD: $M = 3.14$, $SD = 1.66$; without a disability: $M = 3.02$, $SD = 1.58$; $t(84) = 0.33$, $p > 0.05$). Thirdly, most students were enrolled in the Humanities and Social Sciences group (ASD: $n = 26$, 60.5%; without a disability: $n = 27$, 62.8%) and the Science, Engineering and Technology group (ASD: $n = 15$, 34.9%; without a disability: $n = 13$, 30.2%; $\chi^2(2) = 0.36$, $p > 0.05$). Initially, the aim was to match the students based on their enrolment in either a professional or an academic educational programme. Results showed that significantly more students with ASD were enrolled in an academic educational programme ($n = 22$, 51.2%) than students without a disability ($n = 9$, 20.9%; $\chi^2(1) = 8.52$, $p < 0.01$) and thus matching the two groups was not possible.

Furthermore, no other significant differences were found when comparing the two groups of students. On average, all students were enrolled in the second year of the bachelor programme (ASD: $M = 2.14$, $SD = 1.19$; without a disability: $M = 2.35$, $SD = 0.92$; $t(84) = 0.91$, $p > 0.05$) and in their current institution of higher education for approximately two to three years (ASD: $M = 2.67$, $SD = 1.64$; without a disability: $M = 2.37$, $SD = 1.20$; $t(84) = 0.98$, $p > 0.05$).

When looking at the demographic characteristics of the student counsellors, it became clear that the participating counsellors were mainly female ($n = 25$, 83.3%) and had between 1 and 22 years of experience as a student counsellor ($M = 10.20$, $SD = 6.98$). Finally, most student counsellors were employed in different university colleges ($n = 29$; 96.7%), while only one student counsellor was working at a university (3.3%).

## Procedure

Student counsellors of seven different institutions of higher education in Flanders (Belgium) received an information letter by email explaining the design and goals of the study and an invitation to participate. This information letter was forwarded by the student counsellors to students with ASD, who were registered as a student with a disability, and to TDC in their institution of higher education. Additionally, students were also recruited during lectures and via social media. An informed consent invitation to participate was sent to students with ASD, TDC and student counsellors who expressed their interest in participating towards the researcher. The participants were asked to read and sign this document if they agreed to participate in the study. The study was approved by the ethical committee of the department of Applied Psychology, Thomas More University College.

## Measures

A self-constructed questionnaire, administered online using Qualtrics software, was used to answer the research questions. On average, it took about one hour to complete the questionnaire for students with ASD and about 20 minutes for student counsellors and TDC.

## Functional and participation problems

A previous literature review by Jansen et al. (forthcoming) revealed 11 different functioning and participation problems students with ASD can encounter in higher education. Participating students with ASD and students without a disability were asked if they experienced these 11 functioning and participation problems (e.g. 'I experience problems with verbal and nonverbal communication') in order to rate how frequently reported functioning and participation problems occur within both groups of students. Here, a yes-or-no answer was required. In addition, student counsellors had to rate the most common functioning and participation problems (e.g. 'Students with ASD experience problems with verbal and nonverbal communication') of students with ASD enrolled in their institution of higher education on a scale from 1 (totally not present) to 10 (always present). If the answer was equal to or larger than 5, the answer was considered to be a 'yes'-answer. The frequency was calculated based on these yes-answers.

## Teaching and evaluation methods

When students with ASD had given a 'Yes'-answer and thus reported a specific problem in higher education, they were asked during which teaching and evaluation methods this problem usually occurs (e.g. 'During which types of teaching and evaluation methods do you experience this problem with verbal and nonverbal communication?'). The students were given 14 different teaching and evaluation methods, which were described in the European Credit Transfer System (ECTS), for example, a lecture, a multiple choice exam or writing a paper. An overview of these methods can be found in the results section (Table 3). The student with ASD had to tick off during which types of methods these problems emerged for each experienced functioning and participation problem. It was possible to tick off multiple methods.

## Effective reasonable accommodations

Based on a literature study, reasonable accommodations were predetermined (e.g. Harrison et al. 2013; Kettler 2012). However, because the scarcity of literature regarding reasonable accommodations for students with ASD, a panel of six academic and professional experts were invited to supplement the list of reasonable accommodations available for students with ASD on the one hand and to appoint the specific reasonable accommodations to particular functioning and participation problems on the other hand. The accommodations were appointed to the specific problems by taking into account the specific objective of each reasonable accommodation. For example, the problem 'difficulty handling stress' was linked to the following reasonable accommodations: exam deferral (i.e. to reduce their stress level during the exam period), taking the exam in smaller than usual groups and extended examination duration (i.e. to reduce the stress during the exam itself).

Students with ASD received the experienced functioning and participation problems combined with the list of reasonable accommodations. Firstly, students had to indicate whether they effectively used the reasonable accommodation in higher education (e.g. 'Was exam deferral offered to you to deal with your difficulty handling stress?'). Secondly, students with ASD had to rate the experienced (when the reasonable accommodations was offered to them) or the expected (when they were not using the accommodation) effectiveness on a 5-point Likert scale (1 – very ineffective to 5 – very effective). In order to avoid a low sample size and to guarantee a reliable image for students with ASD, reasonable accommodations were perceived to be effective, and therefore listed in the results section, if (1) they had an overall score of 3 out of 5, and if (2) 3 or more students with ASD rated the experienced effectiveness (and thus used the reasonable accommodation).

## Analyses

### Descriptive statistics

In order to analyse the occurrence of the functioning and participation problems (i.e. research question 1) and the perceived effectiveness of the reasonable accommodations (i.e. research question 3), descriptive statistics, namely frequencies, ranges, means and standard deviations, were used. Additionally, to compare the data from the students with ASD to the data of students without a disability and the students counsellors (i.e. research question 1), chi square statistics were used. This comparison was made to explore inter-informant differences and to examine whether the functioning and participation problems are ASD-specific or if they occur in a general population of students in higher education.

### Two-mode partitioning

The probability with which the functioning and participation problems occurred during the different teaching and evaluation methods was examined by a two-mode partitioning (Schepers and Hofmans 2009; Schepers, van Mechelen, and Ceulemans 2006). Since both variables consisted of a large number of items, this statistic was used to reduce the number of functioning and participation problems and the number of teaching and evaluation methods by simultaneously grouping them into different clusters. If two functioning and participation problems are equally likely to emerge during the same teaching and evaluation methods, these problems are assigned to the same cluster. Correspondingly, two teaching and evaluation methods were clustered together if different functioning and participation problems are emerging to a similar extent.

Because the number of clusters in the solution had not been determined previously, the CHull procedure was used, meaning that the best fitting model was selected based on its interpretability and the goodness-of-fit versus the complexity balance (Ceulemans and Kiers 2006; Schepers, Ceulemans, and Van Mechelen 2008). When this model was selected, the two-mode partitioning yields a core matrix. In this core matrix, the strength of the relationship between each cluster of functioning and participation problems and each cluster of teaching and evaluation methods is represented. No rule of thumb has been described in literature with regard to the interpretation of these core values. Here it was decided to interpret these values in terms of probabilities, meaning that, if the core value is 0.65, students with ASD have a 65 per cent chance of experiencing a specific cluster of functioning and participation problems during a specific cluster of teaching and evaluation methods.

## Results

### Functional and participation problems

The results regarding the frequency of experienced functional and participation problems are shown in Table 1.

**Table 1.** Functional and participation problems of students with and without ASD according to the students and student counsellors.

|  | Students with ASD N | Students with ASD % | Students without ASD N | Students without ASD % | Student counsellors N | Student counsellors % |
|---|---|---|---|---|---|---|
| Problems with verbal and non-verbal communication | 29 | 67.4 | 8 | 18.6 | 22 | 73.3 |
| Oversensitivity to change | 29 | 67.4 | 7 | 16.3 | 22 | 73.3 |
| Problems distinguishing gist from detail | 29 | 67.4 | 12 | 27.9 | 16 | 53.3 |
| Problems planning and organising[a] | 26 | 61.9 | 18 | 41.9 | 22 | 73.3 |
| Problems with global information processing | 25 | 58.1 | 8 | 18.6 | 18 | 60.0 |
| Problems with social interaction | 23 | 53.5 | 8 | 18.6 | 22 | 73.3 |
| Problems handling stress | 22 | 53.7 | 11 | 25.6 | 20 | 66.7 |
| Problems with cognitive flexibility | 20 | 46.5 | 3 | 7.0 | 19 | 63.3 |
| Problems directing and shifting attention | 16 | 38.1 | 5 | 11.6 | 12 | 40.0 |
| Problems applying learning strategies[a] | 12 | 29.3 | 9 | 20.9 | 14 | 46.7 |
| Stereotypical, repetitive movements[a] | 9 | 20.9 | 8 | 18.6 | 6 | 20.0 |

[a]Non-significant difference between students with and without ASD ($p > 0.05$).

Two-third of the participating students with ASD mentioned problems with verbal and non-verbal communication, sensitivity to change and problems distinguishing the gist of the syllabus from the detail. When comparing the results of these students with ASD to the answers of student counsellors, no significant differences were found (all: $\chi^2(1) > 0.01$, $p > 0.05$). Finally, when looking at the results of students without a disability, results showed that these students experienced all functioning and participation problems significantly less frequently compared to students with ASD, except for problems with planning and organising ($\chi^2(1) = 3.42, p < 0.05$), problems applying learning strategies ($\chi^2(1) = 0.78, p < 0.05$) and experiencing stereotypical, repetitive movements ($\chi^2(1) = 0.787, p < 0.05$). This indicates that these three functioning and participation problems occurred to the same extent in both groups of students.

## Functional and participation problems during teaching and evaluation methods

The two-mode partitioning resulted in a model with three clusters of functioning and participation problems (Table 2) and five clusters of teaching and evaluation methods (Table 3). This 3 × 5 model accounted for 66.59% of the variance in how often specific functioning and participation problems occurred during particular teaching and evaluation methods.

Table 4 shows the core values that display the chance of occurrence of each cluster of functioning and participation problems during each cluster of teaching and evaluation methods.

**Table 2.** Clusters of functional and participation problems.

| Cluster 1 | Cluster 2 | Cluster 3 |
|---|---|---|
| Social interaction and communication | Inefficient study skills | Coping skills and behaviour |
| Problems with verbal and non-verbal communication | Problems distinguishing gist from detail | Problems handling stress |
| Problems with social interaction | Problems with global information processing | Problems planning and organising |
| Problems with cognitive flexibility | Problems directing and shifting attention | Stereotypical, repetitive movements |
| Oversensitivity to change | Problems applying learning strategies | |

**Table 3.** Clusters of ECTS teaching and evaluation methods.

| Cluster 1 | Cluster 2 | Cluster 3 | Cluster 4 | Cluster 5 |
|---|---|---|---|---|
| Classical teaching methods | Activating teaching methods | Classical evaluation methods | Alternative evaluation methods | Activating evaluation methods |
| Lecture | Excursion | Closed book exam | Multiple choice exam | Self or peer evaluation |
| Practical | Internship | Writing a paper | Open book exam | Process evaluation |
| | | Oral exam | Practical exam | |
| | | | Bachelor or master thesis | |
| | | | Portfolio | |

**Table 4.** Core values of the two-mode partitioning displaying the chance of occurrence of each cluster of functioning and participation problems during each cluster of teaching and evaluation methods.

| | Classical teaching methods | Activating teaching methods | Classical evaluation methods | Alternative evaluation methods | Activating evaluation methods |
|---|---|---|---|---|---|
| Social interaction and communication | 0.46 | 0.41 | 0.22 | 0.18 | 0.22 |
| Inefficient study skills | 0.61 | 0.18 | 0.53 | 0.35 | 0.13 |
| Coping skills and behaviour | 0.42 | 0.37 | 0.59 | 0.43 | 0.22 |

Firstly, the results show that the chances of experiencing social interaction and communication problems are highest during classical and activating teaching methods (probabilities, respectively, 0.46 and 0.41). The probability of encountering social interaction and social communication problems during the three clusters of evaluation methods (probability between 0.22 and 0.18) is lower. Secondly, when looking at the inefficient study skills, it became clear that students with ASD have a high chance of experiencing these problems during classical teaching and evaluation methods (probability of 0.61 and 0.53). The students mentioned lower chances of experiencing these problems during alternative evaluation methods and activating teaching and evaluation methods (probability between 0.35 and 0.13). Finally, it was shown that students with ASD have a high chance of experiencing problems with coping skills and behaviour during classical evaluation methods (probability of 0.59), alternative evaluation methods (probability of 0.43) and classical teaching methods (probability of 0.42), while the chances of experiencing coping problems are low during activating teaching and evaluation methods (probability respectively 0.37 and 0.22).

## *Effective reasonable accommodations*

The perceived effective reasonable accommodations (i.e. if the reasonable accommodation had a score of three or more out of five according to students with ASD who used the reasonable accommodation) for each functional and participation problem were listed in Table 5. For two functioning and participation problems, namely problems with verbal and non-verbal communication and problems with social interaction, no effective reasonable accommodations were found and therefore were not included in Table 5.

With respect to the cluster 'social interaction and social communication', extended examination duration was reported as most effective for students with ASD in higher education experiencing problems with cognitive flexibility, while students with ASD who are oversensitive to change perceived the reasonable accommodation 'receiving the schedule of an excursion in advance' as most effective. When looking at the cluster 'inefficient study skills', students with ASD mentioned that 'extended examination duration' was effective in dealing with all four functioning and participation problems of this cluster. Finally, when looking at the cluster 'coping skills and behavior', exam deferral was perceived as the most effective reasonable accommodation to deal with problems with handling stress and planning and organising according to students with ASD in higher education. Additionally, taking the exam in smaller than usual groups was mentioned as the only effective reasonable accommodation when dealing with stereotypical, repetitive movements. Other reasonable accommodations which were perceived as effective for specific functioning and participation problems can be found in Table 5.

The results also indicated that the experienced effectiveness of reasonable accommodations according to students with ASD who did not use the reasonable accommodation but did experience the specific functioning and participation problem was typically lower than the perceived effectiveness of reasonable accommodations reported by students with ASD who did use the reasonable accommodation. Significant differences were marked in Table 5 using an asterisk (*).

## Discussion

Previous literature already stated that students with ASD are in need of reasonable accommodations in order to provide equal participation chances in higher education for these students (Jansen et al., forthcoming; Van Hees, Moyson, and Roeyers 2015). Before being able to select and implement effective reasonable accommodations, it is important to have insight into both the personal characteristics (i.e. functioning and participation problems) of students with ASD and the environmental characteristics (i.e. teaching and evaluation methods) of the institutions of higher education. With this study we wanted to add to existing insights by examining following research questions: (1) How frequently did the identified functioning and participation problems occur for students with ASD in higher education?, (2) During which teaching and evaluation methods did these problems emerge?, and (3) Which reasonable accommodations were perceived to be effective to deal with the experienced functioning and participation problems?

**Table 5.** Effective reasonable accommodations for the functional and participation problems within each cluster.

| | | n used (%) | M (SD)[a] | Range | M (SD)[b] |
|---|---|---|---|---|---|
| **Social interaction and communication** | | | | | |
| Problems with cognitive flexibility | Extended examination duration | 16 (80.0) | 3.88 (0.96) | 2–5 | 2.50 (1.92)* |
| | Extended time for tasks | 4 (20.0) | 3.75 (0.50) | 3–4 | 3.06 (1.65) |
| Oversensitivity to change | Planning of excursion in advance | 9 (32.1) | 3.89 (0.78) | 3–5 | 3.05 (1.47) |
| | Not staying the night at an excursion | 3 (10.7) | 3.33 (1.53) | 2–5 | 2.16 (1.34) |
| | Designated seating in exam room | 5 (17.9) | 3.00 (1.58) | 1–5 | 2.43 (1.27) |
| | Picture overview of tutors | 3 (10.7) | 3.00 (1.00) | 2–4 | 1.92 (1.08)** |
| **Inefficient study skills** | | | | | |
| Problems distinguishing gist from detail | Extended examination duration | 21 (72.4) | 3.62 (1.24) | 1–5 | 3.00 (1.60) |
| | Extended time for tasks | 3 (10.3) | 3.00 (1.73) | 2–5 | 2.81 (1.33)* |
| Problems with global information processing | Extended time for tasks | 7 (28.0) | 3.86 (1.07) | 2–5 | 2.61 (1.29) |
| | Extended examination duration | 19 (76.0) | 3.79 (1.08) | 2–5 | 2.17 (0.98)* |
| Problems directing and shifting attention | Extended examination duration | 14 (93.3) | 3.71 (1.27) | 1–5 | 1.00 (/) |
| | Exam deferral | 5 (33.3) | 3.60 (1.52) | 1–5 | 2.50 (1.51) |
| | Taking the exam in smaller groups | 8 (53.3) | 3.50 (1.41) | 1–5 | 2.14 (1.35) |
| | Reading exam questions aloud | 3 (20.0) | 3.33 (1.16) | 2–4 | 1.67 (0.99) |
| Problems applying learning strategies | Extended examination duration | 12 (100.0) | 3.42 (1.56) | 1–5 | / |
| | Exam deferral | 4 (33.3) | 3.25 (1.71) | 1–5 | 2.75 (1.28) |
| **Coping skills and behaviour** | | | | | |
| Problems handling stress | Exam deferral | 7 (31.8) | 4.29 (0.76) | 3–5 | 3.33 (1.63) |
| | Taking the exam in smaller groups | 6 (27.3) | 4.33 (0.82) | 3–5 | 2.44 (1.55) |
| | Extended examination duration | 14 (63.6) | 4.14 (1.10) | 1–5 | 3.00 (1.77) |
| | Alternative exam format | 3 (13.3) | 3.00 (0.00) | 3 | 2.74 (1.49)* |
| Problems with planning and organising | Exam deferral | 8 (30.8) | 4.00 (1.31) | 1–5 | 2.89 (1.49) |
| | Support from student counsellor | 17 (65.4) | 3.88 (0.86) | 3–4 | 1.89 (1.05)** |
| | Exam questions one by one | 3 (11.5) | 3.33 (0.58) | 3–4 | 1.87 (0.92)* |
| | Visual time indication | 11 (42.3) | 3.27 (1.27) | 1–5 | 2.67 (1.29) |
| Repetitive movements | Taking the exam in smaller groups | 3 (33.3) | 3.33 (0.58) | 3–4 | 1.50 (0.84) |

[a]Perceived effectiveness rated by students with ASD who used the reasonable accommodation to deal with the specific functioning and participation problem.
[b]Expected effectiveness rated by students with ASD who did not use the reasonable accommodation but did experience the specific functioning and participation problem.
*Significant difference between the experienced and perceived effectiveness of an accommodation ($p < 0.05$). **Significant difference between the experienced and perceived effectiveness of an accommodation ($p < 0.01$).

## Research question 1: occurrence of the functioning and participation problems

To examine the first research question, a multi-informant approach was used and student counsellors, students with ASD and students without a disability were recruited. The results showed that students with ASD mentioned problems with verbal and non-verbal communication, oversensitivity to change and distinguishing gist from the detail as most frequently present. Student counsellors also reported that students with ASD have most problems with verbal and non-verbal communication and that these students are very sensitive to change.

In addition, student counsellors stated that these students also frequently encounter problems with planning and organising and with social interaction. These results are in line with the literature specifying that the most common problems for individuals with ASD are social interaction and communication on the one hand and stereotypical, repetitive behaviours and movements on the other (APA 2013; Billstedt, Carina Gillberg, and Gillberg 2007). When comparing data from the students with ASD with data from the student counsellors, no significant differences were found. This indicates that student counsellors have a good idea of the problems students with ASD generally experience in higher education.

Furthermore, students without a disability were included in order to determine whether the problems, which are experienced by students with ASD, are specific for the included students with ASD or if they occur to the same extent in the general population of students in higher education. By comparing the results of the students with ASD and the answers of students without a disability, three non-significant differences emerged. This means that, according to the students, stereotypical, repetitive movements, problems with planning and organising, and problems with applying learning strategies occur to the same extent for both groups of students. However, other explanations should be considered. It is possible that students with ASD have difficulties with self-insight and thus underreported these problems in the questionnaire (Frith and Happé 1999; Johnson, Filliter, and Murphy 2009). Previous research already suggested that students with ASD could have more problems with planning and organising and applying learning strategies compared to TDC (e.g. Jansen et al., forthcoming). Although it is not reported in this study, when comparing the answers of the TDC with the results of the student counsellors, only a significant difference with regard to stereotypical, repetitive movements was found. Another explanation for the lack of group differences within the student population on these three functioning and participation problems could be that students with ASD already learned how to plan and organise or apply effective learning strategies as a result of previous interventions (e.g. during secondary education). Unfortunately, our data-set does not allow us to test this hypothesis. With respect to stereotypical, repetitive movements, only a small number of students with ASD mentioned that they experienced this specific problem in higher education. Nevertheless, stereotypical, repetitive movements are included in the criteria for diagnosing ASD in the DSM-5 and literature already suggested that this problem is specific for individuals with ASD (APA 2013). However, it has already been shown that the occurrence of stereotypical, repetitive movements decreases when students with ASD age (e.g. Billstedt, Carina Gillberg, and Gillberg 2007).

### *Research question 2: problems during the teaching and evaluation methods*

With respect to the second research question, a two-mode partitioning was used to reduce the number of functioning and participation problems and the number of teaching and evaluation methods. The methods were clustered into five different groups, namely classical teaching methods, activating teaching methods, classical evaluation methods, alternative evaluation methods and activating evaluation methods. In the literature, teaching and evaluation methods are also mostly divided into classical teaching and evaluation methods and activating teaching and evaluation methods (e.g. Struyven, Dochy, and Janssens 2008).

Simultaneously, the functioning and participation problems were divided into three clusters, namely social interaction and communication, inefficient study skills, and coping skills and behaviour. The first cluster corresponds to the first of two diagnostic criteria described in DSM-5 namely 'social interaction and communication' (APA 2013). The second cluster contains inefficient study skills, which are mostly looked at as one subset of skills for students with and without disabilities in higher education (e.g. Mortimore and Ray Crozier 2006). With respect to students with ASD, problems with these study skills were also found by Jansen et al. (forthcoming). The last cluster of functioning and participation problems was the most heterogenic cluster of functioning and participation problems and is related to problems with handling stress and poor coping skills and behaviours of students with ASD. These problems can provoke stereotypical, repetitive movements and cause problems with planning, organising and time management or students with ASD (e.g. Glennon 2001).

Probability indices of the two-mode partitioning indicated that the chance of experiencing social interaction and communication problems is most pronounced during classical (e.g. during a practical) and activating teaching methods (e.g. during an excursion). During these teaching methods, students are challenged to work together, and thus communicate and interact, with other students and the professor. This is very demanding for students with ASD (e.g. Jansen et al., forthcoming; Orsmond et al. 2013). During other teaching and evaluation methods, students with ASD are less forced to work and study together and – as such – can prevent the emergence of specific functioning and participation problems.

Moreover, results showed that the chances of experiencing problems with inefficient study skills were more probable during the classical teaching and evaluation methods. During these teaching methods, lecturers provide large amounts of information when addressing the group of students. It is possible that, because of their problems with directing and shifting attention, students with ASD find it difficult to focus on the important information and are distracted by, for example, other students (Jansen et al., forthcoming). Furthermore, when studying and during classical evaluation methods, students with ASD have problems with selecting good learning strategies, processing information globally and distinguishing gist of the syllabus from the detail (Jansen et al., forthcoming). As a result, they are at risk of answering questions with too much detail and to make more mistakes during the classical evaluation methods. During alternative or activating evaluation methods, this risk is smaller because of the design of these exams. For example, during multiple choice exams students with ASD can only mark the right question while during oral exams or practical exams professors can interrupt the students when they are giving too much detail.

Finally, students with ASD who experience problems with coping skills and behaviour were most likely to encounter these problems during classical teaching and evaluation methods and during alternative evaluation methods. It is possible that students with ASD feel stressed during these teaching and evaluation methods, for example, when following a course together with a large group of students, and that the elevated stress level can provoke stereotypical, repetitive movements (Glennon 2001). Because of their raised stress level, students with ASD are likely not to go to the lectures or have to take some time off to relax. When they experience these elevated stress levels, the planning of students with ASD will change and they risk problems with rearranging their study or leisure time. During exam periods, the stress level of students with ASD is also elevated, causing problems with planning and organising and again leading to stereotypical, repetitive movements.

## *Research question 3: perceived effectiveness of reasonable accommodations*

Results regarding the third research question indicated that, in general, extended examination duration is the most effective reasonable accommodation for social interaction and communication problems and inefficient study skills. In line with the literature, it can be concluded that extended examination duration was also most used by the participating students with ASD (Kettler 2012). In addition, students with ASD perceived exam deferral and taking the exam in smaller than usual groups as most effective to deal with problems with coping skills and behaviours. Here, it is assumed that these students who received the accommodation exam deferral have more time to plan and organise their study time and thus reduce their stress during the exam period. Also, taking the exam in smaller than usual groups can reduce the stress level of students with ASD resulting in less stereotypical, repetitive movements (e.g. Glennon 2001).

Furthermore, it also became clear that a single reasonable accommodation is not effective in dealing with all specific functioning and participation problems. For example, it was shown that support from the student counsellor is only effective in dealing with planning and organising problems and not for other functioning and participation problems (see Table 5: Coping skills and behaviours). Additionally, results indicate that problems that cannot be neutralised by the use of reasonable accommodations in higher education are primarily associated with the (mandatory) social communication and interaction problems of ASD rather than with the (more heterogeneous) restrictive, repetitive behaviours and interests (DSM-5; APA 2013). As such, additional support outside the educational context for ASD core symptoms will be necessary.

In addition, the range of the perceived effectiveness varied for each reasonable accommodation (see Table 5). For example, when looking at the perceived effectiveness of extended examination duration when dealing with problems cognitive flexibility, the effectiveness score ranged from 2 to 5. This showed that there is a large heterogeneity in the perceived effectiveness of each reasonable accommodation for the individual students with ASD experiencing a specific functioning and participation problem. As a result, it can be concluded that the perceived effectiveness of a specific accommodation is individually determined.

Lastly, students with ASD, who experienced a specific functioning and participation problem but were not offered the reasonable accommodation, did rate the expected effectiveness of the accommodation. This expected effectiveness was often rated lower, and in some cases even significantly lower, than the perceived effectiveness rated by students with ASD who were using the accommodation. One explanation could be that the student counsellors tailored the reasonable accommodations perfectly to the needs of the student with ASD meaning that these reasonable accommodations were only effective for students using them and would not be effective for students with ASD who were not offered these reasonable accommodations. Alternatively, it has already been suggested that students with ASD have a hard time imagining which reasonable accommodations would be helpful because of their lack of insight into their own problems and the lack of experience and knowledge regarding accommodations in higher education (Magnus and Tøssebro 2014).

## Limitations

We recognise that this study has its limitations. Firstly, it is noticeable that significantly more students with ASD were enrolled in an academic educational programme in comparison to a professional educational programme than students without a disability. This could mean that the participating students with ASD constitute a specific subset of probably very high functioning individuals that effectively found their way into academic programmes. It is possible that these students experience less or different functioning and participation problems compared to the average student with ASD in secondary education who did not find their way into higher education.

Secondly, the items of functioning and participation problems and of the teaching and evaluation methods were reduced by the use of two-mode partitioning. This statistical analysis was used to make the data more manageable and generally show during which teaching and evaluation methods the problems of students with ASD emerge most. This does not imply that the detailed results are not important and student counsellors should not take into account individual differences between students with ASD in higher education.

Thirdly, classical teaching and evaluation methods are very frequently used in university colleges and universities. As such, the chances of experiencing functioning and participation problems are higher during these methods than during alternative or activating methods. Because of the frequent use of classical teaching and evaluation methods, it is possible that the perception of students with ASD is biased even when various functioning and participation problems occur to the same extent during all methods.

Fourthly, reasonable accommodations were listed in the results section if three or more students with ASD rated the experienced effectiveness in order to avoid a too low sample size. This entailed that some reasonable accommodations were removed from the results because only one or two students used the reasonable accommodation, regardless of whether the accommodation was perceived as effective or not. Because the effectiveness of reasonable accommodations is individually determined, it is important for student counsellors to also take into account other reasonable accommodations that were not listed in the results.

Finally, students with ASD had to rate the perceived or experienced effectiveness of each reasonable accommodation. This is a subjective parameter of effectiveness and does not provide an answer to the question whether the accommodation also has an objective effect on the test scores of students with ASD in higher education. Further research should focus on this objective effectiveness of reasonable accommodations.

## Implications for practice

As pointed out by the results of the first research question, there is a large heterogeneity between students with ASD when it comes to experiencing specific functioning and participation problems. Because of this heterogeneity and these individual differences, it is essential to map the specific functioning and participation problems before selecting and implementing effective reasonable accommodations. The specific problems of each individual student with ASD should be clarified during the intake session with the student counsellor. Additionally, the environmental characteristics, which impact the experienced functioning and participation problems and the selection of reasonable accommodations, should be identified in order to adjust the selection of reasonable accommodations to the context of the institution of higher education. Because of their direct impact on the functioning and participation of individual students with ASD in higher education, teaching and evaluation methods were investigated in this study. It became clear that these environmental characteristics have an influence on the experience of functioning and participation problems. However, also other environmental characteristics such as policy and organisational limitations should be explored before suggesting reasonable accommodations to students with ASD.

When functioning and participation problems and environmental characteristics are mapped, student counsellors can suggest reasonable accommodations. The results of this research goal, which were summarised in Table 5, gave a good indication of which reasonable accommodations are effective when dealing with specific functioning and participation problems. Selection and implementation of reasonable accommodations should be discussed with the student with ASD in order to select accommodations that are tailored to the needs of the individual.

Finally, our data indicated that two specific functioning and participation problems, namely problems with verbal and non-verbal communication and social problems, could not be neutralised by offering a reasonable accommodation. Therefore, it is possible that students with ASD need additional support to help them overcome specific functioning and participation problems. Student counsellors should have a good knowledge about the additional support to be able to refer these students to coaches or therapists, specialised organisations or multidisciplinary teams. Again, it is important that this additional support is tailored to the needs of the individual student with ASD in order to be effective in dealing with the specific problems.

In summary, this study showed that students with ASD frequently experience functioning and participation problems in higher education and that the occurrence of these problems may be different during various teaching and evaluation methods. Reasonable accommodations should be selected based on the personal characteristics (i.e. the experienced functioning and participation problems) of each individual student and the environmental characteristics (e.g. the teaching and evaluation methods) of the educational programmes of each institution of higher education in order to be effective. Therefore, student counsellors should take into account the context of the institution and the large variability between students with ASD when implementing reasonable accommodations in higher education.

## Acknowledgements

This article was performed as part of a research project on reasonable accommodations in higher education, supported by the Education Development Fund of KU Leuven Association.

## Disclosure statement

No potential conflict of interest was reported by the authors.

## References

APA (American Psychiatric Association). 2013. *Diagnostic and Statistical Manual of Mental Disorders*. 5th ed. Arlington, VA: American Psychiatric Publishing.

Barnhill, Gena P. 2016. "Supporting Students with Asperger Syndrome on College Campuses: Current Practices." *Focus on Autism and Other Developmental Disabilities* 31 (1): 3–15. doi:10.1177/1088357614523121.

Berger, Hans J. C., Francisca Aerts, Karel P. van Spaendonck, Alexander R. Cools, and Jan-Pieter Teunisse. 2003. "Central Coherence and Cognitive Shifting in Relation to Social Improvement in High-Functioning Young Adults with Autism." *Journal of Clinical and Experimental Neuropsychology* 25 (4): 502–511. doi:10.1076/jcen.25.4.502.13870.

Billstedt, Eva, I. Carina Gillberg, and Christopher Gillberg. 2007. "Autism in Adults: Symptom Patterns and Early Childhood Predictors. Use of the DISCO-10 in a Community Sample followed from Childhood." *Journal of Child Psychology and Psychiatry* 48 (11): 1102–1110. doi:10.1111/j.1469-7610.2007.01774.x.

Ceulemans, Eva, and Henk A. Kiers. 2006. "Selecting among Three-mode Principal Component Models of Different Types and Complexities: A Numerical Convex Hull Based Method." *British Journal of Mathematical and Statistical Psychology* 59: 133–150. doi:10.1348/000711005X64817.

Frith, Uta, and Francesca Happé. 1999. "Theory of Mind and Self-consciousness: What is it Like to be Autistic?" *Mind & Language* 14 (1): 1–22. doi:10.1111/1468-0017.00100.

Gelbar, Nicholas W., Isaac Smith, and Brian Reichow. 2014. "Systematic Review of Articles Describing Experience and Supports of Individuals with Autism Enrolled in College and University Programs." *Journal of Autism and Developmental Disorders* 44 (10): 2593–2601. doi:10.1007/s10803-014-2135-5.

Glennon, Tara J. 2001. "The Stress of the University Experience for Students with Asperger Syndrome." *A Journal of Prevention, Assessment and Rehabilitation* 17 (3): 183–190. http://content.iospress.com/articles/work/wor00188.

Harrison, Judith R., Nora Bunford, Steven W. Evans, and Julie S. Owens. 2013. "Educational Accommodations for Students With Behavioral Challenges: A Systematic Review of the Literature." *Review of Educational Research* 88 (4): 551–597. doi:10.3102/0034654313497517.

Jansen, Dorien, Elke Emmers, Katja Petry, Saskia van der Oord, and Dieter Baeyens. Forthcoming. "Functioning and Participation of Students with ASD in Higher Education according to the ICF-framework, a Multimethod Design." *Journal of Further and Higher Education*.

Jeste, Shafali S., and Daniel H. Geschwind. 2014. "Disentangling the Heterogeneity of Autism Spectrum Disorder through Genetic Findings." *Nature Reviews Neurology* 10 (2): 74–81. doi:10.1038/nrneurol.2013.278.

Johnson, Shannon A., Jillian H. Filliter, and Robin R. Murphy. 2009. "Discrepancies Between Self- and Parent-Perceptions of Autistic Traits and Empathy in High Functioning Children and Adolescents on the Autism Spectrum." *Journal of Autism and Developmental Disorders* 3 (12): 1706–1714. doi:10.1007/s10803-009-0809-1.

Kettler, Ryan J. 2012. "Testing Accommodations: Theory and Research to Inform Practice." *International Journal of Disability, Development and Education* 59 (1): 53–66. doi:10.1080/1034912X.2012.654952.

Magnus, Eva, and Jan Tøssebro. 2014. "Negotiating Individual Accommodation in Higher Education." *Scandinavian Journal of Disability Research* 16 (4): 316–332. doi:10.1080/15017419.2012.761156.

Mortimore, Tilly, and W. Ray Crozier. 2006. "Dyslexia and Difficulties with Study Skills in Higher Education." *Studies in Higher Education* 31 (2): 235–251. doi:10.1080/03075070600572173.

Olu-Lafe, Olufemi, Jacqueline Liederman, and Helen Tager-Flusberg. 2014. "Is the Ability to Integrate Parts into Wholes Affected in Autism Spectrum Disorder?" *Journal of Autism and Developmental Disorders* 44 (10): 2652–2660. doi:10.1007/s10803-014-2120-z.

Orsmond, Gael I., Paul T. Shattuck, Benjamin P. Cooper, Paul R. Sterzing, and Kristy A. Anderson. 2013. "Social Participation among Young Adults with an Autism Spectrum Disorder." *Journal of Autism and Developmental Disorders* 43 (11): 2710–2719. doi:10.1007/s10803-013-1833-8.

Schepers, Jan, Eva Ceulemans, and Iven Van Mechelen. 2008. "Selecting among Multi-Mode Partitioning Models of Different Complexities: A Comparison of Four Model Selection Criteria." *Journal of Classification* 25: 67–85. doi:10.1007/s00357-008-9005-9.

Schepers, Jan, and Joeri Hofmans. 2009. "TwoMP: A MATLAB Graphical User Interface for Two-Mode Partitioning." *Behavior Research Methods* 41 (2): 507–514. doi:10.3758/BRM.41.2.507.

Schepers, Jan, Iven van Mechelen, and Eva Ceulemans. 2006. "Three-Mode Partitioning." *Computational Statistics and Data Analysis* 51: 1623–1642. doi:10.1016/j.csda.2006.06.002.

Seltzer, Marsha M., Marty W. Krauss, Paul T. Shattuck, Gael Orsmond, April Swe, and Catherine Lord. 2003. "The Symptoms of Autism Spectrum Disorders in Adolescence and Adulthood." *Journal of Autism and Developmental Disorders* 33 (6): 565–581. doi:10.1023/B:JADD.0000005995.02453.0b.

Shattuck, Paul, Sarah Carter Narendorf, Benjamin Cooper, Paul Sterzing, Mary Wagner, and Julie Lounds Taylor. 2012. "Postsecondary Education and Employment among Youth with Autism Spectrum Disorder." *Pediatrics* 129 (6): 1042–1049. doi:10.1542/peds.2011-2864.

Smith, Caroline P. 2007. "Support Services for Students with Asperger's Syndrome in Higher Education." *College Student Journal* 41 (3): 515–531. https://www.questia.com/library/journal/1G1-169306797/support-services-for-students-with-asperger-s-syndrome.

Struyven, Katrien, Filip Dochy, and Steven Janssens. 2008. "Students' Likes and Dislikes regarding Student-Activating and Lecture-Based Educational Settings: Consequences for Students' Perceptions of the Learning Environment, Student Learning and Performance." *European Journal of Psychology of Education* 23 (3): 295–317. doi:10.1007/BF03173001.

UN (United Nations). 2006. *Convention on the Rights of Persons with Disabilities*, December 13. http://www.ond.vlaanderen.be/leerzorg/VN/verdrag.pdf (Dutch version).

University of Leuven. 2014. *Annual Report 2013–2014*. Belgium, Leuven: University of Leuven.

VanBergeijk, Ernst, Ami Klin, and Fred Volkmar. 2008. "Supporting More Able Students on the Autism Spectrum: College and Beyond." *Journal of Autism and Developmental Disorders* 38 (7): 1359–1370. doi:10.1007/s10803-007-0524-8.

Van Hees, Valérie, Tinneke Moyson, and Herbert Roeyers. 2015. "Higher Education Experiences of Students with Autism Spectrum Disorder: Challenges, Benefits and Support Needs." *Journal of Autism and Developmental Disorders* 45 (6): 1673–1688. doi:10.1007/s10803-014-2324-2.

White, Susan, Thomas Ollendick, and Bethany Bray. 2011. "College Students on the Autism Spectrum: Prevalence and Associated Problems." *Autism* 15 (6): 683–701. doi:10.1177/1362361310393363.

WHO (World Health Organization). 2001. *International Classification of Functioning, Disability and Health (ICF)*. Geneva: WHO.

Zürcher, Nicole R., Nick Donnelly, Ophélie Rogier, Britt Russo, Loyse Hippolyte, Julie Hadwin, Eric Lemonnier, and Nouchine Hadjikhani. 2013. "It's All in the Eyes: Subcortical and Cortical Activation during Grotesqueness Perception in Autism." *PloS one* 8 (1): 1–14. doi:10.1371/journal.pone.0054313.

# Developing an inclusive learning environment for students with visual impairment in higher education: progressive mutual accommodation and learner experiences in the United Kingdom

Rachel Hewett, Graeme Douglas, Michael McLinden and Sue Keil

**ABSTRACT**
Drawing on the findings of a unique longitudinal qualitative study, this article investigates the experiences of 32 young people with visual impairment (VI) in higher education (HE) in the United Kingdom (UK) to explore how well they were able to participate on their courses. We propose and apply a Bioecological Model of Inclusive HE to interpret these experiences and examine how accommodations were made to facilitate participation. Focusing specifically on 'curriculum access', the results highlight the importance of accommodations that are progressive and mutual. The accommodations come in many forms and include: the provision of resources through nationally based schemes (e.g. the Disabled Students Allowance in the UK); the support, adjustments and anticipatory adjustments HE institutions should provide; and the study skills and independence skills individual students should be able to act upon. The findings showed that while the majority of participants reported that their HE institution made some adjustments to enable them to access their course, a lack of anticipatory adjustments created barriers. The most common compensation for this barrier was to provide deadline extensions, often resulting in additional pressure on other aspects of the course. Interviews with university staff highlighted limited specialist knowledge and resources within their institutions to enable accommodations for students with VI and, more broadly, understanding of how to develop an inclusive learning experience. The findings also highlighted expectations made of the learner, particularly being able to explain their required adjustments and having well-developed independent study skills. The paper has particular relevance to HE institutions in that it provides a model to aid interpretation of their role in creating an inclusive learning experience for students with VI. It also offers a reference point for professionals supporting young people with a broader range of disabilities in considering how best to prepare them for life after compulsory education.

## Introduction

The UK Equality Act (2010) is central to the support system for students with disabilities in the United Kingdom (UK); it requires education providers to make 'reasonable adjustments' (including *anticipatory* adjustments) to remove barriers and ensure no student is put at a disadvantage.

---

**Box 1.** An overview of the legal responsibility of HE providers to make reasonable adjustments (adapted from the UK Equality Act 2010).

The responsible body in relation to a course to which this section applies must not discriminate against a person

(a) In the arrangements it makes for deciding who is enrolled on the course;
(b) As to the terms on which it offers to enrol the person on the course;
(c) By not accepting the person's application for enrolment.

The responsible body in relation to such a course must not discriminate against a person who is enrolled on the course in the services it provides or offers to provide.

The duty comprises the following three requirements.

(1) The first requirement is a requirement, where a provision, criterion or practice of A's puts a wdisabled person at a substantial disadvantage in relation to a relevant matter in comparison with persons who are not disabled, to take such steps as it is reasonable to have to take to avoid the disadvantage.
(2) The second requirement is a requirement, where a physical feature puts a disabled person at a substantial disadvantage in relation to a relevant matter in comparison with persons who are not disabled, to take such steps as it is reasonable to have to take to avoid the disadvantage.
(3) The third requirement is a requirement, where a disabled person would, but for the provision of an auxiliary aid, be put at a substantial disadvantage in relation to a relevant matter in comparison with persons who are not disabled, to take such steps as it is reasonable to have to take to provide the auxiliary aid.

In relation to the second requirement, a reference in this section or an applicable schedule to avoiding a substantial disadvantage includes a reference to:

(a) removing the physical feature in question,
(b) altering it, or
(c) providing a reasonable means of avoiding it.

---

Underpinned by these requirements, inclusion of students with disabilities in higher education (HE) within the UK is supported by a range of interrelating services and responsibilities including:

- The Disabled Student Allowance (DSA) Gov.UK (2016), a non-means tested scheme available to UK-based students to fund specialist equipment, non-medical support (e.g. note-takers, mobility support) and general expenses associated with a student's disability.
- HE institutional support (including that funded by DSA), often coordinated by a central Disability Support Office (DSO) or equivalent with responsibility for determining and directing the 'reasonable adjustments' required for a student to access their course.

- Departmental support provided by welfare tutors or equivalent with responsibility for ensuring reasonable adjustments are made for individual students in line with the Equality Act.
- Non-medical support provided by external agencies that recruit, train and manage staff.

In July 2015, the UK government's Department for Business, Innovation and Skills (BIS) launched a consultation regarding the future of DSA, proposing a new system where HE providers take greater responsibility (both practically and financially) for the non-medical support disabled students receive (BIS 2015). The rationale provided for this proposal was that:

(1) HE providers should take more responsibility for creating inclusive learning environments by making anticipatory adjustments for students with disabilities in accordance with the Equality Act, and
(2) Students with disabilities can and should make greater use of assistive technology to access their courses.

The proposals by BIS, however, appear to be based upon a number of drivers or assumptions: HE providers are equipped with the necessary resources, knowledge and desire to create 'inclusive' learning environments for all students; and students with disabilities have the necessary skills to embrace a more inclusive learning environment. It is in this context that we examine the inclusion of students with visual impairment (VI) within UK HE institutions.

## Aims

Drawing upon a longitudinal study that has followed a cohort of young people with VI as they left compulsory school education, we examine the experiences of 32 participants who made the transition into HE. Specifically, this paper explores three key questions to investigate the changes proposed by BIS (2015):

(1) To what extent does HE in the UK currently offer an inclusive learning experience for students with VI?
(2) How well equipped are HE providers in the UK at present to enable a more inclusive experience for students with VI?
(3) To what extent are students with VI entering HE equipped with the necessary skills to embrace such changes?

We begin the article with a brief overview of the longitudinal study outlining the background context, methods, participants and format of data analysis. We then propose a Bioecological Model of Inclusive Higher Education (based upon Bronfenbrenner 1979, 2005; Anderson, Boyle, and Deppeler 2014). This model is used as a lens through which we interpret young people's experiences of HE and the *enablers* and *barriers to participation* they faced.

## Longitudinal qualitative study

### Background

The Longitudinal Transitions Study was designed to investigate the transition experience of young people with VI from compulsory education to the labour market. The study was proposed in response to concerns about poor employment outcomes for young people with VI. In 2010 over 80 participants aged between 14 and 16 were recruited to the study through local authority sensory support services and specialist schools based in England and Wales. Whilst it is common for young people with VI to have additional (and often complex) special educational needs, this study focuses on those who met the inclusion criteria of being able to 'independently complete a questionnaire'. The participants have been educated in various educational settings including mainstream and specialist schools. The sample was judged to have a good representation from the population (Hewett, Douglas, and Williams 2011). At the time of writing, participants have been surveyed through semi-structured telephone interviews twice a year for 6 years and 65 young people remain active participants. These interviews have covered both the participant's transition pathways and specific factors believed to be significant for successful transitions of young people with VI (e.g. skills to access information independently, mobility skills and ability to self-advocate). Specifically, interview schedules used with participants in HE included the following topics: application process; support packages; access to the curriculum; assessments; and living independently in HE. A more thorough breakdown is provided in Hewett, Keil, and Douglas (2015a). Prior to initial participant recruitment, the project received ethical approval through University of Birmingham Ethics Committee and additional ethical approval has been sought prior to each data capture. The project followed usual protocols for participant confidentiality, anonymity and informed consent (which were revisited at the beginning of each interview to ensure continued willingness to be involved). An important consideration in this longitudinal study was how to respond to those participants experiencing difficulties who could potentially benefit from some form of intervention. The project adopted a policy to signpost these participants to relevant services (including seeking advice from the project steering group were necessary). These referrals have been recorded as part of the project.

Whilst there are other studies which have investigated the experiences of students with VI and disabilities in HE, this study provides a unique perspective in being, to our knowledge, the first qualitative longitudinal study with this group.

## *Data collected on HE experiences*

Since leaving compulsory education, the participants have followed various routes including FE, HE, apprenticeships, voluntary work and employment (or seeking employment). One common destination has been HE, with half of the participants (32) pursuing this option. Interviews were conducted with the participants in HE at several points: at the time of initial application, shortly after starting their studies and at the end of their first year of study. Further information about these young people is presented in Table 1. The severity of the participant's VI ranged from individuals requiring few adjustments, to individuals who have no vision at all. They attended a variety of HE institutions including 'pre-1992' universities, which tend to demand higher grades, and smaller institutions offering specialist courses. Case study work was also carried out with five participants. This involved site visits and additional interviews with key people who had had a role in their transition into HE, including four parents/carers, five Disability Support (DS) officers and five welfare tutors.

**Table 1.** Overview of participants in HE (*N* = 32).

| Variable | Total (*N*) |
| --- | --- |
| *Gender* | – |
| Male | 18 |
| Female | 14 |
| *Registration type* | – |
| Sight impaired (partially sighted) | 13 |
| Severely sight impaired (blind) | 11 |
| Not registered | 5 |
| Participant does not know | 3 |
| *Preferred reading format* | – |
| Standard font size (up to pt 14) | 4 |
| Large print (Pt 16–22) | 15 |
| Very large print (Pt 24+) | 4 |
| Braille/Electronic | 9 |
| *Type of secondary school education* | – |
| Mainstream school | 19 |
| Special school | 11 |
| Both mainstream and special school | 2 |
| *Type of HE institution attended* | – |
| Pre-1992 institution | 12 |
| Post-1992 institution | 17 |
| Specialist institution | 3 |

**Table 2.** Key terms used in WHO ICF, adapted from WHO (2001, 9, 10).

| Terminology | Description |
| --- | --- |
| Impairment | Problems in body function or structure such as a significant deviation or loss |
| Activity | Concerned with performances in activities at an individual level |
| Participation | Concerned with involvement in life situations on a society level |
| Participation restrictions | Problems an individual may experience in involvement in life situations |
| Environmental factors | Concerned with variables which can be manipulated (whether physical, social or attitudinal) which might improve performance on activities and/or increase participation |
| Barriers | General term describing environmental factors which may cause 'activity limitations' and 'participation restrictions'. Similarly, *facilitators* (or *enablers*) may remove such limitations or restrictions |

## *Data analysis*

The data collected in the study was analysed through both basic summary statistics and thematic analysis (using NVivo 10) following a three-stage approach. Stage 1 involved Author 1 gathering the data into broad sequences of events experienced by the participants and to some extent reflected the structure of the questions used in various interviews. These findings are presented in full technical and summary reports (Hewett, Keil, and Douglas 2015a, 2015b). Stage 2 involved the researchers working together to rearrange and combine codes. The researchers drew upon two frameworks to support their analysis. The first was the World Health Organization's (WHO) International Classification of Functioning, Disability and Health (ICF). We have used this approach extensively in our previous research as 'it keeps "participation" at its centre, and emphasises the importance of removing barriers to disabled people's participation' (Douglas et al. 2012, 19). Key terms are summarised in Table 2, and these terms were being used as a source of language when developing the interview schedules and for analysing and reporting the research findings (as reflected in use of ICF language in the results, in particular identified 'barriers'). The second framework used was the Bioecological Systems Theory of Human Development (BST) described below. Finally, Stage

3 considered how well the system works as a whole, what lessons can be learnt, and what implications of proposed policy changes to DSA these findings might predict.

## Bioecological model of inclusive education in HE

The BST was developed and refined by Bronfenbrenner throughout the course of his career (e.g. Bronfenbrenner 1979, 2005). The theory was originally intended to explore how human development is influenced by the environment in which an individual is situated, with later versions placing greater importance on the role individuals play in their own development (Tudge et al. 2009). The later version of the theory (e.g. Bronfenbrenner 2005) consists of four key interrelated elements: 'process' (human development through interactions with the environment around them); 'person' (personal characteristics that impact on development, e.g. age, skills and temperament); 'context' (the environments in which the person sits); and 'time' (the time in which this process occurs) (Tudge et al. 2009). The context in which the individual sits is described by Bronfenbrenner with reference to five systems: microsystems (factors in the environment immediately around the individual); mesosystems (interactions between factors within the microsystems); exosystems (factors outside the individual's immediate environment that impact upon their development); macrosystems (factors and culture outside the physical environment); and chronosystems (human development over time). A more detailed overview of Bronfenbrenner's work is provided in McLinden et al. (2016) and Anderson, Boyle, and Deppeler (2014).

Anderson, Boyle, and Deppeler (2014) developed BST further to propose a Bioecological Model of *Inclusive Education*. The ecological model outlined by Anderson, Boyle, and Deppeler (2014) has a focus on inclusive education in schools and serves as a useful framework in interpreting the 'complicated, messy and changeable' (31) environments and various influences on a child's participation in education. Given the wide-ranging and interacting influences on a learner's participation in HE, we have found it valuable to use a similar conceptual framework in the form of a Bioecological Model of Inclusive HE as a lens to analyse data from the study. Such application has been found to be beneficial by other academics. For example Anderson, Boyle, and Deppeler (2014) argue that the ecological systems theory provides an 'invaluable framework within which to organise the environmental factors and understand their influence on inclusivity by placing the learner at the centre' with each contributory factor 'located in relation to the learner's educational ecosystem' (28). Similarly, May and Bridger (2010) found it to be 'a useful model to describe the layers of influence operating in a given situation'. Further, not only does the model add a greater sophistication in relation to the educational systems for this analysis, but it also allows us to draw upon the language of the ICF and the concern to identify and remove barriers to participation.

In the next section we outline this model, which has been shaped through our research findings, before presenting findings within this framework.

The application of a Bioecological Model of Inclusive Education to the experiences of students with VI in HE provides an original way to view the experiences of students with disabilities. This is particularly true in the context of the longitudinal qualitative study as we are able to consider the development of the young people over a period of time, rather than at a particular time point.

## Analysis of findings

### *Outlining a bioecological model of inclusive higher education*

At the centre of the model is the learner with VI in HE. Each learner will have particular characteristics and needs, which is important to acknowledge in any analysis of his or her participation in HE. As an example, there are many types of VI affecting individuals in different ways. VI can affect visual acuity and central/field vision (for the criteria used to determine whether an individual can be certified as having a VI, see RNIB 2016), or an individual may have a condition that affects their visual processing. It is not uncommon to have more than one condition causing VI, emphasising the importance of considering individual needs. It is also common for participants with VI to have additional disabilities or learning difficulties. For example, Keil (2012) found that approximately 20% of children and young people with VI in the UK have 'additional' special educational needs and/or disabilities (SEND). Some learners may be restricted in getting around independently and require mobility training/orientation or a sighted guide to get to and from learning facilities. VI learners typically access information using different methods from their sighted peers – e.g. using a larger font size or braille. Technology provides different opportunities for making material more accessible, including screen readers, which verbalise text, and braille devices, which convert electronic material into braille. It is likely that these learners will require adjustments to participate in visual aspects of their courses, such as practical sessions (Douglas et al. 2011).

Situated around the learner are a series of interrelated systems (Figure 1):

- *Microsystem* – factors that directly impact the learner, e.g. DSO, welfare tutors, lecturers, support staff, peers, curriculum and assessment practices, and relevant institution infrastructure.

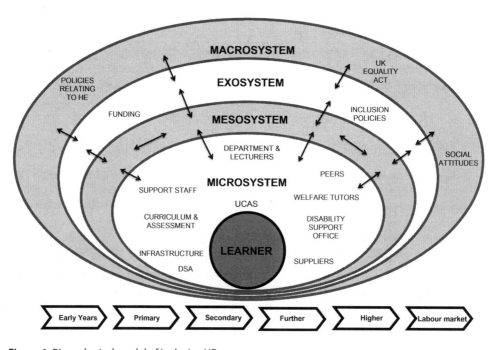

**Figure 1.** Bioecological model of inclusive HE.

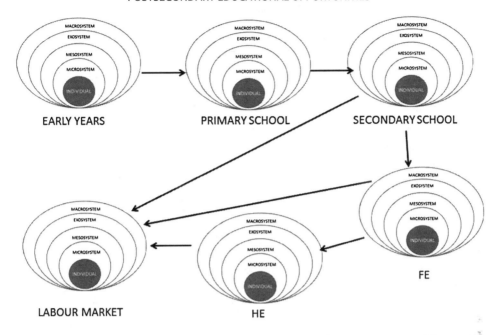

**Figure 2.** The chronosystem illustrating the individual experiences changing systems at different stages of their life.

- *Mesosystem* – representing the interactions that take place between these factors in the microsystem.
- *Exosystem* – factors that do not impact the learner's immediate environment but still affect their experience, e.g. inclusion policies.
- *Macrosystem* – factors external to the HE institution, e.g. the Equality Act, HE funding and societal perceptions of VI.
- *Chronosystem* – time and the development of the individual and their movement through various stages of life and changing systems (e.g. from early years to the labour market, as represented in Figure 2).

## Macrosystem: factors and culture outside the physical environment

### Equality Act

The UK Equality Act requires educational institutions to make reasonable adjustments to enable learners with disabilities to participate on their courses. This is important empowering legislation for students with disabilities. However, a relatively high proportion of participants (25%) was unaware of the Equality Act, whilst others had limited knowledge of its contents. Of 15 participants asked, 8 felt that the institutions had observed the requirements of the Equality Act, whilst 7 did not. One participant in particular believed that institutions' responsibilities are not sufficiently defined:

> In practice, probably not all that well, on paper, fairly good. I think the thing is, it's the problem with the Equality Act in general isn't it – reasonable adjustments is a bit of a loose term, and is very subjective. So they have probably done everything that they possibly could to do [what] they think is a reasonable adjustment. (Blind student, pre-1992 institution)

## Societal attitudes

Whilst difficult to quantify, interviews with DS officers and lecturers illustrated how societal perceptions of VI had an impact upon their initial judgement of the young person they were working with. For example, a DS officer was initially concerned that one severely sight impaired student would not be able to get around independently without a guide dog, showing a misunderstanding about independent mobility. A lecturer shared how he had made the assumption that the student he was working with would not misuse extended assessment deadlines on the basis that they were VI, indicating that he had had different (higher) expectations for this student, to those he had for other students.

## Policies

One DS officer identified how the government policies towards HE were centred on a medical model of disability (making compensations on an individual basis), which can act as a barrier to students who may not wish to identify themselves as disabled:

> ... it's based on the medical model of disability, rather than the social model of disability as well, so for some students that's a struggle as well; they don't want to be providing evidence and all that sort of stuff, but you have to do it to get the support that you require. (DS officer, post-1992 institution)

### Exosystem: factors outside the learners immediate environment

## Approaches to inclusion

Positively, all of the DS officers interviewed reported having published guides for staff to describe reasonable adjustments as part of inclusive learning policies. An Education Support Manager with responsibility for disabled students at a departmental level described how normally the adjustments required for students with learning difficulties and disabilities are covered by their inclusive teaching policy:

> There's quite a lot of students that are covered by our inclusive teaching policy. This is something that the DSO are hoping to run out across the university, and it's something that has been created. So things like copies of lecture notes in advance, quite a lot of student support packages are covered by that. (Education Support Manager, pre-1992 university)

However, DS officers and academic staff highlighted how challenging it can be to meet these requirements due to limited staff resource:

> You talk to most staff and they would say 'yeah, yeah, of course we want to support', but they are busy, and they don't like to be told that they have to do a lot of extra work. (Welfare tutor, pre-1992 university)

## Moving towards more inclusive practice

Both DS officers and students observed that DSOs have limited power in the HE institution (HEI) hierarchy to ensure that student support agreements are adhered to. DS officers suggested that more resources needed to be invested to develop inclusive learning practice, with one officer arguing this needed to be at the core of the institution:

> I think it would be the Pro-Vice Chancellor setting up a team of people, to ensure that the university is fully accessible to anybody, whatever their disability ... Everything that is done, is done with accessibility in mind. (DS officer, pre-1992 university)

## *Microsystem and mesosystem: interacting factors in the immediate environment*

### *Applications*

Prospective HE students submit applications on the Universities and Colleges Admissions Service (UCAS) website. Whilst 17 participants were able to access this process (e.g. by using assistive technology), 13 participants experienced difficulties with the accessibility of the website and in some cases were unable to complete applications independently. Similarly, three participants experienced barriers when applying for DSA, having been sent paper copies of forms, which they could not complete without sighted assistance:

> It's not very accessible. All the forms and stuff we get sent out in print. That was a bit frustrating. We didn't get email copies of anything, and I wasn't able to fill it out myself, so I had to have someone else do it for me or with me, so that was frustrating ... (Young person, screen-reader user)

### *Disabled student allowance*

BIS (2015) states that many of the barriers faced by students with disabilities in HE can be overcome with assistive technology. Despite this, many of the participants were limited in the equipment DSA was prepared to fund. Ten participants received compromised equipment due to the cap on funding, whilst others were not permitted to use DSA to fund certain 'mainstream' equipment like tablet computers, despite their inbuilt accessibility benefits (e.g. Hewett and Douglas 2015). Participants also experienced problems with the reliability of the laptop computers they were given, which was particularly challenging for those reliant on their computer to access information:

> It had ups and downs. Most of the downs you could link very directly to technical issues I had – laptop failure ... I had technical issues in all three terms. The first term it was concerning and worrying. The second time it was 'oh no, not again', but I think the second term was the more problematic one as it left me with days where I didn't have a laptop ... (Young person, screen-reader user)

Despite these challenges, participants emphasised how important DSA was to them, seeing it as an essential means for participation on their course:

> I wouldn't be able to access my course without this equipment that I [purchased] through DSA because I didn't have it otherwise. I couldn't have just bought it off my own back. (Young person, screen-reader user)

### *External agencies*

Many students spoke positively of the external agencies that provided their non-medical support, equipment and training. A particularly positive account came from one student whose university worked with the external agency to identify a research assistant with the necessary expertise to support him in practical sessions. The agency in turn provided training for this research assistant to enable them to support the student.

However, a number of participants experienced problems with external agencies. Several started their first academic year without their equipment in place, making it impossible for them to participate fully in their courses. Others found that despite receiving funding for non-medical support (e.g. a note-taker or library support), the supplier was unable to provide the staff required and almost all participants requiring mobility support (e.g. to learn routes around the university) had difficulties accessing it:

And then last summer I rang up, and I then got blamed for apparently leaving it until the last minute, which I felt really upset and really patronised about because I had done the opposite … it impacted on my studies, rather than it being nice and relaxed, and it was awful. (Young person, long cane user)

The most positive mobility stories came from participants who received their mobility training prior to the start of the term, enabling them to develop their independence:

… I learned how to get to uni [university], how to get around uni, how to get into town, how to get to Sainsbury's, a few places in the first week. [...] I am glad I did that, because it meant that when everyone else arrived I was able to move around, and I think the worst thing you can do is leave it and not get training until after everyone arrives, because otherwise it relies on other people. (Young person, guide dog and long cane user)

## *Disability support office*

The first point of contact for students with disabilities is often the DSO whose responsibility is to develop a support plan (student support agreement) detailing the adjustments the institution will need to make to enable that student to be able to participate in their course. Participants had mixed experiences with regards to how well the DS officer was able to understand their VI:

Terribly, terribly. I think the reason why they had so much trouble providing things for me is because they didn't understand my visual impairment in the first place. (Young person, partially sighted, pre-1992 institution)

## *Implementation of support plans*

Welfare tutors and DS officers reported large numbers of students in receipt of support plans, making it challenging for academic staff to put these plans into effect, e.g.:

… [support plans] get ignored. [...] So it just turned out a lot of times I would be going into lectures and seminars and they wouldn't even know; they would have no idea that there were these issues. (Young person, partially sighted, post-1992 institution)

None of the academic staff interviewed received any institution-led training or guidance on how to adapt their teaching practices to create a more inclusive learning experience. Whilst academic staff looked towards the DSO for such guidance, interviews with the DS officers revealed that none of them had received any specific training on supporting students with VI.

The inclusion plan would make reference to [participant's] condition, and it would say that these are the reasonable adjustments that staff must make. But they largely related to provision of materials, [...] so there wasn't any guidance on how to rethink your lectures. Pedagogically it's quite a big thing to rethink that. (Lecturer, post-1992 university)

One DS officer shared how she felt academics were scared at the prospect of supporting students with severe VI:

They are scared actually, and I don't blame them, I really don't blame them. I would panic if I was in their position, because there is no one to go to … (DS officer, pre-1992 institution)

Case study interviews identified tensions between DS officers and academic staff. DS officers were frustrated at what they perceived to be a lack of engagement by teaching staff, whilst academics found DS officers to be unrealistic regarding the adjustments they expected lecturers to make:

> The problem we are having now is the [department] just haven't done what they need to do, and this is always the frustration, always, always the frustration. (DS officer, pre-1992 university)

> I said 'look, I am going to be honest with you here, I really want to be supportive, but I know what can and can't be done, academic staff won't do these things, so you have to work with us. (Welfare tutor, pre-1992 institution)

## *Accessible curriculum and assessment*

The participants identified various positive adjustments made by lecturers to enable them to participate in teaching sessions. These included describing diagrams in lectures, writing descriptions of visual content on lecture notes and demonstrating equipment through one-to-one sessions. Many of these adjustments were the product of discussions between the student and staff before modules commenced – i.e. anticipatory adjustments.

Barriers students encountered included not having lecture material in accessible formats; no adjustments to visual elements; and fast-paced lectures. In some cases, lecturers were unable to make components or even entire modules accessible to the student. Rather than addressing this, at the start of the academic year, these barriers were sometimes ignored and extended into the assessment period at which point examinations were delayed to enable the student to 'catch-up' and provide the lecturer time to determine how to make the teaching accessible.

> I just spoke to the lecturer and said 'is it worth it?' and most of the time we decided that I just wouldn't bother going [to lectures]. (Blind student, pre-1992 institution)

Some participants required alternative formats for course textbooks. A common challenge faced was obtaining these with sufficient time to be able to participate in lectures and seminars, and complete assignments. These barriers often stemmed from institutions not meeting their responsibility to make anticipatory adjustments by supplying reading lists with sufficient notice. Additionally, some support staff did not understand the format the students required, and sometimes even adjusted material remained inaccessible. Positive accounts came from students who were given copies of reading lists prior to the start of term, allowing sufficient time for library staff to obtain accessible copies of texts. One student described how not having accessible copies of texts made her feel excluded from the course and from her peers. This student's experience illustrates how a lack of anticipatory adjustments can impact upon students in multiple ways. Engagement with peers is an important aspect of HE, as recognised in including peer-to-peer support in the microsystem:

> No, it makes a big difference as well, because it makes you feel more included in what's going on, but it makes you feel more sort of welcome, and gives me more of an incentive to … bother I guess. (Blind student, post-1992 institution)

Additionally, several students experienced barriers when taking exams, including: inaccessible copies of exam papers; not being given the correct room information; not being allocated the correct amount of extra time; and not being given the correct assistive technology.

> … they gave me the wrong [format] paper in picture PDF form. And I had a bit of a meltdown because I was so nervous. It was so frustrating because I have been there for two years now, and it's such a basic thing. It's on every … it's on my inclusion plan, or whatever it is, it's like the first thing that is on it, that I need stuff in Word. (Blind student, post-1992 institution)

In contrast, one student described a very positive experience. Instead of her exam arrangements being communicated on an ad-hoc basis, they were incorporated into the university's main examination system:

> And then when it comes to getting my exams, they automatically factor in the extra time. So it will say start time and end time [on my timetable on the VLE], it will automatically factor in my extra time, and automatically puts me in one of the alternative rooms. (Partially sighted student, pre-1992 institution)

## *Infrastructure*

Positive accounts came from some students of an inclusive teaching experience facilitated by the standard teaching approaches their institutions used. A clear example was when students were able to access course notes in advance of lectures through the institution's virtual learning environment (VLE) and electronic copies of books or journal articles through their library's online database:

> It just meant that I could ... when we were sat in the lecture if I couldn't get close to the front, I didn't have to be sat close to the front, I could sit wherever I liked and could keep up with what was being said. That was quite beneficial. [...] A lot of people took laptops to lectures as well, so it wasn't like in school where you are the only one, it's just normal at uni. (Partially sighted student, post-1992 institution)

However in contrast, some students experienced additional barriers due to inaccessible VLEs. As well as being restricted in accessing course notes, participants had problems with accessing their timetable, email, exam results and module choice forms:

> And I had an issue with picking my modules for next year, because the module selection process wasn't accessible, so I had a delay in being able to do it because I needed sighted assistance to be able to do it. (Blind student, post-1992 institution)

## **Chronosystem and the learner: development over time**

### *Preparation for HE*

When considering transitions and the need for the learner to be prepared to move from one setting to the next, very few participants had received guidance from school teachers or specialist teachers from local authority Sensory Support Services to support their transition to HE. Instead, they tended to rely on the guidance of the DSA assessor to develop a support package. However, eight participants questioned the quality of their assessment.

> It was clear she hadn't worked with a blind person before, and it was clear that ... because she said it herself, basically 'I don't know what I am doing, you have got to tell me what you need', rather than ... I was like 'actually, I think that's your job!' (Blind student, post-1992 institution)

Both university staff and students viewed the transition into HE as an ongoing process, during which the institution developed a better understanding of required adjustments, and the student learned how to manage their support.

> Like I say, there was kind of an acknowledgement, right from the beginning [...] I was quite clear about this, and [participant] was clear about this, that we would come across, there would be a case of adjustments as things developed, because we wouldn't be able to pre-empt and plan for everything. (Welfare tutor, post-1992 institution)

Some students who experienced problems in the first year found that by the second year they had a better understanding of what was needed for them to participate on their courses:

I was much happier because I knew my way around better, and myself and my library assistant had a routine going for getting books done on time, and getting things managed in that way. I think as well, I understood what I needed [better]. So at the beginning of the year I met with all my new tutors and went to talk to them about what I needed and stuff like that. (Blind student, post-1992 institution)

The experiences of the participants also highlighted the necessity of the learner to have an understanding of the types of adjustments they required, the ability to be able to advocate for these adjustments and the skills to benefit from these adjustments. We now consider the importance of the development of these skills for a successful transition into HE by focusing on two specific examples – self-advocacy and accessing information.

## *Self-advocacy*

Interviews with DS officers and welfare tutors revealed how support systems in HE rely on the learner being able to self-advocate and act as 'expert' in their impairment:

I am not a specialist with visual impairment at all, so my knowledge and understanding of what she needs is very limiting. From a general point of view as a disability advisor, I could also do what's needed, but she was able to tell us exactly what, so it was very good. (DS officer, pre-1992 institution)

The interviews also demonstrated a reliance on the student to take responsibility for their learning and to make staff aware if they experienced problems. For example, one DS officer said he assumed that the participant he supported was having a positive experience as he had not heard from her since early on in the first year.

And what we do say to all students, you are an adult now, you have left home, you have come to university, we are going to treat you as an adult ... we do expect you to tell us when there is a problem ... (DS officer, post-1992 institution)

In reality, this student was having a very challenging time as lecturers were not adhering to her support plan. The student was restricted by firstly not having the confidence to address this, and secondly by externalising the responsibility:

Researcher: 'Is there meant to be someone in the department who is responsible for ensuring that people get the support agreements?'

Participant: 'Apparently, but I don't know who they are. I know one student knew who they were because they contacted them, but they have never done anything to contact me.' (Partially sighted student, post-1992 institution)

As previously noted, very few participants had been facilitated to act as self-advocates in HE. Consequently, the participants experienced a number of barriers including not knowing how to explain their impairment and how it affected them and not knowing how to explain to staff how to prepare accessible materials.

... basically, I went from an environment where everyone was visually impaired to an environment where nobody had a visual impairment ... I didn't think about having to explain to people that I was visually impaired, so I didn't quite have a sense of how to do that, that was one of the adjustments that I had to make. (Partially sighted student, pre-1992 institution)

## *Independent access to information*

In comparison with school, studying within HE normally requires students to be more independent learners, able to extend their knowledge through participation in lectures and seminars, supplemented by independent research. Interviews demonstrated that many participants benefited from a range of skills they learned at school including choosing the most appropriate method for accessing information according to the task in hand. For example, whilst most participants with severe VI preferred to use screen-reader technology to listen to large volumes of text, some found it helpful to follow their lecture notes using braille displays, which enabled them to read and make notes and listen to the lecturer at the same time.

However, some participants appeared to have less-developed skills for accessing information, thus restricting their ability to work independently. This included one student who relied on sighted assistance to complete online research and a student who had not received any formal training in using her screen-reader prior to HE. At the most extreme, were a small number of students who had not previously used any assistive technology in school and were finding it difficult to adapt to incorporate these into their normal working practice.

> When I had my training session from DSA, I found I kind of realised quite a lot, but at the same time, I don't know very much if you know what I mean! [I do quite well given that] I never had any training, but in terms of everything that [the technology] has to offer, I know very little, realistically ... The trainer was like 'do you know how to do this?' and I was like 'yeah, yeah', and then she would go 'oh, so you know how to do that?', and I was like 'nooo!' (Blind student, screen-reader user)

## Discussion

The Bioecological Model of Inclusive Education in HE outlined above provides a valuable framework with which to examine the experiences of the participants in HE through a holistic view that takes into account the individual learner and the surrounding systems. By adopting this broader perspective, we have identified a range of potential barriers to inclusion in HE. In discussing these barriers we refer to our original research questions. We then draw the analysis back to the BST and end by considering the future policy context within the UK.

### *Do UK HE institutions offer an inclusive learning experience?*

Anderson, Boyle, and Deppeler (2014) recommend assessing the inclusivity of an educational experience by looking at the three key principles of 'participation', 'achievement' and 'value'.

*Participation*
Having faced barriers in participation on their courses, four of the participants failed to complete their first year. In each case, the HE provider accepted responsibility for not having made reasonable adjustments. Other participants persevered with their courses, but in many cases faced challenges.

The UK Equality Act (2010) requires HE providers to make reasonable adjustments to enable participation for students with disabilities. In many ways the HE providers appear to take this requirement seriously; for example, by providing dedicated teams to devise support plans to facilitate course access. However, from our evidence for students with VI, a significant barrier appears to be a lack of *anticipatory adjustments*. Examples of anticipatory adjustments (as demonstrated by some providers) include ensuring that infrastructure (e.g. the VLE) is accessible to *all* students from the outset, ensuring that *all* relevant documents are produced in accessible formats, and providing reading lists in sufficient time for alternative formats to be sourced. Failure to make anticipatory adjustments led to various challenges such as not being able to discuss a text in seminars, not being able to make module choices and even, in one case, not being able to take an exam.

## Achievement

Many of the participants spoke positively with regards to their achievements, although these did not always follow the same timescales as their peers. It was common for academic staff to rely on students' use of deadline extensions to compensate for the barriers they experienced, thereby adding pressure onto other deadlines and often extending the student's academic year. A small number of participants expressed disappointment at the grades they obtained, which they attributed to the barriers they encountered. Achievement, however, is broader than simply academic attainment per se. For example, one participant was disappointed not to have been able to learn to use statistical software she considered a core component of her course, whilst another participant spoke positively of having had the opportunity to learn to use equipment in practical geography sessions as a result of the careful and considered planning of his department.

## Value

Anderson, Boyle, and Deppeler (2014), citing Aspin (2007), define value as 'being accepted, respected and seen as important and capable of doing' (25). Positively, interviews highlighted that the participants were largely treated in the same manner as their peers, and held to the same expectations. However, whilst many of the participants expressed that they did not feel any different to their sighted peers, this was less true for participants with severe VI. One DS officer described academic staff as 'scared' of working with students with severe VI, substantiated by a parent who observed 'panicked' reactions from staff at open days. Three participants identified times in which they felt left on the fringes during group work with their peers. They attributed this to barriers to accessing course material, as well as their peers' apparent perception of them having a lower ability, and being cautious about interacting with VI students in case of causing offence. Linked to this, the consequences of working to different timescales (e.g. deadline extensions) meant that some connections with peers were lost. Academic staff would have liked to provide greater support to students with disabilities, but felt limited by the resources available to them.

## How prepared are HE institutions for developing an inclusive learning experience?

Interviews with lecturers and DS officers at six institutions highlighted a lack of specialist knowledge of how to make accommodations for students with VI. Whilst DS officers look to the DSA assessment of needs report to shape the support offered, some participants questioned how well equipped DSA assessors are to provide such guidance. Additionally, some participants felt that the DS officers struggled to understand the implications of their VI.

Support plans provide basic guidance on the adjustments that lecturers are expected to make to enable participation. However, two lecturers found these plans did not provide the pedagogical guidance they required in order to create a more inclusive learning environment. Both lecturers and DS officers highlighted that limited resources meant that lecturers were restricted in how much time they could devote to developing an inclusive curriculum.

## *How prepared are learners with VI for the transition into HE?*

Bronfenbrenner (2005) emphasised the importance of considering the role of the developing learner. We have observed that the current support system for students with disabilities relies on the individual entering HE with independence skills in place. Firstly, as in the case of all students, it relies on them having the skills to be able to work relatively independently in comparison with their school education. For students with VI, this can often mean having a range of skills to call upon to enable them to adapt to the demands of a particular task. Whilst most participants generally felt prepared to access information in a variety of ways, some were limited, having received minimal training or experience in using assistive technology. Although the methods that the participants had used in school or college had been sufficient for those contexts, it was noted that some had difficulty with the volume of reading required (both in terms of reading speed and with fatigue), and a small number had difficulties using online academic databases in HE. Secondly, the system relies on the young person being able to self-advocate. In terms of practical implications, Hewett, Douglas and Keil (2016) identified four ways in which students with VI are required to advocate in HE: negotiating support packages; negotiating support arrangements; explaining VI; and challenging if things go wrong. It is partly preparation that enables and empowers students in HE to self-advocate in this way: having had opportunities to self-advocate when younger; having a good understanding of one's own VI; and being well informed of the specialist support and equipment available. Many of the participants did not feel equipped to self-advocate in one or more of these scenarios, and several identified ways in which this had a negative impact upon their experience of HE. Other examples of independence skills include mobility and independent living skills, aspects of this project that will be explored in future publications.

## *Progressive mutual accommodations*

A central tenet of the BST is the notion of *accommodation* within and between the different systems in which the individual is operating over a given timeframe. Bronfenbrenner (2005) referred to this as *progressive mutual accommodation* (107). Different factors within and between systems mutually accommodate one another to ensure successful inclusion and development of the individual. The accommodations in HE come in many forms as outlined in this paper.

Our interest in educational transition and the longitudinal design of the research adds an important dimension to this analysis – *time*. As indicated above, 'mutual accommodation' is necessary for a young person to successfully participate in a given environment. However, implicit to this success is that they are able to develop the skills necessary to transition from one environment to another. Bronfenbrenner (1979) called these 'ecological transitions which are described as occurring whenever a person's position in the ecological environment is altered as the result of a change in role, setting, or both' (26). Gaining a place at an HEI is typically linked to a prospective student gaining appropriate grades in relevant academic subjects. Implicit also is that all students, including those with disabilities, have broader skill sets to enable them to live and study independently when at university, such as skills to self-advocate, access information and live independently. In the context of the education of VI children, these skills come under the umbrella term of what is referred to in the UK as the 'additional curriculum'. This is used to describe all areas that would not typically be taught in schools as part of the core curriculum – see, for example, the review by Douglas et al. (2011) and McLinden et al. (2016). Particular areas highlighted are: mobility (e.g. being able to independently navigate around the school and community); low vision and information access (e.g. using technology and strategies to independently access printed material, the use of low vision aids, learning to read through braille and the use of computers with appropriate access technology); and social skills (e.g. having friendship groups and self-advocacy skills). In the US, the term 'expanded core curriculum' is used in a similar way (e.g. Hatlen 1996).

Importantly, there is evidence that the presence of independence skills is associated with positive progress after school including into employment for people with VI (e.g. Capella McDonnall 2011; Wolffe and Kelly 2011). This is hardly surprising given that systems beyond school have different expectations and make different accommodations. The *progressive* nature of the mutual accommodation in relation to HE is drawn out in two ways in our research presented here: firstly, what takes place before and in preparation for HE; and secondly, what continues while in HE (and beyond).

Examining what takes place before HE involves close attention to the balance of school education throughout childhood as described above. There may also be targeted and specific preparations just prior to going to HE – with occasions where it is necessary for students with VI to learn new skills to enable them to fully benefit from the adjustments made by their HE institution. For example, in the summer prior to entry, one participant committed to learning a new piece of software through which he could access his course notes electronically. In turn, his department produced all course notes in an electronic format compatible with this software.

In terms of continued progressive mutual accommodation whilst in HE, this is clearly illustrated by acknowledgement that things change and develop over time (e.g. the welfare tutor who described 'adjustments as things developed'; the blind student who 'met with all new tutors and went to talk to them about what I needed'). Therefore the skills and requirements of the disabled student will change and develop during their time at university, as will the response and anticipation of the people and systems around them.

## Conclusion

The BIS consultation on changes to DSA in the UK places greater emphasis upon anticipatory adjustments and the use of assistive technology to enable better access to university courses by disabled students. For students with VI at least, the findings presented raise concerns about this strategy. Firstly, there is an assumption that students with disabilities arrive equipped with the skills to use such technology. The research findings, however, identified a number of barriers faced by the participants in doing so, including: having limited knowledge of the equipment available; not being equipped to advocate for equipment; not having received formal training to use specialist equipment; and not having had the experience of incorporating such equipment into their working practice. Linked to this, literature elsewhere raises concern that the teaching of independence skills is often not given appropriate emphasis in school education (e.g. Sapp and Hatlen 2010; Douglas and Hewett 2014). Further, whilst many of the participants identified ways in which they are able to access their courses through assistive technology, several were limited in the amount of funding available to pay for equipment, the quality of equipment provided and the type of equipment they were provided. Therefore, whilst technology does offer some solutions for students with disabilities, this suggests more consideration is required by BIS regarding their funding policies. Secondly, our findings raise concerns about how well equipped HE institutions are to provide a more inclusive learning environment. Our research evidence indicates that many UK HE providers focus on making accommodations on an individual basis (individually focused model approach), rather than ensuring learning is accessible to all (socially focused model approach). As the costs of making individual accommodations will be passed directly to the HE provider, we anticipate such changes would bring about difficulties in the shorter term. In the longer term it may act as a catalyst for bringing about improved access and support for students with disabilities. Nevertheless, given the extra costs involved this would need careful monitoring to ensure the reverse was not the case.

The findings described in this paper mirror the findings of other studies investigating the experiences of students with disabilities in HE. For example, relatively old research by Hall and Tinklin (1998) outlined a number of recommendations for HE institutions to improve their support for students with disabilities (89) and it appears 20 years later much work is still required. More recently, Bishop and Rhind (2011) investigated barriers and enablers faced by visually impaired students at a UK HEI and identified factors at multiple levels, including factors relating to institutional provision, external factors, and factors unique to the individual.

Seale's (2013) analysis of students with disabilities and their experiences also chimes with our findings – not least that both studies highlight the significance of technology to the successful inclusion of these students. A central theme of Seale's analysis was that of 'digital capital' which 'is exemplified by individuals investing time in improving their technology knowledge and competencies through informal or formal learning opportunities, as well as a socialisation into technology use and "techno-culture"' (259). She concluded that while digital capital was not enough to guarantee inclusion, it was a vital component of a broader social and cultural capital people with disabilities need in HE. This concept of an individual's social and cultural capital is a powerful one and it is in keeping with our findings and model because it values the importance of past and ongoing experience in the development of this capital. This supports our argument that whilst it is important to consider the responsibilities of the HEI (including the provision of accessible materials and technology), this must not be done in isolation; prior experiences and education have a critical role.

Although this paper focuses specifically on the experiences of students with VI in the UK, many of the findings are applicable for students with other disabilities in other contexts. Applying Bronfenbrenner's model as a Bioecological Model for Inclusive HE has provided a valuable framework, allowing the researcher to take a more holistic view of the learner's experience in their immediate and broader context, and the progressive mutual accommodation between learner and educator. This approach captures the dynamic nature of HE – while there should be clear expectations of the reasonable adjustments required to be in place and the study skills individual students have, there is also an acceptance that this will develop over time. Such an approach also makes a more explicit link with the transition *into* HE (often from school or college), the student learning journey *within* HE and the eventual transition *from* HE, often into the labour market.

## Disclosure statement

No potential conflict of interest was reported by the authors.

## Funding

The research was funded by Royal National Institute of Blind people (RNIB) between 2009 and 2011, the Nuffield Foundation between 2012 and 2015, and is currently being funded by Thomas Pocklington Trust. The Nuffield Foundation has funded part of this project, but the views expressed are those of the authors and not necessarily those of the Foundation. More information is available at www.nuffieldfoundation.org

## References

Anderson, Joanna, Christopher Boyle, and Joanne Deppeler. 2014. "The Ecology of Inclusive Education-Reconceptualising Bronfenbrenner in Equality." In *Education: Fairness and Inclusion*, edited by Hongzhi Zhang, and Philip Wing, 23–34. Rotterdam: Sense.

Aspin, David. 2007. "The Ontology of Values and Values Education." In *Values Education and Lifelong Learning: Principles, Policies, Programmes*, edited by David Aspin and Judith Chapman, 27–47. Dordrecht: Springer.

BIS. 2015. *Consultation on Targeting Funding for Disabled Students in Higher Education from 2016/17 Onwards*. London: Department for Business, Innovation Skills.

Bishop, Daniel, and Daniel Rhind. 2011. "Barriers and Enablers for Visually Impaired Students at a UK Higher Education Institution." *British Journal of Visual Impairment* 29 (3): 177–195.

Bronfenbrenner, Urie. 1979. *The Ecology of Human Development: Experiments in Nature and Design*. Cambridge, MA: Harvard University Press.

Bronfenbrenner, Urie. 2005. *Making Human Beings Human: Bioecological Perspectives on Human Development*. Thousand Oaks, CA: Sage.

Douglas, Graeme, and Rachel Hewett. 2014. "Views of Independence and Readiness for Employment amongst Young People with Visual Impairments in the UK." *The Australian Journal of Rehabilitation Counselling* 20 (2): 81–99.

Douglas, Graeme, Mike McLinden, Steve McCall, Sue Pavey, Jean Ware, and Ann Marie Farrell. 2011. "Access to Print Literacy for Children and Young People with Visual Impairment: Findings from a Review of Literature." *European Journal of Special Needs Education* 26 (1): 25–38.

Douglas, Graeme, Sue Pavey, Christine Corcoran, and Ben Clements. 2012. "Evaluating the Use of the ICF as a Framework for Interviewing People with a Visual Impairment about Their Mobility and Travel." *British Journal of Visual Impairment* 30 (1): 6–21.

Gov.UK. 2016. "Disabled Students' Allowances (DSAs)." Accessed May 2, 2016. https://www.gov.uk/disabled-students-allowances-dsas/overview

Hall, John, and Teresa Tinklin. 1998. *Students First: The Experiences of Disabled Students in Higher Education*. Edinburgh: The Scottish Council for Research in Education.

Hatlen, Phil. 1996. "The Core Curriculum for Blind and Visually Impaired Students, including Those with Additional Disabilities." *RE: View* 28 (1): 25–32.

Hewett, Rachel, and Graeme Douglas. 2015. "Inclusive Design – It's Impact on Young People with Visual Impairment." *Journal of Technology and Persons with Disabilities* 3: 277–290.

Hewett, Rachel, Graeme Douglas, and Huw Williams. 2011. *Post 14 Transitions Support – A Survey of the Transition Experience of Visually Impaired Young People: Technical Report of Findings to Summer 2011*. Birmingham: University of Birmingham.

Hewett, Rachel, Sue Keil, and Graeme Douglas. 2015a. *Experiences of Blind and Partially Sighted Young People as They Make the Transition into Higher Education*. Birmingham: University of Birmingham.

Hewett, Rachel, Sue Keil, and Graeme Douglas. 2015b. *Summary Report: Experiences of Blind and Partially Sighted Young People as They Make the Transition into Higher Education*. Birmingham: University of Birmingham.

Hewett, Rachel, Graeme Douglas, and Sue Keil. 2016. "The Importance of Self-Advocacy Skills: 'This is What I Can Do, and These Are the Adjustments I Require.'" Conference Proceedings for ICEVI, Orlando.

HM Government. 2010. "Equality Act 2010: Chapter 15." Accessed March 30, 2016. http://www.legislation.gov.uk/ukpga/2010/15/pdfs/ukpga_20100015_en.pdf

Keil, Sue. 2012. "RNIB Survey of VI Services in England and Wales 2012: Report for England. Royal National Institute of Blind People.

May, Helen, and Kath Bridger. 2010. *Developing and Embedding Inclusive Policy and Practice*. York: The Higher Education Academy.

McDonnall, Michele Capella. 2011. "Predictors of Employment for Youths with Visual Impairments: Findings from the Second National Longitudinal Transitions Study." *Journal of Visual Impairment & Blindness* 105 (8): 453–466.

McLinden, Mike, Graeme Douglas, Rory Cobb, Rachel Hewett, and John Ravenscroft. 2016. "'Access to Learning' and 'Learning to Access': Analysing the Distinctive Role of Specialist Teachers of Children and Young People with Vision Impairments in Facilitating Curriculum Access through an Ecological Systems Theory." *British Journal of Visual Impairment* 34 (2): 179–197.

Royal National Institute of Blind People. 2016. "The Criteria for Certification." Accessed March 15, 2015. http://www.rnib.org.uk/eye-health-registering-your-sight-loss/criteria-certification

Sapp, Wendy, and Phil Hatlen. 2010. "The Expanded Core Curriculum: Where We Have Been, Where We Are Going, and How We Can Get There." *Journal of Visual Impairment & Blindness* 104 (6): 338–348.

Seale, Jane. 2013. "When Digital Capital is Not Enough: Reconsidering the Digital Lives of Disabled University Students." *Learning, Media and Technology* 38 (3): 256–269.

Tudge, Jonathan, Irina Mokrova, Bridget Hatfield, and Rachana Karnik. 2009. "Uses and Misuses of Bronfenbrenner's Bioecological Theory of Human Development." *Journal of Family Theory & Review* 1 (4): 198–210.

WHO (World Health Organisation). 2001. *The International Classification of Impairments, Disabilities and Handicaps*. Geneva: WHO.

Wolffe, Karen, and Stacy Kelly. 2011. "Instruction in Areas of the Expanded Core Curriculum Linked to Transition Outcomes for Students with Visual Impairments." *Journal of Visual Impairment & Blindness* 105 (6): 340–349.

# Responding to the needs of students with mental health difficulties in higher education: an Irish perspective

Esther Murphy

**ABSTRACT**
This article presents findings from a recent national study supported by Association for Higher Education Access & Disability and the National Learning Network (2016) to investigate the experiences of students with mental health difficulties in higher education in Ireland. The data investigation was a combination of both survey and qualitative research activities. A total of 22 out of 28 Higher Education Institutions (HEIs) in Ireland participated in a national survey. In addition 14 students and 11 professionals participated in focus groups and semi-structured one-to-one interviews. This article focuses on the qualitative data collected. While the topic of the needs of students with mental health difficulties is an under-researched area in Ireland, this study does recognise and build on recent work both nationally and internationally. The study demonstrates the benefits of a whole campus approach to meeting the needs of students with mental health difficulties combined with specialised supports. It recommends that that individual HEIs review existing policies and practices for students with mental health difficulties.

In Ireland, there are approximately 354,000 full- and part-time students in higher education – in over 30 colleges both in Northern Ireland and in the Republic (HEA, 2015). In the last decade the attitudes in Ireland towards and provision for people with mental health difficulties have become more positive as an outcome of recent legislation such as the Equal Status Acts 2000–2008, the Mental Health Act (2001) and the Disability Act (2005). The Acts aim to promote equality; prohibit certain kinds of discrimination (with some exemptions) across nine grounds; require reasonable accommodation of people with disabilities; and allow a broad range of positive action measures. The Mental Health Act (2001) specifically relates to the care and treatment of adults and young people with mental health difficulties. A key recommendation of the Mental Health Act was the establishment of the Mental Health Commission of Ireland (MHCI) which was involved in the development of critical policy documents on suicide prevention – *Reach out: national strategy for Action on Suicide Prevention 2005–2014* (HSE 2005) and mental health, *A Vision for Change* (HSE 2006).

Underlying these policies is the guiding principle of developing a whole population approach to mental health. To ensure effective implementation of these policies the Irish Health Service Executive (HSE) acknowledge in their report *Mental Health in Ireland: Awareness and Attitudes* (2007) that improvements in public attitudes and awareness of mental health is required at every level of Irish society. While the establishment of the MHCI was welcomed, especially the recognition that the mental health rights of patients require updating, there has been criticism from mental health practitioners about the lack of available data and investigation into the experiences of people with mental health difficulties. In particular, Headstrong, the National Centre for Youth Mental Health raised concern that the data for *A Vision for Change* was mainly based on international data-sets and as stated in the *A Vision for Change* report:

> We do not know the number of individuals nationally who avail of mental health services, the type of interventions or treatments they receive or the effectiveness of those treatments … we have no information on the number of people with mental health problems in the Irish population. (HSE 2006, 53)

Headstrong in conjunction with the University College Dublin School of Psychology aimed to address this gap by establishing an Irish-based data-set in relation to youth who have mental health difficulties (Dooley and Fitzgerald 2012). The 'My World Survey' (MWS, Dooley and Fitzgerald 2012) was the outcome of this initiative. It is the first comprehensive national study of youth mental health in Ireland (up to the age of 25). It reported that a third of Irish young people had experienced mental health difficulties. This insight into the scale of mental health difficulties experienced by young people in Ireland also coincides with an increase in numbers of young people making the transition to third level education, with over 196,000 full-time and part-time students enrolled in Irish Higher Education Authority (HEA) funded institutions in 2011/2012. This also reflects international studies that report students with mental health difficulties are the fastest growing populations in higher education (Belch 2011; Stein 2014).

To gain a complete overview and deeper understanding of the situation of students with disabilities in Ireland, Association for Higher Education Access & Disability (AHEAD) gathers annual participation rates from all twenty-eight Higher Education Institutions (HEIs). For the 2013/2014 national survey twenty-seven institutions in Ireland responded and a total of 9694 students with disabilities, were identified representing 4.7% of the total student population, of which 8769 are studying undergraduate courses and 925 are studying postgraduate courses. This represents a 7% rise in the total number of students with disabilities from 2012/2013, when the figure was 9082. The rise in enrolments means that the number of students with disabilities participating in higher education in Ireland has doubled in the last 5 years. Of these groups 10% represent students with a mental health condition (AHEAD 2015).

## Areas for investigation in this article

This article addresses two specific barriers to supporting students with mental health difficulties in higher education identified in previous research. (1) The rise in the number of students with mental health difficulties not matched by increase in specialised supports on campus; (2) the stigma attached to disclosure preventing students seek support.

Based on these two specific barriers two interrelated facilitators have been: A whole campus approach to mental health combined with sufficient specialised supports tailored to individual needs of students with mental health difficulties. These facilitators have been recommended as good practice in previous studies. In this study several good practices of supporting students with mental health difficulties were reported. This article shares two specific examples from Irish HEIs. This current study builds on international findings and validates the need for implementing these good practices.

## *Inadequate provision of support services on campus*

Over the last decade, the Irish Association for University and College Counselling Service's (IAUCC) annual statistics on numbers of students accessing their services, indicate a significant increase in numbers of students across the country. While the numbers of students with mental health difficulties accessing their services is rising significantly, the supports available in particular from the counselling services on college campuses has not increased. As Broderick (2013) reports the increased numbers of students seeking support is resulting in services being seriously overstretched. Since the IAUCC began collating data in 2006, the numbers of students presenting with mental health concerns have steadily increased. In particular, anxiety disorders have increased from 19 to 32%; depression from 9 to 24%; relationship problems from 11 to 24% and academic-related issues from 19 to 29% (Broderick 2013). This increase in students with mental health difficulties accessing higher education in Ireland is representative of the international context and also the common concern amongst college counsellors of ensuring appropriate responses to the increasing prevalence of serious psychological conditions (Stein 2014). It is recognised that significant progress has been made in the last decade in supporting students with mental health difficulties in HEIs in particular where specialised services for students with mental health difficulties have been established. However, the widely reported increase in the numbers of students with mental health difficulties accessing higher and further education and the complexity of these students' needs has not been matched with an increase in the provision of support services.

In Ireland, 65% of 18-year-olds participate in higher education (Department of Education and Skills 2011). Considering the high proportion of Irish adults who will be in higher education when they experience mental health difficulties it is advocated that robust HEI support institutional infrastructures are in place to ensure these students are appropriately supported (HEFCE 2015; HEA 2015; Royal College of Psychiatrists 2011).

## *Stigma and disclosure of mental health difficulties*

Although mental health difficulties may increasingly be the most common problem for young people on college campuses, less than one in four students seek support (Blanco et al. 2008). The stigma associated with disclosure of mental health difficulties has been identified as a critical barrier for students to seek support. The stigma associated with disclosure of mental health difficulties has been identified internationally as a critical barrier for students to seek support in post-secondary education environments (Venville, Street, and Fossey 2014). Emphasis has been placed on the role of disability and specialist support services on campus and the necessity for students to disclose clinical diagnosis in order to gain access to supports and accommodations (Venville, Street, and Fossey 2014).

## A whole campus approach to mental health

A number of reports including the Higher Education Funding Council for England Report, 'Understanding provision for students with mental health difficulties' conducted by the Institution of Employment Studies (2015), the Royal College of Psychiatrists' (RCP) most recent guides for mental health professionals (RCP 2011, 50) and the UK Mental Well-Being in Higher Education (MWBHE) recognise the benefits for all students to a whole campus approach to mental health and highlight the dangers inherent in the system where HEI departments operate as individual 'silos' rather than as a whole system. MWBHE advise that services move away from a 'silo' approach to establishing a whole and systematic institutional approach. The RCP (2011, 93) states: 'A comprehensive whole-system approach that can map and understand interrelationships, interactions and synergies within higher education settings, with regard to different groups of the population, different components of the system and different health issues'. This kind of approach offers the 'potential to address health in a coherent and coordinated way and to forge connections to both health related and academic targets within higher education'.

In Ireland, many HEIs address mental health as an issue of concern in their policies. For example, in 2016 University College Dublin published a policy document to promote mental well-being across the campus, based on a clear understanding that:

> Mental health and wellbeing is crucial to students' academic performance, capacity to learn, and ability to engage fully with the wider experience of higher education. It is therefore a vital concern of the UCD community. (UCD Registry 2016, 1)

Nevertheless, while many institutions espouse a whole college approach, in reality it can be difficult to achieve (O'Grady 2015).

A common concern identified in Stein's (2014) grounded theory research study with 16 higher education students with mental health difficulties enrolled in a regional public university in the Mid-Atlantic area of the United States, is that owing to poor communication and training, faculty staff are not knowledgeable about campus supports and procedures. This demonstrates a lack of a whole campus approach and the impact for students with mental health difficulties is that their needs are not appropriately supported and accommodated. Moreover, Stein (2014, 59) reports that as a result of faculty staff's lack of 'knowledge or understanding regarding disabilities affected their performance in the course'. Students in this study suggested that faculty staff could assist them by participating in 'professional development for faculty regarding disabilities, more communication between Disability Support Services (DSS) and professors, and providing accommodations when requested' (Stein 2014, 59).

A lack of a whole campus awareness of individuals and services roles and responsibilities on campus in supporting students with mental health difficulties is raised as a concern (HEFCE 2015). Research investigating the needs of students with mental health difficulties has focused on accommodation provision and the need for more coordinated systems between faculty and Disability Support Services (DSS, Stein 2014, 2015). This current study builds on this research and gives evidence to validate the impact of the benefits of adopting a whole campus approach from the perspective of both students with mental health difficulties and the professionals who support them navigate the higher education environment. In particular, one of the challenges identified for DSS is 'how to balance the need to serve as a clearinghouse to ensure students are being provided access and accommodations, while encouraging the rest of the campus community to take ownership for inclusion of students with disabilities' (Myers, Lindburg, and Nied 2014, 8). Recently there has been a shift towards working with students individually across services to structure academic plans for each learner (Haverkos 2011). Individual support is advised within the context of a holistic team approach:

> The blanket approach of working with students to provide standard accommodations does not meet the individual need of each student ... A team approach including faculty, staff, academic advisors student health and counselling and disability services to develop an individual, holistically focused plan for each student would be ideal. (Myers, Lindburg, and Nied 2014, 7)

## *Specialised supports for students with mental health difficulties in higher education*

Access to specialised supports for students with mental health difficulties and assurance of continuity of support during times of transition is critical to mental health well-being (HEFCE 2015; HEA 2015). The Royal College of Psychiatrists (2003) suggested that those with mental health problems required higher levels of support in order to achieve their potential. To ensure continuity of support The University Mental Health Advisors Network (UMHAN) was formed in 2001 in the UK with just 5 members and now has 95. The 58 respondents to the 2003 Mental Wellbeing in Higher Education UK survey reported that 53% of the institutions surveyed employed a mental health advisor. By 2008, around 80% of responding institutions had at least one advisor. The growing number is a sign of confidence that the role is working to meet both staff and student needs (Grant 2011). Above all, there is a recognition that specialised support for students with mental health difficulties that meet individual academic and well-being needs is required (RPC 2011). In Ireland, the role of 'mental health adviser' is currently not formally recognised or nationally implemented. Instead there is evidence of some institutions (e.g. NUIG, Athlone IT) providing a liaison officer (funded by surplus monies from the individual institutions) to facilitate communication between on campus and external agencies on behalf of the student. The need for specialised support and strengthening collaboration with academic faculties has been recently recognised by the HEA's recent Plan 2015–2019 with a commitment to delegate 'access champions' in all HEIs (HEA 2015). This is also reflected in Stein's (2014) study where many students highlighted the need for more coordinated communication between faculty staff and DSS in particular calling for an 'advocate' to support their needs.

## *Specialised supports in Irish HEIs*

In Ireland there are a small number of initiatives providing specialised 'add on' services in the HEI sector to support students specifically with mental health difficulties. Examples featured in this study include Unilink, an accessible one to one client centred service established in Trinity College Dublin in 2004. Since Unilink was set up, there has been a steady increase in the number of students accessing the service with an increase from 30 students in 2004 to over 300 students today. The approach used by Unilink is rooted in the Recovery Model, as espoused by A Vision for Change (2006) and the Person-Environment-Occupation Model (Law et al. 1996) and the social model of disability (Swain and French 2000; Barnes and Mercer 2003; Terzi 2004). The National Learning Network (NLN) has also developed a tailored support service for students with disabilities in a number of HEIs including Maynooth University (NUIM), IT Blanchardstown (ITB) and the National College of Art and Design (NCAD) as well as the City of Dublin Education and Training Board (CDETB) Colleges of Further Education. In 2012, the NLN set up an on campus service called Student Central in Maynooth University. Student Central is available to people who are registered with the University's Disability Office and who have a diagnosis of a Mental Health Difficulty, Attention Deficit Hyperactivity Disorder or Autistic Spectrum Disorder. Students work collaboratively with a psychologist to develop practical self-management skills and strategies that assist them in completing academic work, self-managing wellness and developing key social skills.

## Study rationale and methodology

The rationale to carry out this research is to investigate existing HEI practices of supporting students with mental health difficulties from the perspective of both students and professionals. At the heart of this investigation is the ambition to listen to the voice of students with mental health difficulties accessing support in higher education and to consult widely with professional staff working within the sector to hear their insights and experiences of good practices and views about where improvements may be made to support students with mental health difficulties.

The following core research questions were developed to address the gaps in knowledge about higher education students with mental health difficulties experiences specifically related to the barriers and facilitators to accessing appropriate support.

- What are the support experiences of students with mental health difficulties in higher education?
- How are students with mental health difficulties supported in higher education?
- How could students with mental health difficulties be better supported in higher education?

A qualitative approach was considered the most suitable method as it allows the researcher to explore 'detailed accounts of problematic experiences (presenting) context, emotion and the webs of social relationship that join persons to one another' (Denzin 1989, 83). Qualitative methods are widely advocated for investigative inquiry into issues and topics that have not received considerable attention and to promote participatory research (Oliver 1993, 1994; Stone and Priestley 1996; Shakespeare 1996; Denzin and Lincoln 2003; Barnes and Mercer 2003). This is reflective of the situation of students with disabilities in higher education particularly those with mental health difficulties as mental health encompasses a highly complex range of difficulties. A purposive sampling strategy was selected as it 'allows us to choose a case because it illustrates some feature or process in which we are interested' (Silverman 2001, 104).

Two methods of identifying students for this study were adopted. Firstly, for the student focus group, the project team circulated an invite to participate via DSS in all HEIs and the Irish Association of University and College Counsellors (IAUCC) distributed invite to college counselling services nationwide. For the semi-structured interviews participants were selected and approached in consultation with professionals supporting these young people.

HEI Disability Support Services were invited to participate in an online survey and share with other relevant colleagues on campus (e.g. counselling service). In this survey the final question asked participants to contact AHEAD should they wish to participate in subsequent focus group or interview at a later stage. 16 respondents out of 22 confirmed their interest in participating in the qualitative stage of the research. Subsequently, the research team also directly invited all DSS staff and counsellors via the IAUCC to participate. In total, 8 professionals participated in the focus group. In addition, a further 5 professionals participated in detailed semi-structured interviews.

In advance of taking part in research activities, the nature of the study and voluntary participation was explained in writing (and verbally in the case of focus groups and interviews) to all participants. Consent forms were prepared and distributed in person and/or by email. Prior to commencing each focus group and interview, participants were assured that pseudonyms would be adopted to preserve participant anonymity. Consent to having the qualitative research activity digitally recorded as a memory aide was agreed prior to each activity. Additionally, participants were advised that should they wish to opt out of the process, at any time during or after the research activity their wish would be fully respected.

To assure anonymity and confidentiality of participants, each participant was assigned a pseudonym (McCann and Clark 2003). Higher education students from a range of institutions, college courses and age groups took part in semi-structured interviews and a lengthy focus group. Professionals represented counselling service, disability service, occupational therapist practitioners, mental health advocacy groups, educational psychologists and a community child and adolescent psychologist.

## *Focus group procedure*

Focus groups allow for researchers to bring together a range of individuals who have similar concerns with particular focus on area of research to 'encourage a range of responses which provide a greater understanding of the attitudes, behaviour, opinions or perceptions of participants on the research issues' (Hennink 2007, 6). Madriz (2000, 836) view as 'a collectivistic rather than an individualistic method that focuses on the multivocality of participants' attitudes, experiences, and beliefs' allowing researcher to 'create data from multiple voices' matches this study's goal. It is contended that focus groups are a particularly useful means to engage with people with mental health difficulties who may be reticent to participant in face-to-face interviews.

Two focus groups were coordinated by AHEAD. The first focus group involved students with mental health difficulties and the second was with professionals who support students with mental health difficulties in HEIs. For each focus group activity, the guidelines for focus groups as described in the Mental Health Commission Report (Dunne 2006) were followed. Both focus group sessions took place in the same non-clinical, non-education central Dublin city location. During the initial contact with inviting students to participate, they were given clear guidance on time, venue and offered travel compensation. Each focus group meeting location was scheduled for 2 hours, with time allocated for short breaks at the start and during the session. All participants were advised that should they wish to go beyond this allocated time this could be facilitated. In each focus group the meeting exceeded the set 2 h by approximately 25 min. The student focus group was moderated by the study's Principal Investigator and assisted by two AHEAD staff. One staff member co-moderated while the second staff member provided expert sign language interpreting. An external professional facilitator moderated the focus group with professionals, with minimal assistance from the Principal Investigator. In total, 11 students with experience of mental health difficulties and 8 professionals participated in separate focus groups. Students were invited to share their current educational situation. Professionals were invited to share their professional role in relation to supporting students with mental health difficulties.

## *Semi-structured interview*

Selecting a semi-structured approach permits as Lofland and Lofland (1995, 273) point out offers the: 'possibility of modifying one's line of inquiry, following up interesting responses and investigating underlying motives'. As the focus of this study is to capture the participants' lived experiences in their own words, the semi-structured in-depth interview is an appropriate approach to complement focus groups. In total, six semi-structured interviews took place (three with students, three with professionals). All student interviews lasted approximately 1 hour. Interviews with professionals ranged between 45 min and 1 hour 30 min. All qualitative data was audio recorded digitally and transcribed verbatim. Transcripts were thematically analysed (Braun and Clarke 2006). Core themes include access to appropriate supports for mental health difficulties, whole campus approach, stigma, peer support, professional ownership and disclosure.

## Findings

This current Irish study validates findings conducted internationally related to recommendations for a whole campus approach to mental health, while also links the need for specialised one to one services. It demonstrates the necessity for these practices to be adopted in Irish HEIs. While previous studies have examined topics of concern for students with mental health difficulties individually this article brings key findings to validate and demonstrate the benefit these inclusive practices.

## *A whole college approach to mental health – early engagement correlates with positive outcomes*

In this study, both students and professionals credit early engagement with mental health topics during coordinated whole campus services such as induction with positive outcomes for students. Different methods and levels of engagement across the higher education sector are recorded in this study. A whole campus coordinated is found to be the best practice approach. Sarah, a college counsellor, who personally witnesses the effectiveness of a joined up support services strategy across her campus, shares her college's practice:

> We would go in at induction, which we're doing at the moment. We would go into every classroom and talk very openly about the issues that are presenting. And you can almost see after induction you can nearly track it. It's not kind of 'oh the counselling service over in the corner there, if you have a problem you go to them'. The induction is very even so you're introduced to the academic staff, the career staff, the disability staff, the counselling staff. So all of those services are laid out to you as being equally accessible.

Many students reported that the combination of an engaging tutor and a clear explanation of practical information e.g. office location and protocol for arranging appointments was most helpful. The practical approach adopted by the counsellor is an example of good practice and enabled the students to feel at ease to arrange and to 'normalise the issue of mental health'. Students highlight the need for early engagement and relationship building between students and support services:

> When I started college, the college counsellor, came into the class early on, during the induction in the first few weeks, introduced herself and said, this is where I'm based, and explained that, she was there for the students. I said to myself, well I need to introduce myself to her so I went and made an appointment, I emailed her explained my situation that

For university student, Neil, mental health was not discussed as part of the induction at his large urban university and he feels this was a missed opportunity to tackle the stigma he felt related to mental health difficulties. In Neil's experience, he found it difficult to seek support on campus due to the stigma he felt, identifying the location of the support services including the disability services and counselling services, as a barrier for engagement:

> For me the location of the disability and counselling office in the middle of campus put me off. When I first started in college, there was a kind of induction day. Nobody ever actually talked about mental health, the services that available to people. I think of that was sort of included right from the very beginning, it would be good way to begin to normalize the whole thing and take away the stigma, when it is sort of casually inserted into the normal sort of orientation of university life. Because I think everyone can experience stress and that can have an effect on your mental health.

### *Mental health awareness among academic staff*

For many students who experience mental health difficulties while at college, they are unaware of what is happening to them and are unaware of where to seek support. This was the case for Patrick, as his mental health difficulties emerged in his first year of college, during the end of the first semester. At that time his parents were living abroad. There has been a lot of evidence in the literature about the advantage of having at least one supportive person during times of mental health distress (Dooley and Fitzgerald 2012). In Patrick's case, his tutor was this person. With his tutor's support Patrick successful progressed into second year at college.

> When I first experienced mental illness I didn't know what was going on with me. I started hearing voices and being very paranoid in public. Because so much happened in such a short period of time, I didn't know about the disability service, that they support mental illness. When college started again in semester two, the first person I went to talk about it, was my tutor in first year he had also been my lecturer. I already knew him and there was some trust so it made it easier, I went up to his office and just told him what was going on. When I started talking to him, he told me stories that happened to a friend of his or family people. I had thought it was something very unique just I've had from the beginning. What he said here, 'You have something that is a mental illness,' so he helped me to go through the steps of what to do next. It was hard because my parents aren't living here so I was basically on my own when I first experienced it.

Academic staff members play a significant role in connecting students to appropriate services in a streamlined and systematic manner. The current system appears to be based on the understanding and capacity of individual staff members, such as academic staff to identify a student in crisis and to then refer them to the appropriate service. The services themselves are not necessarily connected and there is an absence of clear information and procedures for ensuring that the students access the services do exist.

The system of early communication between departments such as disability support offices and academic departments proved to be crucial in advocating for students:

> A big help was talking to my supervisors and tutors, just letting them know that I might need some extra time because I couldn't have told them myself. I couldn't have told them myself. It was good that there someone else who actually wrote an email to my supervisor sating, 'She's registered with us now'. I needed that.

### One to one tailored specialised support to meet individual students' needs

Students in this study equate appropriate individualised support provided by their HEIs with positive impacts for their mental health well-being and academic attainment. Students share their positive experiences of specialised services such as the Unilink service, NLN Service including NUIM Student Central. During the focus group with students, the benefits of the individual one to one sessions with professionals with mental health expertise to support students with academic skills was identified by all students who had experience accessing some kind of individual support at their HEI. Those students that did not have this support expressed disappointment and at times anger that this support was not available for them. Systematic referral from disability services to appropriate academic support services was also identified as significant in helping them cope with the challenges their mental health difficulties presented for them in meeting their academic goals. In these services the processes of referral were clear and transparent and all were based on the practice of individualised assessment to identify and appropriate supports. Implementing supports were commonly based structured collaborations with other services such as academic departments.

### Dual academic and mental health support through dedicated service

The UniLink services provide one-to-one occupational therapy support on campus tailored to individual students' needs. Lucy found this individual focus particularly helpful and enjoyed having a time slot set-aside in her timetable to visit her occupational therapist (OT). Lucy was already registered with her university's Disability Support Services for supports related to her physical disability but she had not disclosed her mental health difficulties. It was the academic and counselling support Lucy received through the UniLink service that helped Lucy disclose her mental health difficulties and subsequently cope with and manage her mental health difficulties while in college:

> The disability officer who referred me to Unilink didn't really know anything about me being down in the dumps, she knew that I got tired very easily and I was struggling to keep up with my college work. She thought the OT's in Unilink might be able to help me with coping strategies. It was only when I had my first meeting with the OT that I disclosed about my depression as well, so the help she gave me was kind of in two forms: counselling-ish kind of service and academic help as well.

What works for Jessica, a mature student, is the combined supported of one-to-one sessions with the college counsellor and the dedicated programme run by the NLN at her college. It is this dual support that currently enables Jessica to identify the best ways to maximise her study time.

> I got a structure off my counsellor. She asked me to write down my days of what I was doing. What I learned was to use my long breaks in college and do assignments, catch up on that. We get reading weeks, so when it comes to exams to try and prep for exams. Support with that calmed me down, I'd been all over the place and so stressed.

## Individualised learning agreement

A number of the students identified, an individualised learning agreement system run established by the National Learning Network that is shared with the academic department as a means to reduce their anxiety about access to the course materials. According to one student Sheila:

> If you said you had a mental health problem, they would have the learning agreement There might be 10 in the class that would get the lecture notes at the start of the class, so you would have them, I never needed a print out, that was less stress for me. I didn't have to go around printing them off, I was able to write the notes on my lecture notes there and then at the lecture. It is such a brilliant resource. They don't have that in the other college. It was brilliant for me. I didn't need to have my own notes, my notes were on the lecture note on the day and when I was going to study it was all there.

The students interviewed all mentioned study support sessions as a key support.

## Discussion

The findings outlined in this study involving students with mental health difficulties and professionals resonate with results from other studies that indicate students can be reticent about seeking support or indeed never do due to stigma in relation to disclosure (Eisenberg, Golberstein, and Gollust 2007; Blanco et al. 2008; Downs and Eisenberg 2012). Additionally, the need for specialised supports is recognised as critical in a higher education environment where growing numbers of students with complex learning needs, related to multiple diagnoses e.g. mental health difficulties and learning difficulties, such as students with dyslexia or dyspraxia and/or on the autism spectrum are reported (Royal College of Psychiatrists 2011; Broderick 2013). This study finds that specialised supports can facilitate a students' capacity to disclose a mental health difficulty and seek appropriate support. Furthermore, earlier studies have identified the growth in complex individual diagnoses as an indication of the increased necessity for a student centred integrated services to ensure the most appropriate support provision (HEFCE 2015; O'Grady 2015).

This current study validates this indication that students' capacity to engage with higher education is increased by the provision one-to-one supports that are tailored to both their academic and mental health needs. A dedicated service that provides dual support for students' academic and mental health needs delivered by professionals with mental health expertise is found in this study to ease students' stress and enable their access to their academic work. While the learning agreement system in practice in the NLN helps reduce students' stress in communicating their needs related to their mental health difficulties with academic staff. Therefore, this practice facilitates students' access to their higher education curriculum work and integration into the learning environment.

The student participants in this study all reported that where available study support sessions were a key enabler to reaching their academic potential in HEIs. Academic skills such as time management and goal setting interventions have all been recognised in previous studies to increase on-task behaviours and independent academic and behavioural functioning (Callahan and Rademacher 1999; Ramdass and Zimmerman 2011). The positive experiences of the students in this study where supports provided are based on their individual needs resonates with this earlier research that students learn to manage their anxiety and ensure that they have the practical study skills to deal with the academic demands of the course but additionally there is the added bonus of facilitating communication between staff members which can aid disclosure and reduce stigma. While this current study's findings confirm the link between disclosure and access to support, it also demonstrates that students' opportunities to disclose their mental health difficulties and reach their potential are also dependent upon HEIs implementing a whole campus approach to mental health while also providing access to specialised services.

Large-scale research in the UK (HEFCE 2015; Royal College of Psychiatrists 2011) has highlighted the need for a whole campus strategy this current study can demonstrate this in action in certain HEIs in Ireland and the benefits it has for students with mental health difficulties in overcoming their difficulties. At the same time, the study shines a light on the challenges for students with mental health difficulties who are undertaking their higher education studies in institutions that do not adopt this approach. Therefore this study contributes to the debate surrounding what can be the most effective response to ensuring students with mental health difficulties can reach their potential in higher education. It is critical that student voices are heard and their views on good practice are implemented in policy.

In evaluating the study it is important to point out the inherent limitations of sampling methods and focus group procedures. To address the challenge of ensuring as many diverse student experiences one to one semi-structured interviews were carried out with students who experienced more severe conditions such as schizophrenia, students with a dual diagnosis and a student with a physical disability and mental health diagnosis. In this case, students who were known to the research steering committee directly approached students to invite them to participate. The aim of this approach was to ensure that the multivocality of the group did not dilute the experiences of those with diverse experiences and that diverse student experiences of mental health difficulties was included. In addition, the student focus group session was co-facilitated by a research team member, who has a lived experience of mental health difficulties. Involving this professional with direct experience proved helpful for students to open up about their own experiences and in general throughout the discussion there was respectful sensitivity between the group to hear and learn from the experiences of others. This was particularly notable when a student from a migrant background discussed her 'dual battle' and 'double stigma' experience of adjusting to life in Ireland and her home country's perception of her mental health difficulties. While her experience was not the 'norm' within the group, all participants expressed an interest and willingness to let her expand upon the theme of the barrier of certain cultural perceptions of mental health. This study notes while the topic of cultural perception of mental health was beyond the scope for this study it is an issue that needs to be addressed within higher education. This is true also in the case of students living with a dual diagnosis specifically addiction problems and the experience of students with physical disabilities and mental health difficulties. To address potential professional bias, the focus group with professionals, was managed by an external professional facilitator.

## Concluding comments

In order to ensure equity of access and participation for students with mental health difficulties in higher education it is essential that individual HEIs review their existing policies and practices for students with mental health difficulties. This would aim to identify *'what's working for students and what could be improved'.* This activity needs to be a whole campus initiative led by collaborative effort between HEI Disability Services and Counselling Services to connect all support services. A whole campus approach to inclusion was strongly suggested by all HEI professionals who participated in this study. While a whole campus approach is advocated for in recent research in higher education and mental health in particular UK reports led by the Royal College of Psychiatrists (2011) and the Higher Education Funding Council for England (2015), in Ireland though the concept is written into several HEI policies this current research gives evidence that its implementation is not experienced by all students. The impact for students with mental health difficulties who are participating in HEIs who neglect to take responsibility for a whole campus approach to mental health is that these students experienced reduced opportunities for disclosure, poorer academic and social outcomes and ultimately are at higher risk of dropping out. Developing and implementing a whole campus approach requires collaboration and cooperation across all faculties and support services thus having the added bonus of addressing the issue of 'silo' work practices and improving cross departmental communication which is proven to improve student outcomes as well. The whole campus approach to mental health is in line with broader government policy articulated in A Vision for Change's (2006) recommendation for a whole population approach to mental health.

This study recognises the benefit students report that they receive from specialised services delivered one to one by professionals with mental health expertise and academic supports to assess and meet individual students' needs. It is evident that there is a need for at least one key point of contact to be identified in each support service and additionally that one individual is appointed in the role as mental health champion/advisor. This study therefore validates the need for 'access champions' in all HEIs as recommended in official government policy (HEA 2015).

## Disclosure statement

No potential conflict of interest was reported by the author.

## Funding

This study was funded by the Association of Higher Education Access & Disability and the National Learning Network.

## References

AHEAD (Association for Higher Education Access and Disability). 2015. *Numbers of Students with Disabilities Studying in Higher Education in Ireland 2013–2014*. Dublin: AHEAD Educational Press.
Barnes, Colin, and Geof Mercer. 2003. *Disability*. London: Polity Press.

Belch, Holley. 2011. "Understanding the Experiences of Students with Psychiatric Disabilities: A Foundation for Creating Conditions of Support and Success." *New Directions for Student Services* 2011: 73–94.

Blanco, Carlos, Mayumi Okuda, Crystal Wright, Deborah Hasin, Bridget F Grant, Shang-Min Liu, and Mark Olfson. 2008. "Mental Health of College Students and their Non-college Peers: Results from the National Epidemiologic Study on Alcohol and Related Conditions." *Archives of General Psychiatry* 65 (12): 1429–1437.

Braun, Virginia, and Victoria Clarke. 2006. "Using Thematic Analysis in Psychology." *Qualitative Research in Psychology* 3 (2): 77–101.

Broderick, John. 2013. "Addressing the Mental Health Needs of Third Level Students." *Education Matters Year Book*. Galway: Education Matters.

Callahan, Kevin, and Joyce A. Rademacher. 1999. "Using Self-management Strategies to Increase the On-task Behavior of a Student with Autism." *Journal of Positive Behavior Interventions* 1: 117–122.

Denzin, Norman K. 1989. *The Research Act: A Theoretical Introduction to Sociological Methods*. London: Prentice Hall.

Denzin, Norman K., and Yvonna S. Lincoln. 2003. "Introduction: The Discipline and Practice of Qualitative Research." In *Strategies of Qualitative Enquiry*, edited by N. K. Denzin and Y. S. Lincoln, 1–39. Thousand Oaks, CA: Sage.

Department of Education and Skills. 2011. *Department of Education and Skills Annual Report 2011*. Dublin: The Stationery Office.

Dooley, Barbara, and Amanda Fitzgerald. 2012. *My World Survey My World Survey: National Study of Youth Mental Health in Ireland*. Dublin: Headstrong and UCD School of Psychology.

Downs, Marilyn F., and Daniel Eisenberg. 2012. "Help Seeking and Treatment Use among Suicidal College Students." *Journal of American College Health* 60 (2): 104–114.

Dunne, Elizabeth A. 2006. *The Views of Adult Users of the Public Sector Mental Health Services*. Dublin: Mental Health Commission.

Eisenberg, Daniel, Ezra Golberstein, and Sarah Gollust. 2007. "Help-seeking and Access to Mental Health Care in a University Student Population." *Medical Care* 45 (7): 594–601.

Government of Ireland. 2000. *Equal Status Act, 2000*. Dublin: Stationery Office.

Government of Ireland. 2001. *Mental Health Act, 2001*. Dublin: Stationery Office.

Government of Ireland. 2005. *Disability Act 2005*. Dublin: Stationery Office.

Grant, A. 2011. *The Growth and Development of Mental Health Provision in UK Higher Education Institutions*. Universities UK/Guild HE Working Group for the Promotion of Mental Wellbeing in Higher Education. http://www.universitiesuk.ac.uk/about/Pages/mwbhe.aspx.

Haverkos, Peter J., 2011. "Finding the Union of Success and Access: A Focus on Learning for Students with Disabilities". In *Contested Issues in Student Affairs: Diverse Perspective & Respectful Dialogue*, edited by Peter M. Magolda and Marcia B. Magolda, 309–315. Sterling, VA: Stylus.

Health Service Executive. 2007. *Mental Health in Ireland: Awareness and Attitudes*. Dublin: HSE.

HEA (Higher Education Authority). 2015. *Supporting a Better Transition from Second Level to Higher Education, Implementation and Next Steps*. Dublin: Higher Education Authority.

HEFCE (Higher Education Funding Council for England). 2015. *Understanding Provision for Students with Mental Health Problems and Intensive Support Needs*. Brighton, UK: Higher Education Funding Council for England.

Hennink, Monique M. 2007. *International Focus Group Research: A Handbook for the Health and Social Sciences*. Cambridge: Cambridge University Press.

HSE (Health Service Executive). 2006. *A Vision for Change: Report of the Expert Group on Mental Health Policy*. Dublin: HSE.

HSE (Health Service Executive). 2005. *Reach Out: National Strategy for Action on Suicide Prevention, 2005-14*. Dublin: HSE.

Law, Mary, Barbara Cooper, Susan Strong, Deborah Stewart, Patricia Rigby, and Lori Letts. 1996. "The Person-environment-occupation Model: A Transactive Approach to Occupational Performance." *Canadian Journal of Occupational Therapy*. 63 (1): 9–23.

Lofland, John and Lyne Lofland. 1995. *Analyzing Social Settings: A Guide to Qualitative Observation and Analysis*. Belmont, CA: Wadsworth.

Madriz, Esther. 2000. "Focus Groups in Feminist Research." In *Handbook of Qualitative Research*, edited by Norman K. Denzin and Yvonna S. Lincoln, 2nd ed, 835–850. Thousand Oaks, CA: Sage.

McCann, Terence, and Eileen Clark. 2003. "Grounded Theory in Nursing Research: Part 3 – Application." *Nurse Researcher* 11 (2): 29–39.

Myers, Karen, Jaci Lindburg, and Daniell Nied. 2014. Allies for Inclusion: Students with Disabilities. *ASHE Higher Education Report* Vol. 39 no. 5. San Francisco, CA: Jossey Bass.

National Suicide Review Group, Ireland. Department of Health and Children, Health Service Executive. 2005. *Reach out: National Strategy for Action on Suicide Prevention 2005–2014*. Dublin: HSE.

O'Grady, Mary. 2015. "Moving for a Reactive to Proactive Model in Support of Students with Mental Health Difficulties." *Presentation at Trinity College Dublin's Disability Service Fourth Annual Symposium 2014–15*, Dublin, TCD.

Oliver, Mike. 1993. "Changing the Social Relations of Research Production?" *Disability, Handicap and Society* 7 (2): 101–114.

Oliver, Mike. 1994. "If I Had a Hammer: The Social Model in Action". In *2004 Implementing the Social Model of Disability: Theory and Research*, edited by Colin Barnes, and Geof Mercer, 18–31. Leeds: The Disability Press.

Ramdass, Darshan, and Barry Zimmerman. 2011. "Developing Self-Regulation Skills: The Important Role of Homework." *Journal of Advanced Academics* 22 (2): 194–218.

Royal College of Psychiatrists. 2003. *The Mental Health of Students in Higher Education*. Council Report CR112. www.rcpsych.as.uk.

Royal College of Psychiatrists. 2011. *Mental Health of Students in Higher Education. College Report CR166*. London: Royal College of Psychiatrists. www.rcpsych.as.uk.

Shakespeare, Tom. 1996. "Rules of Engagement: Doing Disability Research." *Disability and Society*. 11 (1): 115–121.

Silverman, David. 2001. *Interpreting Qualitative Data: Methods for Analysing Talk, Text and Interaction*. 2nd ed. London: Sage.

Stein, Kathleen F. 2014. "Experiences of College Students with Psychological Disabilities: The Impact of Perceptions of Faculty Characteristics on Academic Achievement." *International Journal of Teaching and Learning in Higher Education* 26 (1): 55–65.

Stein, Kathleen F. 2015. "DSS and Accommodations in Higher Education: Perceptions of Students with Psychological Disabilities." *Journal of Postsecondary Education and Disability* 26 (2): 145–161 145.

Stone, Emma, and Mark Priestley. 1996. "Parasites, Pawns and Partners: Disability Research and the Role of Non-Disabled Researchers." *The British Journal of Sociology* 47: 699–716.

Swain, John, and Sally French. 2000. "Towards an Affirmation Model of Disability." *Disability and Society* 15 (4): 569–582.

Terzi, Lorella. 2004. "The Social Model of Disability: A Philosophical Critique." *Journal of Applied Philosophy* 21 (2): 141–157.

University College Dublin. 2016. *UCD Student Mental Health and Wellbeing, Policy and Procedures*. Dublin: UCD Registry.

Venville, Annie, Annette F. Street, and Ellie Fossey. 2014. "Good Intentions: Teaching and Specialist Support Staff Perspectives of Student Disclosure of Mental Health Issues in Post-secondary Education." *International Journal of Inclusive Education* 18 (11): 1172–1188.

# Belonging to higher education: inclusive education for students with intellectual disabilities

Kristín Björnsdóttir

**ABSTRACT**
The college experience in Iceland has traditionally been reserved for those who have passed the matriculation examination and meet the admission requirements of higher educational institutions. Since 2007, the University of Iceland has offered a Vocational Diploma Programme for people with intellectual disabilities in inclusive settings. The purpose of this article is to describe the diploma programme as well as exploring students' sense of belonging to the college community. The diploma programme is located at the School of Education and students trained to work at pre-primary schools, after school clubs and within the field of disability such as self-advocacy. Inclusion has been achievable by adapting the general curriculum and learning outcomes to individual needs, flexible teaching methods and the cooperation between academic faculty members, programme coordinators, student mentors and the diploma students themselves. The diploma students receive academic and social support from student mentors who are other undergraduate students at the School of Education. The collaboration with student mentors has proven to be valuable, expanded diploma students' social networks and contributed to a sense of belonging. Regardless of various attitudinal and structural hindrances, there is much evidence that the diploma students are not only tolerated but welcomed at the School of Education and belong to the college community.

This article describes the vocational diploma programme for students with intellectual disabilities offered at the University of Iceland's School of Education as well as exploring students' sense of belonging to the college community. In 2007, the diploma programme was established by the former Iceland University of Education, which has since merged with the University of Iceland (UI) and forms the core of the UI's School of Education, with the support of the National Association of Intellectual Disabilities modelling a programme at Trinity College in Dublin (Stefánsdóttir and Jóhannsdóttir 2011).

The Icelandic education system can be divided into four levels; pre-primary schools, compulsory education, upper secondary schools and tertiary education. Iceland is considered to have a highly inclusive education system with inclusive education as the guiding education policy (Bjarnason and Marinósson 2015; Ólafsdóttir et al. 2014). However, the inclusiveness of the system seems to fade out as students move through it, with all children together at the pre-primary school level but segregated special schools available at the compulsory school level for those children whose needs have been assessed as 'severe' or 'profound' (Ólafsdóttir et al. 2014). Less than 1% of all compulsory aged school children are reported to be enrolled in segregated special schools (Statistics Iceland n.d.). Since 1996, students with intellectual disabilities have had access to self-contained special education classes in Icelandic upper secondary schools, but with few opportunities for participation in inclusive settings (Egilson 2014; Stefánsdóttir and Björnsdóttir 2015).

Access to higher education for people with intellectual disabilities is a novel concept in Iceland and the college experience is traditionally reserved for those who have achieved secondary education qualifications. Post-secondary programmes for students with intellectual disabilities at colleges are offered at campuses in the USA, Canada, Australia and Ireland (Hart et al. 2006; Uditsky and Hughson 2012). The level of inclusion across these campuses ranges from separate special education courses to inclusive individualised academic and social activities, but the most common format is a mixture of segregated and inclusive options (Grigal, Hart, and Weir 2012).

The vocational diploma programme at the UI is a part-time two-year inclusive vocational diploma programme for students with intellectual disabilities who have completed a four-year upper secondary school education and were interested in working in pre-primary schools, after-school programmes or within the field of disability (e.g. self-advocacy). These students do not meet the university's criteria for admission since they have not passed the matriculation examination (Ministry of Education Science and Culture 2008) and the programme is therefore categorised as an experimental or developmental programme or even the 'pet' project of the School of Education.

Students are admitted to the programme every other year and comprise a diverse group of people; while some have been identified by health/human service professionals as having 'mild/moderate' disabilities, others' needs have been assessed as 'severe/profound'. Since 2007, 68 students have graduated from the programme and 14 students are expected to graduate in spring 2017. About 60% of applications for admission have been rejected, based on the limited space available (Stefánsdóttir and Björnsdóttir 2015).

The author of this paper was the faculty coordinator of the programme from 2011 to 2016 and was responsible for the administrative management. In this article, I present a critical analysis of the vocational diploma programme offered by the University of Iceland's School of Education. The analysis is based on documentation that has taken place during the development of the programme from the onset in 2007 and my personal experience of developing and coordinating the programme in cooperation with other faculty members and students at the School of Education.

## Inclusive higher education

The purpose of higher education has been a topic of debate for many years and the worldwide student population is growing fast and has expanded to an estimated 150 million (Jónasson 2008). In recent years, there has been an increasing demand for equal access to education, including higher education. Therefore, the role of universities has changed 'playing a bigger social role than ever before' and to a certain extent reflects changing societies (Jónasson 2008, 17). Most higher education institutions, of the global north, are legally bound to accommodate disabled students who have met the criteria for admission such as passing the matriculation examination but have been criticised for relying on a biomedical definitions of who are eligible for services instead of providing support when and where it is needed (Hutcheon and Wolbring 2012). The UI has appointed a Council for Disability Rights in an effort to ensure that the policy and practice of the university coincide with legislation and disabled student's rights for support (University of Iceland 2015). This is a step forward, but since Icelandic legislation on higher education institutions has not been revised to accommodate students with intellectual disabilities they do not have a formal right to college education.

Across the Atlantic, the US Higher Education Opportunity Act, has been amended, granting higher education institutions a permit and funding for college programmes for students with intellectual disabilities and these students are eligible for federal financial aid. The amendment has opened up doors for more students with intellectual disabilities to attend college with an increased number of inclusive programmes (Papay and Griffin 2013). However, Slee (2011) has pointed out that it is not enough to change legislation; for example, quotas for university enrolments of indigenous students have not turned out to be successful: 'Establishing quotas for university enrolments of indigenous students, devoid of strategies to dismantle Eurocentric curriculum and pedagogy, inexorably reconfirms their identities of failure and drives them out of higher education' (40). Similarly, changing legislation to allow for the enrolment of students with intellectual disabilities in post-secondary education institutions is not enough by itself, there need to be strategies for including them in educational and social activities. The theoretical discussion on inclusive education has mainly been focused on primary education, but with increased emphasis on human rights in all spheres of society, inclusive education systems at *all* levels have been identified as essential for the pursuit of equal educational opportunities (United Nations 2007, Article 24).

A simple definition of inclusion is the 'process of a person or group of people being *included* within *something*. They are to be included within its processes, structures and everyday typical experiences' (Rix 2015, 4) which raises the question what the diploma students are being included in. The vocational diploma programme for people with intellectual disabilities at the UI is categorised in the course catalogue as inclusive in instances where the courses at the School of Education are offered to disabled students and non-disabled students studying at the undergraduate level (University of Iceland 2016).

## The diploma programme at the School of Education

The vocational diploma is a part-time non-credit bearing a two-year programme that does not provide access to further education or the labour market. On the one hand, the aim of the programme is to prepare students for specific jobs within the field of education, in pre-primary schools, after-school clubs and within the field of disability and self-advocacy (occupations in which the School of Education provides training). Previously, students were also trained to work at libraries but this has, since 2015, been discontinued due to lack of training sites and relevant courses at the university. On the other hand, the aim of the programme is to give students with intellectual disabilities an opportunity for college education and practical knowledge and skills in inclusive education settings in order to promote their participation in society (University of Iceland 2016).

The programme structure comprises both mandatory courses and free electives. There has never been a 'special' curriculum for the diploma programme; the learning outcomes for each course are adapted to meet the needs of each diploma student who also receives support from student mentors who are undergraduate students at the School of Education. Mentors assist students, individually or in small groups, with assignment participation and accessing the course material and lectures (Stefánsdóttir and Björnsdóttir 2015, 2016).

All first-year diploma students enrol in the same courses which consist of career guidance/practicum and two large mandatory courses offered across different undergraduate programmes at the School of Education, with over 100 students, including 15–20 diploma students (depending on the size of each class). The second year of study the diploma students spread out and have free electives which are smaller courses with 20–30 students, including one to three diploma students. They select courses depending on the scope of their training (early education, leisure studies or social education) and consequently these courses also include students who are being trained as pre-primary school teachers or are earning BA-degrees in leisure studies and social education. All of these courses are inclusive in principle, with an individualised and adapted curriculum. The level of adaptation differs depending on the needs of each student, the subject and the teaching methods and in some instances the diploma students successfully undergo assessment without any adaptations (Stefánsdóttir and Björnsdóttir 2015).

The two large mandatory courses offered to the first-year diploma students have been redesigned as cooperative learning with the aim of making the courses more accessible to all students. Although collaboration and teamwork is common in college education, programmes and courses are generally not organised in the tradition of cooperative learning which involves students working in groups on assignments that cannot be completed by individual students within the given time frame (Johnson, Johnson, and Smith 2007). The redesign of these courses as cooperative learning means that there has not been a need for student mentors as academic support during the first year; there is less emphasis on lectures and more on cooperative assignments where the contribution of all is valued regardless of physical or cognitive ability (Stefánsdóttir and Björnsdóttir 2016). Nevertheless, the student mentors have proven to be a valuable asset for the inclusion process, which will be discussed in detail in a subsequent section.

About a third of the programme comprises career guidance and practicum. These are separate or segregated courses which suggest that the programme should be categorised as a mixed programme instead of inclusive. Ideally, the diploma students would be included in the BA/BEd. practicum courses but the nature of their field training, for example, responsibilities and hours spent in the field has led to smaller, separate courses with emphasis on individualisation. Rix (2015) warns that even though an institution is committed to inclusion it can rapidly lead to marginalisation with an emphasis on individualisation. Different tasks, different curricula and even segregated courses are justified by the intention to meet the needs of the individual. The separate career guidance courses and practicum have been justified by the fact that other programmes at the School of Education do not share their practicum, therefore it is reasonable to offer separate courses for the diploma students.

The aim of the programme is to go beyond the physical placement of students within the university buildings and classroom to create an inclusive atmosphere. It is relatively simple to get information about the academic and social participation of diploma students within the university community, and to observe how other students and lecturers respond to them which generally has been positive (Stefánsdóttir and Björnsdóttir 2015, 2016). However, it is more difficult to identify how being a college student makes the students with intellectual disabilities feel, i.e. if they have achieved sense of belonging to the college community.

## Belonging

There are many barriers to full inclusion and people with intellectual disabilities have limited access to social networks and social institutions and participation in areas such as education and employment (Björnsdóttir and Traustadóttir 2010). Community integration and physical placement alongside non-disabled people does not guarantee social contact and access to social networks (Ager et al. 2001; Björnsdóttir and Traustadóttir 2010; Hall 2010). However, research has demonstrated that students with intellectual disabilities who have been enrolled in inclusive college programmes have opportunities to participate in various social and academics activities (Paiewonsky 2011). Furthermore, people with intellectual disabilities who live in community settings often use its resources, wish to participate in society and have the opportunity to engage in various community activities (Abbott and McConkey 2005; Björnsdóttir and Traustadóttir 2010; Kampert and Goreczny 2007; O Rourke et al. 2004).

The meaningful participation of disabled students in general education has been identified as a critical element of inclusion since it goes beyond the physical placement of students (Voltz, Brazil, and Ford 2001). Similarly, people with intellectual disabilities who live in community settings are more likely to be involved in 'meaningful' day-to-day activities than those who live in institutional settings (Walker and Rogan 2007). There is however some ambiguity in these writings regarding what constitutes meaningful activity and who defines it as meaningful, i.e. teachers, professionals, researchers or people with intellectual disabilities. The voices of people with intellectual disabilities have been absent from the inclusion discussion, but research indicates that people with intellectual disabilities are able to communicate their wishes regarding involvement in society (Björnsdóttir and Jónsson 2015).

Related to the idea of meaningful participation is the notion of belonging, i.e. students should share a sense of belonging in inclusive settings (Voltz, Brazil, and Ford 2001). The sense of belonging has been identified as another critical element of inclusion (Mahar, Cobigo, and Stuart 2014; Voltz, Brazil, and Ford 2001). As noted above, community or physical placement does not automatically provide a sense of belonging and it has been suggested that segregated settings for people with intellectual disabilities could provide access to specialised services or offer friendship and a sense of belonging which some seem to lack in the community or general education settings (Hall 2010; Norwich 2008). There is also some ambiguity in these suggestions and it is difficult to pinpoint what exactly constitutes as a sense of belonging and how it is achieved in segregated settings and not inclusive settings.

Mahar, Cobigo, and Stuart (2013) have developed a transdisciplinary conceptualisation of social belonging with the aim of evaluating the effectiveness of community-based programmes for disabled people which relies in part on active input from the service users. As mentioned above, much of the research addressing the inclusion of people or students with intellectual disabilities has been from the perspectives of teachers, professionals and parents. It is therefore important to include the input of the diploma students when attempting to determine whether the vocational diploma programme has the potential of providing a sense of belonging in an inclusive educational environment.

**Table 1.** Overview of the five principles of belonging.

| Principles | Definition |
| --- | --- |
| Subjectivity | A perception that is unique to the individual that centres on feelings of value, respect and fit. Sense of belonging corresponds to the personal and important qualities of how membership in a relationship, group or system makes the individual feel |
| Groundedness | An appropriate understanding of a sense of belonging requires that a referent group for belonging is provided to anchor the subjective feeling. One belongs to something |
| Reciprocity | A sense of relatedness or connectedness that is shared by the individual and the external referent. Similar physical, intellectual or behavioural characteristics are alone insufficient to engender a feeling of belonging. A label lacks the weight to define the perception of belonging |
| Dynamism | Physical and social environments may contribute to or detract from an individual's sense of belonging. Physical barriers include geographic area and disability. Social barriers may include behaviours of a group towards an individual, prejudice and discrimination. The dynamic interplay between enablers and barriers needs to be recognised in any formal definition of sense of belonging |
| Self-determination | The right of the individual to choose to interact with referents and their perceived power in the interaction. An individual's ability to feel a sense of belonging and their subsequent decision to feel that they do or do not belong is an interesting intricacy of belongingness. Individuals who feel powerless to belong as the result of physical or environmental factors may otherwise 'qualify' for group membership, yet never successfully achieve a sense of belonging |

Source: (Mahar, Cobigo, and Stuart 2013).

Mahar, Cobigo, and Stuart (2013) offer a criteria for belonging based on five principles; subjectivity, groundedness, reciprocity, dynamism and self-determination. I use that criteria as a framework for my analysis and compare the vocational diploma programme to these five principles. Table 1 offers an overview of the five principles of belonging.

The first principle, *subjectivity*; 'a sense of belonging is a perception that is unique to the individual that centres on feelings of value, respect and fit' (1030). During the first years of the programme, there were some reports of negative attitudes. For example, a young man said: 'At first, when we were supposed to be working on group assignments with other [non-disabled] students it felt as if nobody wanted to work with us' (Stefánsdóttir and Björnsdóttir 2015, 8). The student interprets the passive responses of the non-disabled students as disrespectful which makes him feel unwelcome. There has however been a noticeable and positive change in other students' attitudes and perspectives towards the diploma students who have in return reported perceptions of value, respect and fit both socially and academically (Stefánsdóttir and Björnsdóttir 2015, 2016). They have made friends, been encouraged to participate in social events and generally feel that they are being treated as equals which contributes to the feeling of fitting in (Stefánsdóttir and Björnsdóttir 2015).

Periodically, from the onset of the programme, a discussion regarding a separate curriculum or special course identification numbers has taken place among administrative staff and faculty members. The students would still participate in the same courses as the undergraduate students but in the official course catalogue there would be two separate course numbers, one for undergraduate students and another for the diploma students. This raises the question what it would mean to a diploma student to be the only student enrolled in a course under a different course number and how it would affect his/her sense of belonging. Perhaps in real life none of the students would be aware that there were two course numbers, but symbolically this arrangement documents students as 'regular' students and 'special' students. One who belongs to the university when the other is a special guest.

Second, a *groundedness* is required; that is, belonging to something. The diploma students referred to themselves as college students, diploma students and belonging to the School of Education. The main campus is in the city centre, but the School of Education is located a few kilometres off the main campus with a small student population of approximately 2000. This has led to a small but close knit community where people know each other well and faculty members have reported that the diploma students contribute to the multicultural atmosphere of the School of Education; they are visible in the hallways, in the library, in the food court which influences the environment in a positive way (Stefánsdóttir and Björnsdóttir 2015).

The third principle that Mahar, Cobigo, and Stuart (2013) offer as criteria for sense of belonging is *reciprocity*:

> or the sense of relatedness or connectedness that is shared by the individual and the external referent ... While similar physical, intellectual or behavioural characteristics may be used to exclude someone from a social group; alone they are insufficient to engender a feeling of belonging. While an identifying characteristic or label may place an individual within a social group or system, they lack the weight to define the perception of belonging. (1030)

While the diploma students did refer to themselves as diploma students they seldom referred to their impairment and it did not seem to anchor any form of belonging. Some of the diploma students were friends before entering the programme and some formed friendships with other diploma students, while yet others only made friends with non-disabled students. For many of the diploma students, college was their first experience of being in an inclusive classroom and a diploma student said:

> The biggest change for me is being in college and not labelled and segregated from others. We participate in courses with other students, it does not matter who you are or what you look like, and this way we meet a lot of people. Just like in real life and work, you have to interact with and work with all sorts of people and not only disabled people. I think that was the biggest lesson for me. (Stefánsdóttir and Björnsdóttir 2015, 7)

Many of the student mentors had never been in school with their disabled peers and described how they were too timid to initiate contact with the diploma students but after working together on assignments and taking the same courses their friendship grew mainly because they had much in common, e.g. being at similar age and studying together and having similar interests (Stefánsdóttir and Björnsdóttir 2016). The student mentors have become essential for providing support to diploma students and lecturers and also for encouraging social participation.

International research has demonstrated that mentoring programmes at colleges where student mentors support other students socially and academically are beneficial for all inclued (Hafner, Moffatt, and Kisa 2011). Research carried out with the diploma students and student mentors at the UI has shown that the mentoring project has expanded the social networks of the diploma students. They, for example, often choose to sit with their mentors at the food court and through them meet other university students, leading to invitations to join them in other circumstances and social events (Stefánsdóttir and Björnsdóttir 2015, 2016). Furthermore, since 2011 the diploma students formally belong to the School of Education student association, which has had a positive effect on the social participation of the diploma students. Many participate in off and on campus activities but the level of individual social participation depends on the support available to students outside of school settings. The formal student association membership and the mentoring feature of the programme seem to enhance reciprocity between students with intellectual disabilities and non-disabled students.

Fourth, Mahar, Cobigo, and Stuart (2013) identify *dynamism* as a principle for sense of belonging where 'both physical and social environments may contribute to or detract from an individual's sense of belonging' (1031). In principle, during the third and fourth semesters, the diploma students can select any undergraduate course that does not have prerequisites. However, some of the academic faculty of the School of Education have had, especially in the beginning, some reservations about the programme. Those faculty members have argued that the vocational programme is a fake and voiced their fear that enrolling students with intellectual disabilities to the university involves 'dumbing down' higher education (Stefánsdóttir and Björnsdóttir 2015). This has resulted in the programme's coordinators steering students away from certain elective courses, but forming close alliances with other faculty members who are willing to provide opportunities for full inclusion. These lecturers employ flexible teaching methods, emphasise collaboration between all students and through their pedagogy contribute to student's sense of belonging (Stefánsdóttir and Björnsdóttir 2016).

Since there are only a couple of European colleges that offer programmes for students with intellectual disabilities, none of which are inclusive there is no consensus as to what constitutes access to the general courses and what an adapted curriculum truly means. The Student Registration oversees enrolment of students, registration of students for courses at all faculties at the university, and are responsible for all certificates and transcripts. From the onset of the programme, the Student Registration has voiced concerns regarding the mobility of the diploma students, whether they could transfer to other departments within the UI or another university. To prevent diploma students' mobility, the university has incorporated the label of intellectual disabilities in the title of their diploma and on their transcripts it states: 'NOT TERTIARY EDUCATION', instead of providing information on the adapted general curriculum. Graduated diploma students have claimed that they feel embarrassed because of it.

Offering students with intellectual disabilities a non-credited diploma is in many instances unfair, especially since the needs of the diploma students vary greatly and some have been able to undergo the same assessments as the undergraduate students with no adaptation or similar accommodation available to students, for example, those with anxiety and dyslexia. It is extremely unfair to these students that their effort is not valued equally to others because they have been labelled as having intellectual disabilities and have bypassed the admission process and entered the university without a matriculation exam.

The lecturers have identified assessment as the biggest obstacle in relation to the adapted curriculum (Stefánsdóttir and Björnsdóttir 2015). Since the vocational diploma programme is a non-credited degree the issue of student evaluations has not been prioritised leaving both lecturers and students uncertain. It is important to provide the lecturers with support so that they are able to construct individualised goals for the students with intellectual disabilities based on the general learning outcomes of the course. Insufficient support could lead to tokenistic physical placement of the diploma students and limited access to the course content. An inclusive programme with an adapted general curriculum means that not only do the diploma students share the physical experience of participating in courses they also have opportunities to acquire knowledge and skills. Limited access to the curriculum is among factors that could detract from sense of belonging and it is crucial for the success of the diploma programme that the issue of student assessment should be resolved.

Finally, Mahar, Cobigo, and Stuart (2013) identify *self-determination* as the fifth principle of sense of belonging, since a feeling of powerlessness can hinder people from achieving this. Graduated students generally regard the programme to be a positive and authentic experience (Stefánsdóttir and Björnsdóttir 2015) which coincides with international results, where students report higher self-esteem and self-worth at the point of graduation (Hart et al. 2006; Uditsky and Hughson 2012). The graduating class of 2013 also demonstrated through self-advocacy that they were able and willing to speak up. With the support of the student council, they fought for the access of diploma students to the general shared graduation ceremony held for all undergraduate students at the UI. The university offers several diploma programmes that do not lead to a bachelor degree and these students do not participate in the graduation ceremony. The School of Education, however, preferred to wish the diploma students with intellectual disabilities a formal farewell in a small separate graduation ceremony. The diploma students felt excluded by these arrangements since they had been included in general courses; they protested publicly and arranged meetings with the Dean of the School of Education. Even though their demonstrations were supported by the student council and caught the attention of the media they were not granted access to the general ceremony on the grounds that it would be unfair to other diploma students who had not been labelled as having intellectual disabilities. Two years later when the next class graduated, the governing board of the School of Education decided to conduct a shared graduation ceremony for all the diploma programmes. A graduated diploma student was contacted by the local media and she described how she felt they had made progress and influenced some changes at the university: 'I am extremely proud … this is the best solution' (Jakobsdóttir 2015).

During their studies, the diploma students have opportunities to acquire knowledge on disability and human rights which are topics of discussion in various courses available to them. Through courses like career guidance and the practicum, efforts are made to provide them with the requisite skills to build their self-determination. When comparing the diploma programme to the five principles for sense of belonging, many indications suggest that the diploma students belong to the UI, therefore, the inclusive initiative of the School of Education has turned out to be successful. However, there are also certain factors, mainly within the structure of the university, which could detract from students' sense of belonging and need to be further addressed. Also, although such a framework for sense of belonging can be a useful tool it only provides general information about the programme and individuals can still experience marginalisation even though the programme has generally been positive for the whole student cohort.

## Conclusion

The difficult economic environment in Iceland, combined with reports of Icelandic students not performing well on the Programme for International Student Assessment, has fuelled the debate on inclusive education (Björnsdóttir and Jónsson 2015). Similarly, in 2006 the UI set itself the ambitious long-term goal of becoming one of the top 100 universities in the world (University of Iceland 2011) which may have contributed to an atmosphere where there is limited space for students labelled as having intellectual disabilities. While the School of Education has provided a small group of students so labelled with the opportunity to further their education there are others who would welcome the opportunity of studying at different departments such as business or tourism studies. For that to become reality, the UI needs to expand its role and aims and the diploma programme needs to be owned by the university and not only the School of Education. I am of course not suggesting that the standards of the education system should be lowered, but rather raised, with inclusion as an ethical project, not to be carried out on a 'discrete population …, but rather something we must do to ourselves' (Allan 2005, 293). Inclusion as an ethical project brings the focus away from the individual student onto the environment and to the structural flaws of the education system and forces us to acknowledge how international assessments and rankings affect our system, teaching and learning. Inclusive higher education provides us with the opportunity to reconstruct the college community and expand the meaning of higher education.

Through the diploma programme, inclusion has been achievable by adapting the general curriculum to individual needs, flexible teaching methods, and the cooperation between academic faculty members, programme coordinators, student mentors and the diploma students themselves. Since the university's resources are limited the programme relies heavily on support from the student mentors who have proven to be valuable both academically and socially. Their shared experience of going through courses and working towards accruing knowledge and skills related to their future fields of employment (pre-primary schools, after-school clubs, the field of disability) has contributed to a sense of belonging. However, there are issues that need to be solved, such as student assessments and how diploma students could accumulate credits if they undergo general assessments without adaption. Regardless of various barriers, there is much evidence that the diploma students are not only tolerated but welcomed at the School of Education and belong to the college community.

## Disclosure statement

No potential conflict of interest was reported by the author.

## References

Abbott, Susan, and Roy McConkey. 2005. "The Barriers to Social Inclusion as Persceived by People with Intellectual Disabilities." *Journal of Intellectual Disabilities* 10 (3): 275–287. doi:10.1177/1744629506067618.

Ager, Alastair, Fiona Myers, Patricia Kerr, Susan Myles, and Ann Green. 2001. "Moving Home: Social Integration for Adults with Learning Disabilities Resettling into Community." *Journal of Applied Research in Learning Disabilities* 14: 392–400.

Allan, Julie. 2005. "Inclusion as an Ethical Project." In *Foucault and the Government of Disability*, edited by Shelley Tremain, 281–297. Ann Arbor: The University of Michigan Press.

Bjarnason, Dóra S., and Gretar L. Marinósson. 2015. "Salamanca and Beyond. Inclusive Education Still up for Debate." In *Inclusive Education Twenty Years after Salamanca*, edited by Florian Kiuppis and Rune Sarromaa Hausstätter, 133–143. New York: Peter Lang Publishing Inc.

Björnsdóttir, Kristín, and Steindór Jónsson. 2015. "Social (in)Equality: Collaborative Reflection." *Icelandic Journal of Education* 24 (2): 99–118.

Björnsdóttir, Kristín, and Rannveig Traustadóttir. 2010. "Stuck in the Land of Disability? The Intersection of Learning Difficulties, Class, Gender and Religion." *Disability & Society* 25 (1): 49–62. doi:10.1080/09687590903363340.

Egilson, Snæfríður Thóra. 2014. "School Experiences of Pupils with Physical Impairments over Time." *Disability & Society* 29 (7): 1076–1089. doi:10.1080/09687599.2014.902363.

Grigal, Meg, Debra Hart, and Cate Weir. 2012. "A Survey of Postsecondary Education Programs for Students with Intellectual Disabilities in the United States." *Journal of Policy and Practice in Intellectual Disabilities* 9 (4): 223–233. doi:10.1111/jppi.12012.

Hafner, Dedra, Courtney Moffatt, and Nutullah Kisa. 2011. "Cutting-Edge: Integrating Students with Intellectual and Developmental Disabilities into a 4-Year Liberal Arts College." *Career Development for Exceptional Individuals* 34 (1): 18–30.

Hall, Edward. 2010. "Spaces of Social Inclusion and Belonging for People with Intellectual Disabilities." *Journal of Intellectual Disability Research* 54: 48–57. doi:10.1111/j.1365-2788.2009.01237.x.

Hart, Debra, Meg Grigal, Caren Sax, Donna Martinez, and Madeleine Will. 2006. "Postsecondary Education Options for Students with Intellectual Disabilities." *Researc to Practice* 45: 1–4.

Hutcheon, Emily J., and Gregor Wolbring. 2012. "Voices of 'Disabled' Post Secondary Students: Examining Higher Education 'Disability' Policy Using an Ableism Lens." *Journal of Diversity Higher Education* 5 (1): 39–49. doi:10.1037/a0027002.

Jakobsdóttir, Nanna Elísa. 2015. "Sameiginleg útskriftarathöfn diplómanema: 'Ég er rosalega stolt.'" [Joint Graduation Ceremony for Diploma Students: 'I Am Extremely Proud.'] In *Fréttablaðið*. http://www.visir.is/sameiginleg-utskriftarathofn-diplomanema-eg-er-rosalega-stolt-/article/2015150429503.

Johnson, David, Roger Johnson, and Karl Smith. 2007. "The State of Cooperative Learning in Postsecondary and Professional Settings." *Educational Psychology Review* 19 (1): 15–29. doi:10.1007/s10648-006-9038-8.

Jónasson, Jón Torfi. 2008. *Inventing Tomorrow's University: Who is to Take the Lead?, Observatory for Fundamental University Values and Rights*. Bologna: Bononia University Press.

Kampert, Amy L., and Anthony J. Goreczny. 2007. "Community Involvement and Socialization among Individuals with Mental Retardation." *Research in Developmental Disabilities* 28 (3): 278–286.

Mahar, Alyson L., Virginie Cobigo, and Heather Stuart. 2013. "Conceptualizing Belonging." *Disability and Rehabilitation* 35 (12): 1026–1032. doi:10.3109/09638288.2012.717584.

Mahar, Alyson L., Virginie Cobigo, and Heather Stuart. 2014. "Comments on Measuring Belonging as a Service Outcome." *Journal on Developmental Disabilities* 20 (2): 20–33.

Ministry of Education Science and Culture. 2008. "Act on Public Higher Education Institutions." *85.*

Norwich, Brahm. 2008. "SPECIAL SCHOOLS: What Future for Special Schools and Inclusion? Conceptual and Professional Perspectives." *British Journal of Special Education* 35 (3): 136–143. doi:10.1111/j.1467-8578.2008.00387.x.

Ólafsdóttir, Steingerður, Sigrún Sif Jóelsdóttir, Lára Rún Sigurvinsdóttir, Dóra S. Bjarnason, Anna Kristín Sigurðardóttir, and Kristín Erla Harðardóttir. 2014. *Skóli án aðgreiningar: samantekt á lögum og fræðilegu efni* [Inclusive Education: Summary of Legislation and Research]. Reykjavík: The Educational Research Institute, University of Iceland and The Ministry of Education, Science and Culture.

O Rourke, Anne, Ian M. Grey, Ray Fuller, and Brian McClean. 2004. "Satisfaction with Living Arrangements of Older Adults with Intellectual Disability: Service Users' and Carers' Views.'" *Journal of Learning Disabilities* 8 (1): 12–29.

Paiewonsky, Maria. 2011. "Hitting the Reset Button on Education: Student Reports on Going to College." *Career Development for Exceptional Individuals* 34 (1): 31–44. doi:10.1177/0885728811399277.

Papay, Clare, and Megan Griffin. 2013. "Developing Inclusive College Opportunities for Students with Intellectual and Developmental Disabilities." *Research & Practice for Persons with Severe Disabilities* 38 (2): 110–116.

Rix, Jonathan. 2015. *Must Inclusion Be Special? Rethinking Educational Support within a Community of Provision*. Oxon: Routledge.

Slee, Roger. 2011. *The Irregular School: Exclusion, Schooling and Inclusive Education*. Abingdon: Routledge.

Statistics Iceland. n.d. "Grunnskólanemendur eftir bekkjum og skóla 2001–2014." [Primary School Students 2001–2014.]. Accessed May 16. http://px.hagstofa.is/pxis/pxweb/is/Samfelag/Samfelag__skolamal__2_grunnskolastig__0_gsNemendur/SKO02102.px/

Stefánsdóttir, Guðrún V., and Kristín Björnsdóttir. 2015. "'I Am a College Student' Postsecondary Education for Students with Intellectual Disabilities." *Scandinavian Journal of Disability Research*: 1–15. doi: 10.1080/15017419.2015.1114019.

Stefánsdóttir, Guðrún V., and Kristín Björnsdóttir, 2016. "'Við lærum af þeim og þau af okkur' Mentorar í starfstengdu diplómunámi fyrir fólk með þroskahömlun." ['We Learn from Them and They from Us' Student Mentors in PSE Program for Students with Intellectual Disabilities] In *Skóli margbreytileikans: Menntun og manngildi í kjölfar Salamanca*, edited by Dóra S. Bjarnason, Ólafur Páll Jónsson, and Hermína Gunnþórsdóttir, 133–143. Reykjavík: Háskólaútgáfan.

Stefánsdóttir, Guðrún V., and Vilborg Jóhannsdóttir. 2011. "A Semi Professional Diploma Program for People with Intellectual Disabilities at the School of Education, University of Iceland." *Netla – Online Journal on Pedagogy and Education*. Accessed May 16. http://netla.hi.is/greinar/2011/ryn/003.pdf

Uditsky, Bruce, and Elizabeth Hughson. 2012. "Inclusive Postsecondary Education – An Evidence-Based Moral Imperative." *Journal of Policy and Practice in Intellectual Disabilities* 9 (4): 298–302. doi:10.1111/jppi.12005.

United Nations. 2007. *Convention on the Rights of Persons with Disabilities*. New York: United Nations.

University of Iceland. 2011. *Policy of the University of Iceland 2011–2016*. Reykjavík: University of Iceland.

University of Iceland. 2015. "Council for Disability Rights." Accessed May 16. http://english.hi.is/university/council_disability_rights

University of Iceland. 2016. "Vocational Diploma Program for Students with Intellectual Disabilities." Accessed June 7. https://ugla.hi.is/kennsluskra/index.php?tab=skoli&chapter=content&id=34347&kennsluar=2016

Voltz, Deborah L., Nettye Brazil, and Alison Ford. 2001. "What Matters Most in Inclusive Education: A Practical Guide for Moving Forward." *Intervention in School and Clinic* 37 (1): 23–30. doi:10.1177/105345120103700105.

Walker, Pam, and Patricia M. Rogan. 2007. *Make the Day Matter!: Promoting Typical Lifestyles for Adults with Significant Disabilities*. Baltimore, MD: Paul H. Brookes.

# Re-visiting the role of disability coordinators: the changing needs of disabled students and current support strategies from a UK university

Mujde Koca-Atabey

**ABSTRACT**
This study aimed to investigate the system designed to support disabled university students from the perspective of disability coordinators. The research on this topic specifically is limited. Disability coordinators from a particular UK university were interviewed to better understand the support system from their own perspective. Interpretative Phenomenological Analysis (IPA) was conducted to reveal themes related to supporting students. IPA is a tool to understand participants' social and emotional world. The final themes were: interest in and internal motivation regarding disability issues; flexibility and disability; personal experiences of disability; good practices; and finally, time and disability. The theme time and disability appeared as a separate theme but also was embedded within the whole analysis. In addition, the results indicated that the support issue is dynamic in nature and that student needs continuously change as new needs emerge. The demographic characteristics of disabled university students have changed over time. Students are also increasingly more competent at using technology. Consequently, disability coordinators should be more active and provide faster solutions to meet higher expectations. The results and policy implications of this study are discussed with reference to the impact of time, change and context.

This study investigated the university support structure provided to disabled university students by disability coordinators. Disability can be defined in a number of ways and its complex nature is emphasised extensively (Corner 2011; Olney and Brockelman 2003; Valeras 2010). Generally, it is considered as a heterogeneous phenomenon (Winn and Hay 2009). The social model defines disability as a social problem that values collective responsibility, choice, rights and social change (Oliver 1996). Therefore, rather than being a clinical issue and personal problem (as the medical model suggests) (e.g. French and Swain 2004), disability is conceptualised within the social context.

Recent legislation has led to a more compatible environment for disabled university students. The Equality Act (2010) stated that 'a person has a disability if they have a physical or mental impairment, and the impairment has a substantial and long-term adverse effect on his or her ability to carry out normal day-to-day activities'. All universities within the UK have legal responsibilities for equality and diversity. The Act has a national enforcement component and also has an international impact. Although this is the case, still there are students who have to make their own personal adjustments (Goode 2007). Sachs and Schreuer (2011) have argued that these students should be studied regarding their experiences and levels of satisfaction with university life. They also assert that disabled students may experience either psychological distress or stress-related growth dependent upon their coping skills. Daily hassles and helpless coping are associated with symptoms, and problem-solving coping is linked to growth (Koca-Atabey et al. 2011). Disabled university students face a number of problems, such as issues relating to accommodations, transportation, accessing course information, environmental barriers and inconsistency in support systems (Holloway 2001; Koca-Atabey 2016; Soorenian 2013). Students may also have limited social opportunities and physical or attitudinal barriers that hinder their academic performance (Goode 2007). Further, fear of stigmatisation may be a barrier to seeking support (Demery, Thirlaway, and Mercer 2012). Hopkins (2011) argued that disabled university students face numerous barriers in higher education settings compared to non-disabled peers. However, both disabled and non-disabled students have been found to experience similar problems in learning and assessment. Thus, both groups would benefit from barrier removal practices (Madriaga et al. 2010).

The present study investigated the university support structure from the perspective of disability coordinators. Although the term 'coordinator' is the widely used expression, other terms are also available. Examples include 'college counselor' (US) (Goad and Robertson 2000), 'disability officer' (Cyprus) (Hadjikakou, Polycarpou, and Hadjilia 2010) 'disability liaison officer' (Australia) (Meredith, Packman, and Marks 2012) or 'staff towards individuals towards disabilities' (Canada) (Mullins and Preyde 2013). Terminology is important because it reflects the conceptualisation of disability in relation to time and context. The structure of the role or job description is also diverse and might depend mainly upon the institutional policies, rules, regulations and needs. Parker (2000) stated more than a decade ago, this area of study was relatively new and – and remains so today – substantial variability exists in terms of staffing, policies and practices. Some students have articulated that they had positive experiences and attained accurate and firm support from disability coordinators (e.g. Fuller et al. 2004; Koca-Atabey 2013) however, this might not be always the case, and students might feel disappointed with the work that the coordinators did. This might stem from a communication-related problem or a failure to adopt an individualised approach, which most students' request (Milic Babic and Dowling 2015). On the other hand, what the coordinators think about the university support system and their role has received little attention. The role of disability coordinators is essential because they are the key actors in the relationship, or the liaison, between the student and his or her department. Therefore, this study aims to re-visit the role of the disability coordinator as they are key actors in the whole process (Parker 2000).

## Method

Disability coordinators from a certain UK university were interviewed in order to understand the nature of the support system. The specific university was selected for the study because it hosts a large disability studies centre that is one of the pioneers in the field both nationally and internationally. Of the seven coordinators, four agreed to participate (see Table 1). The

**Table 1.** Disability coordinators.

| Pseudonym | Specialisation | Education | Experience |
|---|---|---|---|
| Amanda | Students with autism spectrum conditions | MS degree | Had experience at different levels of disability support (e.g. note taker, mentor, disability coordinator) at the university level |
| Mary | Students with mental health conditions | Currently doing a course in mental health counselling | Had community-based experience in relation to mental health counselling |
| Hilary | Deaf and hard of hearing students | MA in Deaf Studies | Had experience as a sign language interpreter and worked in schools, colleges and universities |
| Valerie | Blind and partially sighted students | BS degree | Had RNIB (Royal National Institute of Blind People) experience |

other three coordinators were either unavailable or declined the invitation which was made via emails. An important ethical issue that arises relates to the limits of confidentiality. This is especially important because there were a few universities with a large number of coordinators, which risks easy identification. This possibility was explained to all participants prior to the interviews and they all agreed to participate. The interview questions were about their experiences as a disability coordinator (e.g. the support structure within the university, difficult cases, departments' responses to student needs, etc.) and anonymity was kept when specific student cases were discussed. The interviews lasted for 35–45 min and were recorded and transcribed verbatim. All coordinators who participated in the study were women.

Interpretative Phenomenological Analysis (IPA) is an appropriate tool to reveal participants' personal and social worlds. Although the number of participants in this study was relatively small, IPA recognises the danger of sacrificing breadth for depth (Smith and Osborn 2003) and supports smaller samples (up to 10) with the underlying assumption that 'less is more' (Reid, Flowers, and Larkin 2005). IPA has two important components. The first one is the phenomenological requirement, which means 'giving voice' to the participants, and the second one is the interpretive requirement, which is 'making sense' of the data (Larkin, Watts, and Clifton 2006). Thus, IPA was used to reveal the superordinate themes and subthemes in the interview transcripts. The transcripts were reviewed a number of times, themes were identified and the cases were integrated (Langdridge 2004).

## Results

The university organises disability support services based on types of disabilities. Although all coordinators were somewhat knowledgeable about all disability areas, they each specialised in one broad area. Their training and/or experiences were associated with their area of specialisation.

The superordinate themes were those which appeared to be important and frequent. These themes were: (1) Interest in and internal motivation regarding disability issues, (2) Flexibility and disability, (3) Personal experiences of disability, (4) Good practices and (5) Time and disability. The time and disability theme was further divided into two subthemes: the changing nature of the disability phenomenon and becoming disabled during university life.

### *Interest in and internal motivation regarding disability issues*

All coordinators revealed that their job choice was based on internal motivation and that it was an area of personal interest. Their journey towards becoming a disability coordinator emerged as an inspirational matter:

> My degree… was French and pure maths, absolutely bored… I just happen to see an ad for RNIB (Royal National Institute of Blind People) wanting people to learn how to produce braille, particularly, if they had French language and maths. It was just so exciting and so different. (DC-Valerie)

> I started learning sign language at the same time as the jobs using sign language… My interest in sign language led me to work in schools with some deaf children … it is an interesting issue really… (DC-Hilary)

It was inspiring to realise that all the participants had positive evaluations about their jobs, considering that being a disability coordinator is not always something that is straightforward. They might feel caught in the middle as employees of the university and student advocates (Parker 2000).

### *Flexibility and disability*

The coordinators had to be flexible in many ways and stated that their jobs inevitably required flexibility:

> Our old head of service [said]: 'Everything will be a lot better if people would just [be] more flexible, you just didn't think there is one way to do things'… people being more inclusive or just accepting diversity. (DC-Hilary)

> Specialist Mentor Scheme… again it is a flexibility, team of support workers and I assign usually one mentor to one student… helping the student organizing their time… keeping [on] top of the deadlines… helping to sending an e-mail to a staff… (DC-Amanda)

### *Personal experiences of disability*

The participants declared personal experiences with disability, all of which occurred during the course of their careers as disability coordinators. The relationship was reciprocal, as their job may have contributed to their personal experiences:

> I suppose it come it time really, when I first start with job… I have no experience with disability but now 50% of my friends have visual impairment. Now my mum has age-related macular degeneration… Each time I see her, how much worse her eye-sight has gone but equally I hope that I have been able to know lots of useful suggestions to her… (DC-Valerie)

### *Good practices*

The coordinators stated that there were examples of good practices wherein both academic standards and student needs were met. For optimal solutions, departmental cooperation is essential:

> We had a student with anorexia who was hospitalised… The hospital was not keen for her to come out to do exams so we organized with the department, an additional four essays, instead of exams… delivered to her in the hospital and it worked well. (DC-Mary)

> A student who had difficulties with, anxiety with presentations, so we had to discuss that and see what the anxieties were and liaise with the department what we will do about that... not to do group presentations... do individual presentation and instead of... give it to the group... (DC-Amanda)

In addition to being helpful to the students, these examples of good practices are important to the coordinators in reinforcing their job satisfaction. Another important fact about the coordinators' role is that their duties started in the students' application stage. Fortunately, examples of good practice were exemplified even in this initial phase. These were proactive in nature:

> I got a letter [from a prospective student] who is applying to do music... and a braille user. There is not anyone in my team that can produce braille music but I have enough notice to find a supplier and that is probably available for that student... (DC-Valerie)

Another example of a good practice included the element of time:

> The other important factor about this particular group of customers we have is the material tends to get republished quite frequently. ...the students do want to read the current edition, that is one the recommended, the page references in the reading lists will refer to the latest edition... (DC-Valerie)

> [Note: When textbooks and other instructional materials are revised sometimes a previous version is the one that has been recorded or translated to braille and this can create confusion for the student.]

## *Time and disability*

Consistent with the above analysis, time appeared as an embedded theme within the whole discussion and was related to all other master themes. Similar to examples given earlier reflecting 'good practices-time' and 'personal experiences-time,' time is also related to the themes of interest and internal motivation. Specifically, interest in the disability issue was a continuous factor for participants. Time was also related to the disability framework due to the tendency of needs to change over time and the possibility of students who would become disabled during the course of their studies.

### *Changing nature of disability phenomenon*

Changes in relation to disability are twofold: change of jobs due to time and changes in terms of current students (i.e. the new generations of students are different than the previous ones). Types of disabilities, numbers, percentages and the students' qualifications are different than they were previously. Specifically, the new disabled student often has less severe impairments. The disability coordinators stated that the number of students who are blind or deaf has decreased substantially. It is an important difference because older studies listed blindness or partial sightedness as the most common type of impairments (e.g. McConnell 1981). Currently, there are more students with psychological impairments (i.e. mental health difficulties), autism spectrum conditions and dyslexia or dyspraxia than in previous years:

> In the last ten years we see a rapid decline in the use of audio and braille. Possibly in the last five years maybe only 2% of our outputs be in braille or audio. ...they used assistive technology at school. ...already know how to access electronic material. Relatively speaking we have very few visually impaired students, about 30... (DC-Valerie)

> There are increasing numbers of students diagnosed with mental health conditions… There was no mental health coordinator and it was causing a lot of problems… Since we had the post, I think more people are coming forward. (DC-Mary)

## *Becoming disabled during university life*

The coordinators were also responsive to the needs of students who became disabled during their course of study. In some cases, it could be a completely new issue for the students or their condition may fluctuate:

> For some it has been a long-standing problem and for others they will develop the illness when they are here…. The difficulty of mental health is people become unwell when they arrive at the university because of all sorts of factors; they are in an age group… that is vulnerable to mental health difficulties and the stress of university… (DC-Mary)

> I see quite a lot of people who for a variety of reasons are losing their sight now or their sight is deteriorating… if they are coming with a new sight loss just to alert them to all the support that is available… (DC-Valerie)

## Discussion

As previously discussed, all coordinators mentioned a personal interest in disability-related issues and had an internal motivation to do their jobs. During their interviews they were questioned about the potential for burnout, but it was clear that burnout was not a primary issue. Although it is a demanding job and the workload is substantial, especially during the first semester, the coordinators stated that they would like to continue their jobs in the future. Therefore, it can be concluded that they are satisfied employees and being a coordinator is a 'career' or may be a 'calling' for them (Seligman 2003).

Another key issue was that of flexibility. In particular, the coordinators indicated that the nature of the job and the population (i.e. disabled university students) requires a substantial amount of flexibility to be effective. Flexibility is also emphasised by other researchers in the literature and the case has been made that flexibility and inclusive curriculum are the key elements within the university setting (Hopkins 2011; López Gavira and Moriña 2015; Sciame-Giesecke, Roden, and Parkison 2009). The results also revealed that what constitutes a disability and how it affects students is continuously changing. Each day, there may be new needs from a different population of disabled students. Inevitably, the issues surrounding disabled students are dynamic. Consequently, coordinators must be more active than they have in the past and should be ready to provide faster solutions to meet ever-changing higher expectations.

Moreover, Zimbardo and Boyd (2008) discuss the importance of time in relation to managing one's life. Similarly, time appeared to be an integral part of working with disabled university students. This is not surprising because what is a disability and what is not is also determined by time. As stated by Seymour (2002), a life with a disability is dominated by time, or time–space and disability are interrelated (Schillmeier 2008). Similarly, Compton-Lilly (2016) argued that time also contributes to who we are and who we become.

Due to the well-established nature of the social model within the UK context, it has undoubtedly affected the structure of disability-related services. However, although the university, in this study, hosts a well-established disability studies centre, which is one of the pioneers of the social model of disability, the unit of the coordinators had little connection to this centre. The paths of practice and education-research are different. For instance, research within the centre is primarily grounded in the social model of disability, some researchers feel that this orientation disregards the bodily experience of the disabled individuals (Morris 1991) and denies the pain of impairment as a pragmatic reality (Oliver 1996). The unit of the coordinators, on the other hand, based their organisations according to categories of disabilities, perhaps recognising that in practice the area of disability has an impact on the specific needs of the student. Additionally, although all coordinators acknowledge the centre's role within the field, none of them had any education or research-based collaborative relationship with the centre.

While this study is based on a single UK university, thus limiting its generalisability and comparability, it provides the benefit of in-depth analysis. The results of the study indicate a number of system-related suggestions including the hiring of more coordinators that specialise in dyslexia or other coordinators might be hired as non-categorical support coordinators to reduce the workloads of existing coordinators. This might also be also useful because similar to language (e.g. Bolt 2005; Hutcheon and Wolbring 2012; Morris 1993), a categorisation based on impairment types could be disabling. Making disability-related services available to students who are otherwise not aware of them is also a key issue. A disability coordinator who is responsible for coordinating with each school or faculty might also be an alternative, which may provide faster solutions. Additionally, it is important to find ways to encourage disabled university students who are reluctant to access the available services. It should not be forgotten that disclosure is the important first step in the whole support process (Stampoltzis and Polychronopoulou 2009). One other important suggestion for this institution and other universities within the UK or beyond might be implementing the principles of the social model. Providing records, establishing a support structure and hiring coordinators might be the initial steps for the countries that do not have such a structure. Institutions with an established structure might use student feedback as a source of input to examine areas for improvement. University students might be regarded as the cream of the crop so appropriate support is essential.

Overall, the coordinators' interpretations of their experiences were either neutral or positive. Within a broader perspective, their attitudes are promising and indicate that long-term and active engagement with disabled university students could result in favourable outcomes. Looking back to Elton's (1981) analysis that change is not easy for universities, it might be stated that although difficult and slow, universities *must* change in relation to both time and context.

## Acknowledgements

The author would like to thank Professor Mark Priestly for his comments to an earlier version of this article. Also, author would like to thank the anonymous reviewer of the part following, Due to the well-established nature of the social model within the UK context, it has undoubtedly affected the structure of disability-related services.

## Disclosure statement

No potential conflict of interest was reported by the author.

## Funding

The author was supported by the British Academy-Visiting Scholars scheme and the study was conducted when author was a scholar at the University of Leeds, Centre for Disability Studies.

## References

Bolt, D. 2005. "From Blindness to Visual Impairment: Terminology Typology and the Social Model of Disability." *Disability and Society* 20 (5): 539–552.

Compton-Lilly, C. 2016. "Time in Education: Intertwined Dimensions and Theoretical Possibilities." *Time and Society* 25 (3): 575–593.

Corner, G. T. 2011. "What Disability Studies Has to Offer Medical Education?" *Journal of Medical Humanities* 32 (1): 21–30.

Demery, R., K. Thirlaway, and J. Mercer. 2012. "The Experiences of Students with a Mood Disorder." *Disability and Society* 27 (4): 519–533.

Elton, L. 1981. "Can Universities Change?" *Studies in Higher Education* 6 (1): 23–33.

Equality Act. 2010. "Advancing Equality and Diversity in Universities and Colleges." Equality Legislation. Accessed November 22, 2015. http://www.ecu.ac.uk/guidance-resources/equality-legislation/

French, S. and J. Swain. 2004. "Controlling Inclusion in Education: Young Disabled People's Perspectives." In *Disabling Barriers-Enabling Environments*, edited by J. Swain, S. French, C. Barnes, and C. Thomas, 169–175. London: Sage.

Fuller, M., M. Healey, A. Bradley, and T. Hall. 2004. "Barriers to Learning: A Systematic Study of the Experience of Disabled Students in one University." *Studies in Higher Education* 29 (3): 303–318.

Goad, C. J., and J. M. Robertson. 2000. "How University Counseling Centers Serve Students with Disabilities: A Status Report." *Journal of College Student Psychotherapy* 14 (3): 13–22.

Goode, J. 2007. "'Managing' Disability: Early Experiences of University Students with Disability." *Disability and Society* 22 (1): 35–48.

Hadjikakou, K., V. Polycarpou, and A. Hadjilia. 2010. "The Experiences of Students with Mobility Disabilities in Cypriot Higher Education Institutions: Listening to their Voices." *International Journal of Disability, Development and Education* 57 (4): 403–426.

Holloway, S. 2001. "The Experience of Higher Education from the Perspective of Disabled Students." *Disability and Society* 16 (4): 597–615.

Hopkins, L. 2011. "The Path of Least Resistance: A Voice Relational Analysis of Disabled Students' Experiences of Discrimination in English Universities." *International Journal of Inclusive Education* 15 (7): 711–727.

Hutcheon, E. J., and G. Wolbring. 2012. "Voices of 'Disabled' Post Secondary Students: Examining Higher Education 'disability' Policy Using an Ableism Lens." *Journal of Diversity in Higher Education* 5 (1): 39–49.

Koca-Atabey, M. 2013. "A Personal Validation of the Social Nature of Disability: Different Environments, Different Experiences." *Disability and Society* 28 (7): 1027–1031.

Koca-Atabey, M. 2016. "Becoming a Blind Teacher in Turkey: A Long Journey." *Work: A Journal of Prevention, Assessment and Rehabilitation* 54 (3): 759–764.

Koca-Atabey, M., A. N. Karancı, G. Dirik, and D. Aydemir. 2011. "Psychological Well-Being of Turkish University Students with Physical Impairments: An Evaluation within the Stress-Vulnerability Paradigm." *International Journal of Psychology* 46 (2): 106–118.

Langdridge, D. 2004. *Introduction to Research Methods and Data Analysis in Psychology*. London: Pearson.

Larkin, M., S. Watts, and E. Clifton. 2006. "Giving Voice and Making Sense in Interpretative Phenomenological Analysis." *Qualitative Research in Psychology* 3 (2): 102–120.

López Gavira, R., and A. Moriña. 2015. "Hidden Voices in Higher Education: Inclusive Policies and Practices in Social Science and Law Classrooms." *International Journal of Inclusive Education* 19 (4): 365–378.

Madriaga, M., K. Hanson, C. Heaton, H. Kay, S. Newitt, and A. Walker. 2010. "Confronting Similar Challenges? Disabled and Non-Disabled Students' Learning and Assessment Experiences." *Studies in Higher Education* 35 (6): 647–658.

McConnell, D. 1981. "Helping Students with a Disability Achieve their Academic Aims." *Studies in Higher Education* 6 (1): 35–45.

Meredith, G., A. Packman, and G. Marks. 2012. "Stuttering, Disability and the Higher Education Sector in Australia." *International Journal of Speech-Language Pathology* 14 (4): 370–376.

Milic Babic, M., and M. Dowling. 2015. "Social Support, the Presence of Barriers and Ideas for the Future from Students with Disabilities in the Higher Education System in Croatia." *Disability and Society* 30 (4): 614–629.

Morris, J. 1991. *Pride against Prejudice. Transforming Attitudes to Disability*. London: Women Press.

Morris, J. 1993. *Independent Lives. Community Care and Disabled People*. London: Macmillan Press.

Mullins, L., and M. Preyde. 2013. "The Lived Experience of Students with an Invisible Disability at a Canadian University." *Disability and Society* 28 (2): 147–160.

Oliver, M. 1996. *Understanding Disability. From Theory to Practice*. New York: Palgrave Macmillan.

Olney, M. F., and K. F. Brockelman. 2003. "Out of the Disability Closet: Strategic Use of Perception Management by Select University Students with Disabilities." *Disability and Society* 18 (1): 35–50.

Parker, V. 2000. "Developing a Code of Practice for Disability Coordinators." *European Journal of Special Needs Education* 15 (3): 275–284.

Reid, K., P. Flowers, and M. Larkin. 2005. "Exploring Lived Experience." *Psychologist* 18 (1): 20–23.

Sachs, D. and N. Schreuer. 2011. "Inclusion of Students with Disabilities in Higher Education: Performance and Participation in Student's Experiences." *Disability Studies Quarterly* 31 (2). Accessed March 21, 2015. http://dsqsds.org/article/view/1593

Schillmeier, M. 2008. "Time-Spaces of In/dependence and Dis/ability." *Time and Society* 17 (2/3): 215–231.

Sciame-Giesecke, S., D. Roden, and K. Parkison. 2009. "Infusing Diversity into the Curriculum: What Are Faculty Members Actually Doing?" *Journal of Diversity in Higher Education* 2 (3): 156–165.

Seligman, M. E. P. 2003. *Authentic Happiness*. London: Nicholas Brealey Publishing.

Seymour, W. 2002. "Time and the Body: Re-embodying Time in Disability." *Journal of Occupational Science* 9 (3): 135–142.

Smith, J. A., and M. Osborn. 2003. "Interpretative Phenomenological Analysis." In *Qualitative Psychology. A Practical Guide to Research Methods*, edited by J. A. Smith, 51–80. London: Sage.

Soorenian, A. 2013. "Housing and Transport: Access Issues for Disabled International Students in British Universities." *Disability and Society* 28 (8): 1118–1131.

Stampoltzis, A., and S. Polychronopoulou. 2009. "Greek University Students with Dyslexia: An Interview Study." *European Journal of Special Needs Education* 24 (3): 307–321.

Valeras, A. B. 2010. "'We Don't Have a Box': Understanding Hidden Disability Identity Utilizing Narrative Research Methodology." *Disability Studies Quarterly* 30 (3/4). Accessed March 21, 2015. http://www.dsqsds.org/article/view/1267/1297

Winn, S., and I. Hay. 2009. "Transition from School for Youths with a Disability: Issues and Challenges." *Disability and Society* 24 (1): 103–115.

Zimbardo, P., and J. Boyd. 2008. *The Time Paradox: The New Psychology of Time that will Change your Life*. New York: Free Press.

# Dual PowerPoint presentation approach for students with special educational needs and note-takers

Nitin Naik

**ABSTRACT**

In higher education, supporting students with special educational needs (SEN) necessitates an understanding of these needs, additional teaching aids and innovative ideas. The teacher must be an integral part of this support process, and this is difficult for the majority of teachers, due to their lack of core understanding of SEN. However, teachers can focus on their core skills and content knowledge, and have immense alacrity to explore potential options to support their students with SEN. I decided to support my students with SEN by adapting my PowerPoint presentations according to their requirements. PowerPoint presentations usually provide concisely summarised information to students that often lead to confusion in their pre-lecture or post-lecture review. This lack of comprehensive subject information within PowerPoint presentations can have serious implications for students with SEN and their note-takers if no other teaching resources or aids are available to help them. Students with SEN and note-takers reported this concern to me at Aberystwyth University, UK. Consequently, I began to explore ways to make my PowerPoint presentations extra helpful for my students with SEN. After a review of best practices for students with SEN based on universal design for learning and a few trials, I developed a dual PowerPoint presentation (DPP), lecture handouts and comprehensive lecture notes. Subsequently, I successfully employed this approach in the delivery of some of the undergraduate modules of a BSc computer science programme. Feedback from students with SEN, note-takers and the student support department, and examination results showed the success and potential of this DPP approach.

## Students with special educational needs, PowerPoint presentation and motivation for dual PowerPoint presentation (DPP) approach

In higher education (HE), numbers of students with special educational needs (SEN) have been growing in classes and they require additional learning aids to accomplish their learning tasks. I believe that teachers need to remember 'teaching is about fostering student connections to content, not just presenting content to students' (Hlynka and Mason 1998) and therefore, as a teacher, I always want to make my lecture content extra helpful and useful for my students. PowerPoint presentations are one of the most common teaching aids used by the majority of teachers in the classroom. However, PowerPoint presentations usually provide only concisely summarised information for students, and this often leads to confusion during the pre-lecture or post-lecture review. The lack of comprehensive subject information could have serious implications for students with SEN and their note-takers if no other teaching resources or aids are available to help them.

I have made several changes in my PowerPoint presentations over the years, but they mostly focused on the academic content and styles of my slides. When, however, I encountered a severe learning issue related to my students with SEN and their note-takers, I realised that my changes had not gone far enough. One day, our Computer Science department at Aberystwyth University, UK received an emergency email from the student accessibility adviser quoting two problems related to the same issue:

(1) 'We are currently experiencing problems recruiting note-takers for lectures in both Computing Science and Institute of Mathematics and Physics (IMAPS) – we have sufficient note-takers, but not with the appropriate skills.'
(2) 'Some students may be struggling to keep up with lecture information so we'd be grateful if staff could post as much information as possible on Blackboard.'

Though it was a general email to the department, I concluded that some students with SEN had likely been struggling with my lecture notes too. Soon after, I discussed this issue with students with SEN, note-takers, and the student support department and came to realise that insufficient PowerPoint notes and study materials are one of the biggest hurdles for students with SEN to overcome. I realised that I should rethink my PowerPoint presentations based on the feedback provided by students with SEN, note-takers and the student support department. As a result of my analysis, after reviewing PowerPoint best practices for students with SEN based on universal design for learning and a few trials, I developed a DPP approach for inclusive teaching.

## PowerPoint best practices for students with SEN based on universal design for learning (UDL)

If the designed PowerPoint presentation is helpful to students with SEN, then it is most likely extra helpful to all students. Teachers develop the PowerPoint presentation based on their skills and experience. However, the majority of teachers do not receive basic training to support students with SEN (Hartley 2010). Consequently, their PowerPoint presentations may not be focused on providing additional support to students with SEN. For designing the SEN PowerPoint presentation, every teacher should require a basic understanding of some main learning difficulties such as literacy difficulty (dyslexia), developmental coordination disorder (DCD/dyspraxia), handwriting difficulty (dysgraphia), specific difficulty with mathematics (dyscalculia), speech language and communication difficulty (SLC), hearing impairment (SNHL), visual impairment (NVI) or physical difficulties.

There is no single rule-of-thumb for making effective SEN PowerPoint presentations. However, UDL framework facilitates equal opportunities to learn for everyone and is one of the most effective ways to develop SEN PowerPoint presentations. UDL framework is based on scientific insights into how humans learn and offers a blueprint for creating instructional objectives, methods, materials, and assessments that work for everyone (*About Universal Design for Learning* 2016). UDL offers flexible approaches that can be customised and

**Table 1.** Best practices for PowerPoint development based on UDL framework.

| PowerPoint best practices | Targeted learners with SEN profiles | Benefits for learners with SEN profiles |
|---|---|---|
| Use of additional images, audios, videos and multimedia content | Learners with strong visual learning styles or print related difficulties | Illustrates concepts and subjects easily by avoiding the text only dependence |
| Readable font size and typeface | Learners with dyslexia and those who are partially sighted | Improves the readability of slides |
| Colour and brightness contrast | Learners with dyslexia and colour-blindness | Improves the visibility of contents of slides |
| Emphasising text | Learners with visual impairments and dyslexia | Highlights the text/concept to attract learners' focus |
| Use of appropriate words, sentences, alignment and justification | Learners with dyslexia, dyspraxia and dyscalculia | Avoids confusion and complexity due to certain types of text or appearance |
| Numbers, arithmetic and maths simplification | Learners with poor memory and dyscalculia | Supports learners by simplifying mathematical concepts |
| Special SEN handouts | All SEN learners (different types of SEN handouts for different SEN learners) | Offers additional learning aids that can be helpful for various purposes |
| Physical action, expression and communication | All SEN learners (different types of delivery methods for different SEN learners) | Communicates effectively the well-prepared lecture notes based on the above best practices |

adjusted to individual needs. According to UDL principles, the design of effective SEN PowerPoint presentations requires some crucial consideration depending on the target SEN group. These adjustments may vary from one SEN group to another or even from one SEN student to another. However, some common guidelines can make our PowerPoint presentations more effective for early-stage or less-affected students with SEN. Table 1 shows some of the best practices, which I have adopted in my PowerPoint presentations.

## DPP approach

In this DPP approach, I designed two versions of the same PowerPoint presentation: handouts for teaching/summarising and comprehensive lecture notes to be used as a guide to SEN students/note-takers. In addition to the teaching aid to students with SEN and note-takers, these DPPs can be used for a variety of purposes. The handouts were useful for my teaching and students' revision, and the comprehensive lecture notes sometimes were useful for me to use in class and also for many students who forgot part of the lecture or missed the lecture; or who found the topic difficult at the time of delivery.

### *Lecture handouts*

My PowerPoint handouts for students with SEN were traditional bulleted PowerPoint slides based on the PowerPoint best practices (see Table 1). Every single slide contains five to seven lines and around up to seven words per line. There must be enough space between lines to prevent crowding effects during reading. The use of graphics, tables and charts was enhanced to help students with SEN. Mathematics was simplified using pictures and real-life examples. Despite focusing on the SEN group, the handouts were used in classroom teaching in order to support those students whose learning styles did not favourably dispose them to the comprehensive lecture notes. The handouts were also useful for all students and note-takers as a note-taking tool and during the exam season, for revision purposes.

### Comprehensive lecture notes

I learnt from my discussion and analysis that many SEN students with issues such as handwriting difficulty, reading difficulty, hearing impairment, SLC had been struggling to prepare detailed notes for their learning. If they could receive the detailed lecture notes, then it could solve their problem with note-taking and avoid the dependence on multiple sources. It could also save a huge amount of time that they could otherwise spend on their actual learning. Again, in this design, I applied most of the PowerPoint best practices (see Table 1) for students with SEN, except adding supplementary content. The comprehensive PowerPoint lecture notes covered the topic in detail, including all terminology, definitions, explanations, simplified mathematics, diagrams, tables and charts. I adopted more graphical content than text; therefore, it could support many students with SEN such as those with dyslexia and visual impairments. Overall, this detailed version was particularly helpful to students with SEN who cannot prepare proper notes due to various reasons and note-takers who take vague notes due to their lack of understanding of topics/concepts.

## Results and feedback

The most interesting thing about the comprehensive lecture notes was that it was developed against the standard PowerPoint practice. The standard PowerPoint practice does not advise us to make a large number of slides with additional contents. However, this was one of the possible solutions I considered during my investigations. Furthermore, some teachers may argue about the need to design second comprehensive lecture notes and prefer the 'notes page' in a single PowerPoint. My opinion is that the 'notes page' is a very basic text editor where you can add your teaching notes to remind yourself of what the slide is all about, and what points you should be covering. This might be helpful for some students but not for students with SEN because it does not provide the enhanced presentation environment to cover all necessary content which may be needed. The foremost aim of my comprehensive lecture notes was to satisfy the need of students with SEN and their note-takers.

I tested this dual PowerPoint approach first in a BSc final-year computer science module (CS35810) 'Further Issues In System and Network Services Administration' and subsequently, in some other modules. I taught primarily by using the lecture handouts and referred to the comprehensive lecture notes when necessary. Extensive feedback from students with SEN, note-takers and the student support department, alongside examination results, showed the threefold success of this new DPP approach. First, it fostered the learning of students with SEN and, in some cases, motivated them to become independent learners (e.g. '... I know I have got everything for my study that gives me the confidence to learn and overcome my difficulties in the modules because I cannot manage on my own'). Mainly, it was because of both PowerPoint presentations were based on the PowerPoint best practices for students with SEN, which offered them preferred lecture notes depending on their specific requirements. Consequently, it eliminated the dependence on multiple sources and saved an enormous amount of time that they could now spend on their actual learning. Second, it helped note-takers to capture notes accurately and align with the actual subject (e.g. '... The comprehensive notes were extraordinary in the sense of capturing lectures precisely as a note-taker'). This was because of the majority of note-takers were not from the same subject areas and having the lack of understanding of topics/concepts. However, in particular, comprehensive lecture notes offered them detailed subject materials related to lectures, which clarified the complex topics and helped to verify their captured lectures precisely. Third, it also helped other students whose grasping of the subject was slow and who were shy to ask anything in the classroom. Additionally, it improved the pass rate by 29.5% and average marks by 15.61%, revealing that DPP approach worked not only for students with SEN but also for the rest of the class. However, in my opinion, the improvement in the module's results was not merely due to the use of this new DPP approach and further in-depth analysis was required to assess the actual contribution of this DPP approach.

The most important finding of this project is that the best practices for students with SEN actually help *all* students. This is an effective presentation teaching approach and learning aid that I developed as a common tool for modules where lecture notes are particularly important. I will not discuss the nature of the academic content since that will be discipline-specific and must remain an issue for the academic staff alone (Jones 2003). I wish to emphasise that this approach may not be helpful for some modules where lecture notes are not vital teaching material. Therefore, it is a context-specific approach and not a universal one.

## Discussion

The UK Equality Act 2010 enforces additional reasonable adjustment for students with SEN in higher education (*Equality Act 2010* 2010). Therefore, it is a legal requirement to make additional reasonable changes to the way things are done, to the built environment and to provide auxiliary aids and services (*Equality Act 2010* 2010). Every university has been providing educational and non-educational services to students with SEN to overcome the barriers to their learning. However, in my opinion, working for students with SEN should not depend on the legal requirement alone, as meeting student needs is a teacher's moral obligation and the duty of society. As a teacher, the main aim of my dual PowerPoint approach was to discover an effective lecture notes provision strategy, particularly for students with SEN and note-takers. I believe that PowerPoint presentations are an important resource for teaching and learning within HE. However, the use of PowerPoint on its own does not guarantee success in teaching and learning. I think my students' assessment success was not solely due to the use of this new type of PowerPoint presentation. I believe that a full evaluation of this approach would accord some credit to the new PowerPoints, while my teaching style, other classroom activities, and students' hard work would also be contributing factors to their success.

Students with SEN need a variety of support at different levels in university. If DPPs were not the most desirable type of support, then it still provided some lecture notes to support students, in particular for students with handwriting difficulty, reading difficulty, hearing impairment, SLC, mathematics difficulty or some other physical difficulties, which prevent them from preparing lecture notes by themselves. Almost all universities provide note-takers to students with SEN. However, these note-takers often do not come from the same subject area, and/or they have very little understanding of the assigned subjects. In this situation, students with SEN who depend on their note-takers may not receive precise notes and this may negatively impact their overall performance. This DPP approach was undoubtedly beneficial for note-takers as they managed to produce better quality lecture notes.

## Limitations of DPP approach

The scope of any research on students with SEN and note-takers will always be limited in numbers. In each class, students with SEN and note-takers are small in number; therefore, it is difficult to make a balance between the learning of students with SEN and the rest of the class. Also, PowerPoint is what you make of it: it is a teaching tool and can be used badly or well (Schulten 2010). I changed my PowerPoint presentations to contribute towards students' learning and this helped my students with SEN. My challenge and my pleasure are teaching my students what they need to do, how they should go about it, and to do it well. Most importantly, research tells us that students learn more by what they do than from what is explained to them (*Using Presentations to Help Students Learn* 2014).

I applied the several PowerPoint best practices in my PowerPoint presentations for students with SEN, and it seems to be helpful for students with mild dyslexia and other mild learning difficulties. However, dyslexia could be more severe when it overlaps with any of the other specific learning difficulties: dyscalculia, dysgraphia, dyspraxia, attention deficit disorder/attention deficit hyperactivity disorder, Asperger syndrome/autism spectrum disorder. In this situation, I do not think any PowerPoint presentation alone would be sufficient for learning. Nonetheless, note-takers can play their part for students with SEN and undoubtedly this DPP will help them.

Though the DPP approach has the potential to support students with SEN and note-takers, it may not be appropriate for subjects where lecture notes are not vital. Preparation of comprehensive lecture notes is a marathon task for teachers, and it can only be possible when teachers have enough extra time to do this work. Furthermore, this DPP approach was tested in a particular module and with a particular class of students, including some specific students with SEN. Critical analysis of the success or failure of this DPP approach needs further testing in various modules and with different levels of students with SEN. This project also does not provide an analysis between the two types of notes and perceptions of the rest of the class in addition to the students with SEN. Therefore, it is still not clear which type of notes worked more effectively for students in general.

## Conclusion

This paper has presented the DPP approach, particularly for students with SEN and their note-takers. However, I developed it as a common tool for modules where lecture notes are of the greatest benefit. Development was based upon and prompted by feedback obtained from students with SEN, note-takers and the student support department. I discovered that students with SEN needed comprehensive notes to understand and review the subject more efficiently. I derived my own PowerPoint best practices for students with SEN based on the UDL. Eventually, I formulated two types of PowerPoint notes: (1) Lecture Handouts (short notes for teaching, summarising topics and note-taking) and (2) Comprehensive Lecture Notes (detailed notes for students with SEN and in-depth studies). Initially, I fused and tested these new types of lecture notes in the BSc final-year module: CS35810: 'Further Issues In System and Network Services Administration'. At the end of the term, I achieved better students' examination results as compared to the last year's results and positive feedback from students with SEN, note-takers and the student support department.

In the future, this DPP approach needs to be tested in various modules and with different groups of students with SEN and their note-takers. Another future task is to perform a comprehensive survey to gather comparison data between the two types of notes and perceptions of the rest of the class. Providing an inclusive learning environment is an important responsibility for the staff at any academic institution and making reasonable adjustments for students with SEN is a vital part of this inclusive learning. The good news is that these adjustments are also likely to benefit all of our students.

## Disclosure statement

The research and views contained in this document are those of the author and should not be interpreted as representing the official research and policies, either expressed or implied, of the UK Ministry of Defence or the UK Government.

## ORCID

*Nitin Naik* http://orcid.org/0000-0002-0659-9646

## References

*About Universal Design for Learning.* 2016. Accessed April 10, 2016, from cast.org: http://www.cast.org/our-work/about-udl.html#.V4oLOzkrL_Q

*Equality Act 2010: What Do I Need To Know? Disability Quick Start Guide.* 2010. Accessed April 16, 2014. https://www.gov.uk/government/uploads/system/uploads/attachment_data/file/85011/disability.pdf

Hartley, R. 2010. *Teacher Expertise for Special Educational Needs.* Accessed April 16, 2014. http://www.policyexchange.org.uk/images/publications/teacher%20expertise%20for%20sen%20-%20jul%2010.pdf

Hlynka, D., and R. Mason. 1998. "'PowerPoint' in the Classroom: Where is the Power?" *Educational Technology* 38 (5): 42–45.

Jones, A. M. 2003. "The use and abuse of PowerPoint in Teaching and Learning in the Life Sciences: A Personal Overview." *Bioscience Education E-Journal* 2(1): 1–13.

Schulten, K. 2010. *Is PowerPoint in the Classroom 'Evil'.* Accessed April 16, 2014. http://learning.blogs.nytimes.com/2010/05/03/is-powerpoint-in-the-classroom-evil/?_php=true&_type=blogs&_r=0

*Using Presentations to Help Students Learn.* 2014. Accessed April 16, 2014. http://www.tltgroup.org/flashlight/Handbook/Presentation/Ideas.htm

# From the voice of a 'socratic gadfly': a call for more academic activism in the researching of disability in postsecondary education

Jane Seale

**ABSTRACT**
In this article, I use the lens of voices and silences to frame my review of research in the field of disability and postsecondary education. I argue that we need to view research in this field as a necessarily political act that seeks to turn voices of silence into voices of change. Researchers therefore need to rethink their role in order to understand how they can use and direct their political voices. In order to persuade researchers to heed my call for more academic activism, adopt the role of a 'socratic gadfly' to identify six political areas of research where I argue that voices and silences need more critical examination. In discussing these six areas, I hope to illuminate the implications for 'genuinely investigative' research in the future.

## Introduction

The purpose of this article is to critically review research relating to disabled students in postsecondary education (PSE) in order to examine what we know and don't know and to highlight implications for future research in the field. For the purposes of this article, the term postsecondary education is used very broadly to mean education which is normally delivered by a university or college. More specifically, the focus is on the learning experiences of disabled students registered for undergraduate or postgraduate degree programmes. In using the term 'disabled student' I am aware that there are differences of opinion regarding which term or label is the most appropriate to use. My justification for using this term in preference to others such 'students with disabilities' is that the term 'people with disabilities' implies that the person's impairment or condition causes them to be 'disabled' (and consequently that it is their responsibility to overcome it), whereas 'disabled person' implies that the person is disabled not necessarily by their condition or impairment, but by society and its inability or reluctance to cater effectively for that person (and consequently that society must effect change to remove that disability) (Phipps, Sutherland, and Seale 2002, iii). I acknowledge that not everyone in the field will agree with me and will return to the tensions around labelling later in this article.

To provide a comprehensive review of all possible literature in the field would be difficult and so I propose to place a boundary on my review by using one specific lens: that of voices and silences. Drawing on Freire's (1972) concept of 'cultures of silence', it is my contention that we need to give voice in a more expansive way than has currently been achieved. For Freire, breaking the culture of silence within education was about giving voice to the marginalised (students) and seeking a means whereby the dominant (teachers) could critically respond to the culture (e.g. of discrimination and prejudice). Where Freire offered critical pedagogy as a tool to break the silence within teaching; in this article I will offer academic activism as a tool to break the silences within the field of disability and PSE. Drawing on the arguments of Barton (2001), I position this academic activism as a political act that creates space for fundamental questions to be explored regarding whether disabled students are valued in PSE and viewed as having the same rights as non-disabled students. This political act is inspired by a desire to transform the oppressive environments in which disabled students find themselves.

## *Giving voice to disabled students as a political act: navigating the silences*

The use of voice as a lens with which to examine disability in PSE is not new. There is a relatively long and strong tradition of research in this field using a range of qualitative methods in order to 'give voice' to or 'amplify' the voice of disabled students and find out more about their experiences of PSE (Hall and Tinklin 1998; Fuller, Bradley, and Healey 2004; Vickerman and Blundell 2010; Brandt 2011). The main justifications for giving voice to disabled students are that their voices are hidden or lost (López-Gavira and Moriña 2015) within research and because the power structures within PSE silence the voices of disabled students and deny their experiences of inequalities (Luna 2009; Beauchamp-Pryor 2012). The purpose of giving voice to disabled students in research is therefore to:

- Illuminate the barriers facing disabled students and the impact they have: Denhart (2008), Hopkins (2011), Redpath et al. (2013), Stein (2013) and López-Gavira and Moriña (2015).
- Identify appropriate and helpful ways of reducing such barriers and inform pedagogical practices: Webster (2004), Quinlan, Bates, and Angell (2012), Redpath et al. (2013), Kubiak (2015) and Lourens and Swartz (2016).

The commitment is therefore to present alternative ways of doing things; 'voices of silence' become 'voices of change' (Hutcheon and Wolbring 2012). A key consequence of the proposed move to give space to 'voices of change' is that researchers will need to rethink their role in order to understand how they can use and direct their own political voices.

## *Research as a political act: directing the focus of our political voices*

In order to outline the role, I believe that researchers need to adopt in order to focus their political voice I will draw on the work of Allan (2010) who argued that the foregrounding of the responsibility to 'the Other' (the marginalised) makes the academic's role explicitly a political one; with a number of specific duties. The first duty for the academic involves the articulation of new political subjectivities, by privileging the voices of minorities and marginalised groups. The second duty, according to Allan is to open up to 'the Other' and be ready to respond to what is forthcoming. Allan (2010) argues that the third duty is to design and undertake research that is genuinely investigative. Allan argues that this requires approaching the research without ready solutions or tricks of the trade. The fourth duty is to 'show oneself' through writing and act as a ' Socratic gadfly' provoking and persuading readers to 'see something other than their own view of the world'. In this article I intend to adopt the role of a 'socratic gadfly' by identifying six key 'political' areas where I will argue voices and silences need critical examination. In doing so, I hope to illuminate the implications for 'genuinely investigative' research in the future.

## Privileging the voices of minorities and marginalised groups

It is my contention that one of the main reasons that researchers like myself need to adopt a political voice and act like 'socratic gadflies' is the significant evidence that exists regarding the marginalisation of significant stakeholders. The most obvious marginalised group is disabled students; but in this section I will also argue that the voices of disabled faculty as well as disability support staff have also been marginalised in both practice and research.

### *The need to privilege the voices of disabled students*

There is evidence to suggest that disabled students experience a lack of understanding and acceptance of their needs from both students (Kowalsky and Fresko 2002; Quick, Lehmann, and Deniston 2003) and academic and support staff (Ryan 2007; Denhart 2008). This lack of understanding can manifest itself in failure to provide accommodations in teaching (Bishop and Rhind 2011; Claiborne et al. 2011) and in assessments (Hammer, Werth, and Dunn 2009; Vickerman and Blundell 2010). Furthermore, such lack of understanding is attributed to negative attitudes towards disability and has been documented in a range of academic spaces including placements and vocational training (Cunnah 2015; Clouder et al. 2016). The experience of negative attitudes and lack of understanding can lead disabled students to feel stigmatised (Stein 2013; Nolan et al. 2015) which can lead them to monitor how they present themselves publically and to be reluctant to speak in public spaces such as seminars or placements (Cameron 2016).

A major area where stigmatisation can silence disabled students voices is in the disclosure of disability in order to obtain the legal right to support and accommodations (Evans 2014; Nolan et al. 2015). For disabled students, disclosure can be viewed as risky because they do not know how faculty will respond (Quinlan, Bates, and Angell 2012); they don't want faculty to think differently of them or misunderstand their difficulties (Baker, Boland, and Nowik 2012; Stein 2013); they are concerned that faculty will not believe they have a real disability (Olney and Brockelman 2003); they don't want to be perceived as not trying hard enough to succeed without support (Hammer, Werth, and Dunn 2009); they are afraid that disclosure might impact on their ability to gain employment (Venville, Street, and Fossey 2014); they have a desire to forge an identity free of disability (Lightner et al. 2012) or they do not wish information about their private identity to become public property (Borland and James 1999; Claiborne et al. 2011).

It is important to acknowledge that there are other reasons (not necessarily linked to stigma) why disabled students choose not to disclose their disability. For example wanting to be treated like other students (Hall and Tinklin 1998) or training for professions where tensions between professional standards and equality exist (see for example Hargreaves et al. 2014). Furthermore, even in a climate that is 'positive', where no obvious prejudice exists, disabled students may still choose not to disclose (Baker, Boland, and Nowik 2012). Nevertheless, the literature on disclosure reveals that many disabled students feel unable or reluctant to voice their rights and advocate for their support needs. This has led for a call for more research into how academics and support staff can develop and encourage self-advocacy skills in disabled students (Stein 2013; Summers et al. 2014). Other researchers are more radical, and view self-advocacy as a political rights issue, drawing parallels with gay and black civil rights movements (Anderson 2009; Stodden 2015). The drawing of such parallels brings with them a call for disabled students organisations or 'collectives'. In addition to promoting self-advocacy, such collectives are argued to encourage interaction and networking that might serve to counteract isolation and stigma (Anderson 2009; Argawal, Calvo and Kumar 2014). Anderson (2009, 1), a blind student, recounts his experiences of an approach towards collectivism called 'The Salon;' at the University of British Columbia (UBC):

> UBC does not provide the infrastructure or environment necessary to encourage the interaction and networking of students with disabilities aside from the odd, start of the year mixer. My fellow disabled students have been cast as passive receivers of services, not active agents of change. … During the three months of the Salon Series, I have felt like an active agent of dialogue, inquiry, and engagement with a large, unruly and dynamic community that has not often come together on campus in such a powerful and all-inclusive manner.

More research is needed into the kind of student organisations and collectives that are needed in order to promote self-advocacy skills of disabled students. More research is also needed to collect the evidence that such initiatives do actually bring about a change in the nature and frequency of disclosure behaviours.

Promoting disclosure behaviour however, does not challenge the policies and systems in PSE that require disabled students to disclose before their needs will be taken seriously and addressed through accommodation. For some, it is the disclosure system that needs changing, not students behaviour. Therefore, a second priority for research is the need to design, develop and evaluate student voice initiatives specifically aimed at engaging disabled students in policy transformation (Redpath et al. 2013). Student voice in PSE is quite well established (See for example Seale 2010) and has a number of purposes, including encouraging students to participate in governance structures. Very little work has been specifically aimed at disabled students however, suggesting they are invisible and silenced in yet another key sphere of PSE. Beauchamp-Pryor (2012) calls for the identification of barriers that are likely to impede the participation of disabled students in the development of higher education policy and provision within the UK, at both a national and institutional level.

### *The need to privilege the voices of other relevant stakeholders*

Researchers have in many regards been exemplary in giving voice to disabled students' academic experiences in recognition of the lack of voice they have in their educational lives and contexts. The same cannot be true for other stakeholders. As Díez, López, and Molina (2015, 148) point out: 'only on rare occasion are other members of the HE community given a voice'. Two stakeholder groups I would like to highlight as being particularly deserving of voice amplification are disabled staff and disability support staff.

There is very little research devoted to understanding the experiences of disabled staff (including graduate students). What stories that are told, tell of difficulties in preserving jobs and in having to manage without accommodations (Abram 2003; Damiani and Harbour 2015). There is a real need therefore, for more privileging of the voices of disabled staff, particularly with regards to whether or not they feel able to disclose their disability. It would seem logical that creating inclusive environments for disabled students would involve the need to recognise and support disabled staff. It is argued, for example, that disabled staff can act as important role models: modelling to disabled students how it is possible to succeed in a postsecondary environment and modelling best teaching practices to fellow and future educators (Anderson 2006; Higbee and Mitchel 2009). It is also argued that through their interactions with non-disabled students, disabled staff can raise the students' disability-awareness and open them up to the acceptability of 'otherness' (Michalko 2001); Sheridan and Kotevski (2014, 1170) argue:

> Disabled teachers embody pedagogies of justice, interdependence, and respect for differences. Teaching (with) disability reveals spaces in education that often get silenced.

In the US, the Council for Exceptional Children has recently published a policy on disabled educators which acknowledges the benefits that disabled educators can bring to learning and teaching environments but also highlights the challenges they face. It calls for the 'provision of strategic supports during recruitment, hiring, practice, and evaluation for educators with disabilities across all educational environments' (CEC 2016, 1). It would be good to see postsecondary institutions producing similar high-profile documents, which do more than pay lip service to their legal obligations in respect to discrimination and equality.

Alongside disabled staff, it is my contention that the voices of disability support staff are missing from research. This might seem an odd claim given that research has sought to document the perceptions of disability support staff regarding the experiences of disabled students (Reed and Curtis 2012) as well their views regarding the knowledge and attitudes of academic staff (Harrison and Holmes 2014). However, there is little research that seeks to document the experiences of disability support staff and the impact that trying to advocate for disabled students and change practices across an institution has on them. This is despite the acknowledgement that they face significant challenges in their work (Hurst 2015). One particular area that I would argue needs further investigation is whether disability support staff are stigmatised by their association with disabled students. Such 'courtesy stigma' has been documented in other fields. For example, Broomhead (2016) documented how teachers employed by schools for pupils with behavioural, emotional and social difficulties felt stigmatised and treated as if they were not as clever as other teachers.

## Opening ourselves up to the other

Another reason that researchers like myself need to adopt a political voice and act like 'socratic gadflies' is the tension that exist surrounding the construction of disability and difference; constructions that can prevent an 'opening up to the other' and that can place institutions at odds with their students and researchers at risk of having their research highjacked by opponents of inclusion.

### *Being sensitive to tensions regarding the construction of disability*

One of the consequences of equality and disability discrimination legislation is that it has produced legal definitions of disability have been 'administratively useful' to PSE institutions and individual tutors in identifying who may need support and accommodations (Jacklin et al. 2007). It is argued however that these legal definitions are based on a medical or deficit model of disability (Berggren et al. 2016). Furthermore, it is claimed that PSE institutions operate a model of compensation in which disabled students have to prove their eligibility for support and accommodations based on the label assigned to their medical diagnosis (Fuller et al. 2009). Not only do disabled students have to submit themselves to a formal diagnosis process, they have to submit themselves to a seeming lottery of whether the institution will accept or contest the diagnosis.

Dyslexia is a particular example where universities and tutors have questioned whether the disability is real or something artificially constructed. In an Irish study examining the experiences of physically disabled and dyslexic students, Hanafin et al. (2007) found that sometimes dyslexia was viewed as a strategy that dyslexic students used to gain unfair advantages. Hanafin et al. (2007) also noted an occasion where a deaf student reported that one of their lecturers would not believe that they were deaf; the student postulated that it may be because the lecturer assumed that deaf people could not talk; a personal construction of disability underpinned by a lack of awareness. Luna (2009) examined how an Ivy League university in the US constructed learning disabilities. Her examination revealed negative stereotypes about students with learning disabilities based on scepticism about the existence of learning disabilities, the competence of students with learning disabilities, the validity of their diagnosis and the fairness of providing accommodations based on this diagnosis.

I would argue that students with other characteristics that are legally protected against discrimination such as age, gender, race, and socio-economic status are not subjected to such a contestation of their legal status. It is difficult imagining a faculty member arguing against accommodating a student's learning needs because the student is 'not really' black, or male or socially deprived. Further sensitivities around how institutions construct disability centre on whether these 'institutional categories are apposite to an understanding of the ways in which students perceive themselves' (Hughes, Corcoran, and Slee 2016, 488). While some students accept labels applied to them, others reject them preferring alternative labels (Griffin and Pollack 2009) or refusing to be marked out as a 'special' or different by the label (Madriaga et al. 2011).

The differences in how institutions construct and understand disability compared to disabled students suggest that researchers need to be sensitive to how they construct disability in their own research. Through such sensitivity, researchers can both open themselves up 'to the other' and to the politics underpinning constructions of disability in PCE. Two examples of such opening up that I wish to discuss in more detail are: being aware of the politics being the labelling of student and being sensitive to the politics of 'ableism'.

## *The labelling of disabled students as a political act: navigating the cacophony of voices*

The majority of literature that I have reviewed in preparation for writing this article uses the term 'student with a disability' (see for example Baker, Boland, and Nowik 2012; Calvo and Kumar 2014; Damiani and Harbour 2015; Díez, López, and Molina 2015; Hurst 2015; Kubiak 2015; López-Gavira and Moriña 2015; Hughes, Corcoran, and Slee 2016). The remaining literature uses the term 'disabled student' (see for example: Vickerman and Blundell 2010; Hopkins 2011; Beauchamp-Pryor 2012; Hutcheon and Wolbring 2012; Wray 2012; Redpath et al. 2013; Hargreaves et al. 2014; Riddell and Weedon 2014; Berggren et al. 2016). In the introduction I gave my justification for why I felt that referring to 'disabled students' was preferable to referring to 'students with disabilities'; arguing that the term 'people with disabilities' implies that the person's impairment or condition causes them to be 'disabled' (and consequently that it is their responsibility to overcome it), whereas 'disabled person' implies that the person is disabled not necessarily by their condition or impairment, but by society and its inability or reluctance to cater effectively for that person (and consequently that society must effect change to remove that disability). This approach has been adopted by others (Richardson 2010; Brandt 2011) in recognition that is more consistent with a social model of disability; but the practice is not universal; indeed some students have rejected its use (see Evans 2014 for example). Ryan (2007) acknowledges that definitions in this field are characterised more by disagreement than agreement, but rightly argues that debate is needed in order to combat prejudice and ignorance. Such debate would hopefully open researchers up to the need to openly justify their use of terms, rather than assume that they are not contested.

## *Being sensitive to the politics of 'ableism'*

One of the key areas of prejudice that students experience is linked to assumptions (often unfounded) that disabled students are not as capable as non-disabled students. These assumptions can lead to an overemphasis in research literature on what disabled students cannot do; their deficits and vulnerabilities and what they require from educational institutions in terms of support or accommodation to address such difficulties. The viewing of disabled students through what (Hutcheon and Wolbring 2012) call a 'hegemonic ableism' lens can result in too little attention being paid to disabled students' abilities and capabilities and how barriers can result in disabled students being unable to demonstrate their competences (Griffin and Pollack 2009; Claiborne et al. 2011). This risk became evident to me during my research into the strategies that disabled university students employ in order to use technologies to support their learning (Seale, Draffan, and Wald 2010). Analysis of 30 in-depth case studies revealed that the disabled students in our study were very technically competent and confident; something which we chose to call 'digital agility'. This finding provoked me into re-evaluating how I could use these data to influence practice within academia. Rather than focusing on what supports were needed by disabled students in order to enable them to access and use technologies; the data enabled me to focus on how collectively, we as non-disabled students and faculty, could learn from the technology strategies that disabled students adopted. It is for this reason that I endorse the label that Irving (2013, 1042) adopted – that of 'dis/ability':

> Here dis/ablement takes on a different hue and adopts a less concrete form. Thus, rather than measure the degree of impairment against a normative white, male, and able-bodied stereotype, and judge it in relation to an individual's productive potential, the dis/abling of students should, in an ideal world, melt away in response to positive social change in which all citizens are valued for who they are, and their human contribution.

In separating out the 'dis' from the 'ability' there is an intention to emphasise both the disabling effect of educational environments and the agency and potential of the student to contribute to that environment and the wider society (Riddell and Weedon 2014). This is attractive to me because it reflects the call made by Connor and Gabel (2013, 100) for 'academic activism that counters the 'master narrative of deficiency'.

## Being aware how examinations of constructions of difference might reveal new insights

Many of the discourses surrounding the inclusion of disabled students in PSE invoke powerful concepts such as rights, social justice and equality. The emphasis on equality is particularly interesting because it has in my view resulted in an unhelpful emphasis on sameness and therefore a denial of difference that may not be in the best interests of disabled students. The right to equal opportunities (to access PSE) and equal outcomes (graduation success and employment) is increasingly translated as having to treat all students the same. In treating non-disabled and disabled students the same, each group is viewed as homogenous. It is my contention that this ignores important dimensions of difference and how they might potentially interact.

One example of how dimensions of difference might interact within groups is in data that reveal that students with multiple disabilities can be more disadvantaged than students categorised as having just one disability. For example, Richardson (2010) compared attainment in 196,405 students with and without disabilities who were taking courses by distance learning with the Open University in the United Kingdom in 2009. He found that the presence of additional disabilities led to poorer attainment in different respects in students who were blind or partially sighted, students who were deaf or hard of hearing, students with impaired speech, and students with unseen disabilities. Richardson used these data to argue that accommodations to support disabled students in distance education need to be focused on different groups of students with particular disabilities. Guardino and Cannon (2015, 347) have argued that there is a 'dearth of information' on theory, research and practice related to students who are deaf with additional disabilities such as learning disability, autism and attention deficit hyperactivity disorder.

Another example of how dimensions of difference might interact between groups is in data that reveal intersections between disability and other minority categories such as low income, race and speaking English as a second language (Cheatham et al. 2013; Liaisidou 2014). Banks (2014) reports that in the US some African-American students with disabilities experience difficulty accessing disability support services and appropriate accommodations. Wagner et al. (2005) report that disparities in postsecondary enrolment trends between European American and African-American youth with disabilities remain disproportionately high and that college degree attainment of African-American students with disabilities is less than half that for European American students with disabilities. Booth et al. (2016) argue that for African-American males with learning disabilities, barriers to education and employment include the disenfranchisement precipitated by the cumulative effects of exposure to racism.

In this article, I have argued that researchers need to engage with diverse voices, those of disabled students, disabled staff and disability support staff. Research in the field of disability and PSE therefore needs to be polyvocal. Having considered the insights that research into the intersectionality of dimensions of difference offer us, it is important also to stress that we cannot assume that each voice has just one story to tell; voices may be multi-tonal and we need to think carefully about what methods we can employ in order to be sensitive to each tone.

## Approaching research without ready-made solutions or tricks of the trade

In the research literature there are two frequently repeated narratives. The first narrative focuses on pedagogical barriers to inclusion and argues that if disabled students are experiencing barriers to inclusive learning in PCE then the solution to this problem is to implement universal design and to teach academics about universal design (see for example Dallas, Sprong, and Upton 2014; Kraglund-Gauthier, Young, and Kell 2014; Liaisidou 2014). The second narrative focuses on wider institutional barriers to inclusion and adopts a social model of disability lens to examine what can be done to reduce barriers to participation for disabled students (See for example Damiani and Harbour 2015; Díez, López, and Molina 2015; López-Gavira and Moriña 2015; Booth et al. 2016). There is a tendency for universal design and the social model of disability to be uncritically presented as ready-made solutions within PSE. In this section I will argue that this tendency needs to be challenged.

### *Critiquing universal design as a ready-made practical solution*

There are three different variants of Universal Design in education. Universal Design as advocated by the DO-IT Program at the University of Washington (DO-IT n.d.); Universal Design for Learning as advocated by the Center of Applied Special Technology (2007) and Universal Design for Instruction as advocated by the Centre on Postsecondary Education and Disability (Mcguire, Scott, and Shaw 2006). These three variants differ in the number and nature of design principles they espouse but at the core of all three is the need for proactivity (Burgstahler 2010). Firstly, Universal Design is about anticipating the needs of a diverse group of learners. Secondly, Universal Design is positioned as inclusive because it values diversity and equity; thirdly, disabled students are not required to continually advocate for access or accommodations. Possibly because there are different variants of Universal Design, it is common for the principles of Universal Design to be quite severely misinterpreted. Edyburn (2010) provides an excellent analysis of ten key ways in which he feels the principles have been universally misinterpreted and uses his analysis to warn that it may be impossible to implement something that cannot be consistently defined. I think this warning is appropriate, but what I wish to focus on is something different; not how Universal Design is implemented but the grounds upon which it is implemented.

Whilst it is unwise to treat any group of stakeholders in PSE as homogenous; generally speaking, one thing I learnt through my experience working in an educational development unit was academics have been trained to look for evidence and to question the evidence. Therefore, if we wish to persuade them to change their practice, in this case implement Universal Design principles; we should probably show them the evidence that it works. But the reality is that Universal Design advocates rarely engage in any depth with such evidence. They are often uncritical in their acceptance of Universal Design. This silence and lack of critical voice concerns me. Writing in the context of e-learning in higher education I have argued that a major area in which Universal Design needs critical examination is the lack of proof that Universal Design principles bring about their intended effects (Seale 2013). I gave three detailed examples to support my argument. Here in this article, I will give two additional examples.

In an article focusing on how faculty embed universal in their practice and the need for professional development in this area, Kraglund-Gauthier, Young, and Kell (2014, 7) argue:

> By increasing student choice and making connections with students' prior knowledge, student motivation to participate and to learn is also increased. (Orr and Bachman-Hammig 2009; Lombardi, Murray, and Gerdes 2011)

A closer inspection of the references given to support the claim for increased student motivation, however reveals that the Lombardi, Murray, and Gerdes (2011) paper is reporting a study on faculty attitudes to Universal Design and therefore offers no evidence regarding improvements in student motivation due to implementation of universal design. The Orr and Bachman-Hammig paper does offer some evidence in that it provides a review of studies that pertain in some way to the Universal Design principles. The review distilled out key themes across the studies and drew some tentative conclusions based on this analysis. As much research in the field is qualitative, we are unlikely to be able to conduct the kind of review where effect sizes and similar quantitative data can be tested across studies. However, I would argue that we do need to have some accepted process for interrogating this qualitative evidence. For example, the review by Orr and Bachman-Hammig included studies where Universal Design was not a specific focus and therefore not embedded in the aims or research questions of the studies in question. It is not clear to me therefore that their inclusion was appropriate in a review seeking to 'test' Universal Design. One example is the inclusion of the study by Beacham and Alty (2006) which was an investigation into the effects that digital media can have on the learning outcomes of individuals who have dyslexia. In the abstract, the authors state that the 'purpose of the study was to obtain data that informed the development and design of e-learning and distance learning materials for universal use'. I would argue that 'universal use' should not be confused with Universal Design. In the beginning of the paper, there is a small paragraph that acknowledges that there are different approaches to design and the work of the Centre for Applied Special Technology is cited but they conclude by stating:

> However, it does seem from our observations that very little extra learning material is being produced for adult dyslexic learners and none concerning assessment. We therefore set up a more detailed study, centred entirely on addressing the effects that computer-based media can have on adult learners who have dyslexia. (Beacham and Alty 2006, 75)

Based on this, I would argue that Beacham and Alty are not positioning their research as being about Universal Design. Furthermore, as Edyburn (2010) argues; using technology does not automatically mean that you are using Universal Design. One approach to reviewing research evidence on Universal Design that I consider to be more rigorous is the systematic review conducted by Pino and Mortari (2014) who synthesised the available evidence on how the inclusion of dyslexic students can be fostered in higher education. In reviewing this evidence they argued for a flexible combination of Universal Design for Learning and individualised support. While the reviews by Orr and Bachman-Hammig and Pino and Mortari both contribute in some way to the collation of evidence regarding whether Universal Design works, it does raise questions about what the community counts as valid or robust evidence that will be convincing enough to persuade academics to change their practice. In addition, I would suggest that it is incumbent on advocates of Universal Design to be more critical of the evidence they are relying on to make their case.

In a study seeking to measure the attitudes of postsecondary faculty towards inclusive teaching strategies, Dallas, Sprong, and Upton (2014, 14) state:

> Applying UDI principles may lessen the need for individual accommodations (Ketterlin-Geller and Johnstone 2006), therefore this could be a positive change in the inclusion of people with disabilities in higher education.

The cited paper by Ketterlin-Geller and Johnstone (2006, 167) discusses applying the principles of Universal Design to assessments. Because it is a discursive paper it offers no direct evidence for Universal Design, but it does cite one source of evidence:

For example, Dolan et al. (2005) have found that students are more successful when flexible options (such as read-aloud approaches) are available to all students in an on-demand fashion.

Interestingly, this is a rare empirical paper, mixed methods in nature, in which two conditions are compared. In a counterbalanced design, students were administered a traditional paper and pencil test or a test using a computer-based system with optional text-to-speech (reflecting principles of Universal Design in terms of flexibility of delivery). What I like about this study was that it combined quantitative performance data with qualitative data to show that not only did the students perform better in the second condition; they preferred the second condition. It is really good to see studies like these; although we do need to be aware that it was conducted by researchers from the Centre for Applied Special Technology. Not that I am suggesting that they are biased. Indeed many of the originators of Universal Design have been much more cautious than their advocates in terms of the claims they make. For example, in addressing the question:' can we develop the UD construct in a rigorous way?' Mcguire, Scott, and Shaw (2006, 172) warn against the dangers of perceiving Universal Design as a magical solution before it is more widely developed and proven:

> The fields of architecture and design have called for the development of a 'critical theory' of UD involving the testing of suppositions (i.e. UD principles) engaging in serious discourse and critical practice, implementing ongoing projects to document exemplars, and refining and validating the UD principles. In contrast to the quick solutions assumed to result from the application of UD to educational environments, this type of iterative theory building is essential to avoid the danger of yet another short-lived panacea for special education.

Ten years on from this, I would argue that the research field is still too prone to viewing Universal Design as a magical solution and that we need to apply a much more critical lens to the presumed evidence. I acknowledge that it might be hard to be the critical voice in a sea of positive voices, particularly when Universal Design has gained such influence over legislation and associated government funding programmes and policies. For example in Norway, one objective of the 2003 'Quality Reform' policy was to ensure that learning environments complied with the principles of Universal Design (Brandt 2011). With such high-level governmental support, the motivation to critically examine whether or not Universal Design is as effective as claimed may be, for some, quite limited. Hence, my call for more 'socratic gadlfies'.

## *Critiquing the social model of disability as a ready-made theoretical solution*

The social model of disability views disability as stemming from failure of the social and physical environment to take account of disabled peoples' needs (Oliver 1990). Disability is deconstructed as a social and political process (Ewens and Williams 2011). In the original model, the problems of disabled people are therefore not seen as within the individual person, but within society. In the field of disability and post-compulsory education the social model has been very influential. It has influenced the debate on labelling (see earlier discussion) and it has influenced approaches to research, with many researchers adopting a barriers lens to the design and analysis of their work. Stodden (2015) for example talks of the need for campuses to be 'barrier-free' and welcoming. Wray (2012) talks about 'barriers and enablers to success'; while others talk of barriers to participation (Damiani and Harbour 2015; López-Gavira and Moriña 2015). Much of the barrier-related work has focused on attitudinal barriers (Díez, López, and Molina 2015; Booth et al. 2016) and institutional barriers such as lack of curricular adaptations (Díez, López, and Molina 2015) or the quality of service provision (Redpath et al. 2013). This work reflects the original version of the social model in that the overarching aim is to investigate how attitudinal and institutional contexts shape disabled 'disabled students' experiences of equal opportunities in higher education' (Berggren et al. 2016). There is however growing evidence that attitudinal and institutional factors on their own are not the sole influences on successful participation of disabled students in PSE.

Some studies have identified environmental factors not related to the institution that appear to have an influence. For example, in a qualitative study, Babic and Dowling (2015) identified that support from family members was significant because they increased the individual's sense of security, belonging and self-esteem. There are also studies that seem to suggest an interaction between different enablers and barriers. Fichten et al. (2014) sought to develop a model to predict which disabled students will drop out before graduation and to investigate the drop out pattern of disabled students. Their analysis revealed that person-specific factors (such as disability, health, career direction uncertainty and lack of interest/motivation); social factors (e.g. financial constraints) and institutional factors (e.g. inadequate disability accommodations) contributed to academic persistence and drop-out. O'Neil, Markward, and French (2012) conducted an exploratory study designed to determine which set of student characteristics and disability-related services explained graduation success among college students with disabilities. The final model they constructed included predictors related to gender, age, disability type and disability-related services.

Studies such as these suggest that it is time to acknowledge that the social model of disability, as it is applied in PSE, offers too narrow a field of view. We need lenses that can expand our understanding of enablers and barriers to success for disabled students and in particular cope with multiple factors that interact in a multitude of ways. Some researchers have begun to demonstrate how this might be done. For example McLean, Heagney, and Gardner (2003), draw on Murray-Seegert's ecological theory of diversity to examine successful transition of students with a disability into the higher education sector in recognition that cultural factors, the 'things outside' an institution, have a significant influence on the opportunities available to young disabled people. One example they give is how culture and ethnicity mould family attitudes and peer relations to disability.

Once we have acknowledged that the social model has served its political purpose in highlighting environmental barriers to inclusion, we can move forward and pay attention to different theoretical voices that offer us ways of not just identifying barriers, but understanding why they exist and predicting successful ways to remove them. In other words, research in the field can become more investigative, rather than simply seeking to confirm what we already know; that barriers to inclusion exist.

## Conclusion

In this article, I have taken on the role of a 'socratic gadfly' to argue that researchers in the field of disability and PSE need to take become academic activists and take on more a political voice in their examination of exclusion and inclusion. Drawing on Julie Allan's (2010) framework, I have identified six key areas where voices and silences in post-compulsory education need critical examination. If more researchers do not take up the call for academic activism, my fear is that the field will become stagnant. We need brave and creative new thinking about how we research and what we research. We need what Wright-Mills (1959) called a 'sociological imagination'; an ability to pull away from the situation and think from an alternative point of view. In doing so, it is my hope that research in the field of disability and PSE can do more than describe current oppression. It is my hope that we can chart paths to achievable alternative futures (Peters 2010).

## Disclosure statement

No potential conflict of interest was reported by the author.

## References

Abram, S. 2003. "The Americans with Disabilities Act in Higher Education: The Plight of Disabled Faculty." *Journal of Law and Education* 32: 1–20.

Allan, J. 2010. "The Sociology of Disability and the Struggle for Inclusive Education." *British Journal of Sociology of Education* 31 (5): 603–619.

Anderson, R. C. 2006. "Teaching (with) Disability: Pedagogies of Lived Experience." *The Review of Education, Pedagogy, and Cultural Studies* 28: 367–379.

Anderson, A. 2009. "Afterward: Celebration, Eulogy, or Pride in Disability Scholarship and Community?." *Review of Disability Studies: An International Journal* 5 (1): 732–737.

Argawal, N., B. Calvo, and V. Kumar. 2014. "Paving the Road to Success: A Students with Disabilities Organization in a University Setting." *College Student Journal* no. 1 (Spring): 34–44.

Babic, M. M., and M. Dowling. 2015. "Social Support, the Presence of Barriers and Ideas for the Future from Students with Disabilities in the Higher Education System in Croatia." *Disability & Society* 30 (4): 614–629.

Baker, K. Q., K. Boland, and C. M. Nowik. 2012. "A Campus Survey of Faculty and Student Perceptions of Persons with Disabilities." *Journal of Postsecondary Education and Disability* 25 (4): 309–329.

Banks, J. 2014. "Barriers and Supports to Postsecondary Transition: Case Studies of African American Students with Disabilities." *Remedial & Special Education* 35 (1): 28–39.

Barton, L. 2001. "Disability, Struggle and the Politics of Hope." In *Disability, Politics and the Struggle for Change*, edited by L. Barton, 1–10. London: David Fulton.

Beacham, N., and J. Alty. 2006. "An Investigation into the Effects That Digital Media Can Have on the Learning Outcomes of Individuals Who Have Dyslexia." *Computers and Education* 47: 74–93.

Beauchamp-Pryor, K. 2012. "From Absent to Active Voices: Securing Disability Equality Within Higher Education." *International Journal of Inclusive Education* 16 (3): 283–295.

Berggren, U. J., D. Rowan, E. Bergbäck, and B. Blomberg. 2016. "Disabled Students' Experiences of Higher Education in Sweden, the Czech Republic and the United States – A Comparative Institutional Analysis." *Disability & Society* 31 (3): 339–356.

Bishop, D., and D. J. A. Rhind. 2011. "Barriers and Enablers for Visually Impaired Students at a UK Higher Education Institution." *British Journal of Visual Impairment* 29: 177–195.

Booth, J., M. K. J. Butler, T. V. Richardson, A. R. Washington, and M. S. Henfield. 2016. "School-faculty-community – Collaboration for African American Males with Disabilities." *Journal of African American Males Education* 7 (1): 87–97.

Borland, J., and S. James. 1999. "The Learning Experience of Students with Disabilities in Higher Education. a Case Study of a UK University." *Disability and Society* 14 (1): 85–101.

Brandt, S. 2011. "From Policy to Practice in Higher Education: The Experiences of Disabled Students in Norway." *International Journal of Disability, Development and Education* 58 (2): 107–120.

Broomhead, K. E. 2016. "They Think That if You're a Teacher Here ... You're not Clever Enough to be a Proper Teacher: The Courtesy Stigma Experienced by Teachers Employed at Schools for Pupils with Behavioural, Emotional and Social Difficulties." *Journal of Research in Special Educational Needs* 16 (1): 57–64.

Burgstahler, S. 2010. "Universal Design of Instruction: From Principles to Practice." In *Universal Design in Higher Education: From Principles to Practice*, edited by S. Burgstahler, and R. C. Corey, 23–44. Cambridge, MA: Harvard Education Press.

Cameron, H. E. 2016. "Beyond Cognitive Deficit: The Everyday Lived Experience of Dyslexic Students at University." *Disability & Society* 31 (2): 223–239.

Center of Applied Special Technology. 2007. "Universal Design for Learning." Accessed March 1. http://www.advocacyinstitute.org/UDL/

Cheatham, G. A., S. J. Smith, W. Elliott, and T. Friedline. 2013. "Family Assets, Postsecondary Education, and Students with Disabilities: Building on Progress and Overcoming Challenges." *Children and Youth Services Review* 35: 1078–1086.

Claiborne, L. B., S. Cornforth, A. Gibson, and A. Smith. 2011. "Supporting Students with Impairments in Higher Education: Social Inclusion or Cold Comfort?" *International Journal of Inclusive Education* 15 (5): 513–527.

Clouder, L., A. Adefila, C. Jackson, J. Opie, and S. Odedra. 2016. "The Discourse of Disability in Higher Education: Insights from a Health and Social Care Perspective." *International Journal of Educational Research* 79: 10–20.

Connor, D. J., and S. L. Gabel. 2013. "Cripping the Curriculum Through Academic Activism: Working Toward Increasing Global Exchanges to Reframe (Dis)ability and Education." *Equity and Excellence in Education* 46 (1): 100–118.

CEC (Council for Exceptional Children). 2016. Policy on Educators with Disabilities. Accessed October 4. https://www.cec.sped.org/Policy-and-Advocacy/CEC-Professional-Policies

Cunnah, W. 2015. "Disabled Students: Identity, Inclusion and Work-based Placements." *Disability & Society* 30 (2): 213–226.

Dallas, B. K., M. E. Sprong, and T. D. Upton. 2014. "Post-secondary Faculty Attitudes Towards Inclusive Teaching Strategies." *Journal of Rehabilitation* 80 (2): 12–20.

Damiani, M. L., and W. S. Harbour. 2015. "Being the Wizard Behind the Curtain: Teaching Experiences of Graduate Teaching Assistants with Disabilities at US Universities." *Innovation in Higher Education* 40: 399–413. doi:10.1007/s10755-015-9326-7.

Denhart, H. 2008. "Deconstructing Barriers: Perceptions of Students Labeled with Learning Disabilities in Higher Education." *Journal of Learning Disabilities* 41: 483–497.

Díez, A. M., R. G. López, and V. M. Molina. 2015. "Students with Disabilities in Higher Education: A Biographical-Narrative Approach to the Role of Lecturers." *Higher Education Research & Development* 34 (1): 147–159.

DO-IT n.d. "Applications of Universal Design." Accessed February 26, 2012. http://www.washington.edu/doit/Resources/udesign.html

Dolan, R. P., T. E. Hall, M. Banerjee, E. Chun, and N. Strangman. 2005. "Applying Principles of Universal Design to Test Delivery: The Effect of Computer-based Read-aloud on Test Performance of High School Students with Learning Disabilities." *Journal of Technology, Learning & Assessment* 3 (7): 1496–1528.

Edyburn, D. V. 2010. "Would You Recognize Universal Design for Learning if You Saw it? Ten Propositions for New Directions for the Second Decade of UDL." *Learning Disability Quarterly* 33 (Winter): 33–41.

Evans, W. 2014. "'I Am Not a Dyslexic Person I'm a Person with Dyslexia': Identity Constructions of Dyslexia among Students in Nurse Education." *Journal of Advanced Nursing* 70 (2): 360–372.

Ewens, D., and J. Williams. 2011. *Enabling Equality: Furthering Disability Equality for Staff in Higher Education: Literature Review*. London: ECU & Foundation for Higher Education.

Fichten, C. C., M. N. Nguyen, R. Amsel, S. Jorgensen, J. Budd, M. Jorgensen, J. Asuncion, and M. Barile. 2014. "How Well Does the Theory of Planned Behaviour Predict Graduation Among College and University Students with Disabilities?" *Social Psychology of Education* 17: 657–685.

Freire, P. 1972. *Cultural Action for Freedom*. Harmondsworth: Penguin Books.

Fuller, M., A. Bradley, and M. Healey. 2004. "Incorporating Disabled Students Within an Inclusive Higher Education Environment." *Disability and Society* 19 (5): 455–468.

Fuller, M., J. Georgeson, M. Healey, A. Hurst, K. Kelly, S. Riddell, H. Roberts, and E. Weedon. 2009. *Improving Disabled Students' Learning: Experiences and Outcomes*. London: Routledge.

Griffin, E., and D. Pollack. 2009. "Student Experiences of Neurodiversity in Higher Education: Insights from the BRAINHE Project." *Dyslexia* 15: 23–41.

Guardino, C., and J. E. Cannon. 2015. "Theory, Research and Practice for Students Who are Deaf and Hard and Hearing with Disabilities: Addressing the Challenges From Birth to Postsecondary Education." *American Annals of the Deaf* 160 (4): 347–355.

Hall, J., and T. Tinklin. 1998. *Students First: The Experiences of Disabled Students in Higher Education*. SCRE Research Report No. 85. Glasgow: The Scottish Council for Research in Education.

Hammer, S., S. Werth, and P. Dunn. 2009. "Tertiary Students with a Disability or Chronic Illness: Stigma and Study". In *Enabling Pathways: 3rd National Conference of Enabling Educators*, November 25–27, 2009, Toowoomba, Australia.

Hanafin, J., M. Shevlin, M. Kenny, and E. McNeela. 2007. "Including Young People with Disabilities: Assessment Challenges in Higher Education." *Higher Education* 54: 435–448.

Hargreaves, J., C. Dearnely, S. Walker, and L. Walker. 2014. "The Preparation and Practice of Disabled Health Care Practitioners: Exploring the Issues." *Innovations in Education and Teaching International* 51 (3): 303–314.

Harrison, A. G., and A. Holmes. 2014. "Mild Intellectual Disability at the Postsecondary Level: Results of a Survey of Disability Service Offices." *Exceptionality Education, International* 23: 22–39.

Higbee, J. L., and A. A. Mitchel, eds. 2009. *Making Good on the Promise: Student Affairs Professionals with Disabilities*. Lanham, MD: University Press of America, and American College Personnel Association.

Hopkins, L. 2011. "The Path of Least Resistance: A Voice-relational Analysis of Disabled Students' Experiences of Discrimination in English Universities." *International Journal of Inclusive Education* 15 (7): 711–727.

Hughes, K., T. Corcoran, and R. Slee. 2016. "Health-inclusive Higher Education: Listening to Students with Disabilities or Chronic Illnesses." *Higher Education Research & Development* 35 (3): 488–501.

Hurst, A. 2015. "Developing and Implementing an Accreditation Scheme for Disability Services Staff in Post-Compulsory Education in the United Kingdom." *Journal of Postsecondary Education and Disability* 28 (1): 9–24.

Hutcheon, E. J., and G. Wolbring. 2012. "Voices of 'Disabled' Postsecondary Students: Examining Higher Education Policy Using an Ableism Lens." *Journal of Diversity Higher Education* 5 (1): 39–49.

Irving, B. A. 2013. "Access, Opportunity, and Career: Supporting the Aspirations of Dis/abled Students with High-end Needs in New Zealand." *International Journal of Inclusive Education* 17 (10): 1040–1052.

Jacklin, A., C. Robinson, L. O'Meara, and A. Harris. 2007. *Improving the Experiences of Disabled Students in Higher Education*. York: HEA.

Ketterlin-Geller, L. R., and C. Johnstone. 2006. "Accommodations and Universal Design: Supporting Access to Assessments in Higher Education." *Journal of Postsecondary Education and Disability* 19 (2): 163–171.

Kowalsky, R., and B. Fresko. 2002. "Peer Tutoring for College Students with Disabilities." *Higher Education Research and Development* 21 (3): 259–271.

Kraglund-Gauthier, W. L., D. C. Young, and E. Kell. 2014. "Teaching Students with Disabilities in Post-secondary Landscape: Navigating Elements of Inclusion, Differentiation, Universal Design for Learning and Technology." *Transformative Dialogues: Teaching and Learning Journal* 7 (3): 1–9.

Kubiak, J. 2015. "Using 'Voice' to Understand What College Students with Intellectual Disabilities Say about the Teaching and Learning Process." *Journal of Research in Special Educational Needs*. http://onlinelibrary.wiley.com/doi/10.1111/1471-3802.12098/abstract. doi:10.1111/1471-3802.12098.

Liaisidou, A. 2014. "Critical Disability Studies and Socially Just Change in Higher Education." *British Journal of Special Education* 41 (2): 121–135.

Lightner, K. L., D. Kipps-Vaughan, T. Schulte, and A. D. Trice. 2012. "Reasons University Students with a Learning Disability Wait to Seek Disability Services." *Journal of Postsecondary Education and Disability* 25 (2): 145–159.

Lombardi, A. R., C. Murray, and H. Gerdes. 2011. "College Faculty and Inclusive Instruction: Self-reported Attitudes and Actions Pertaining to Universal Design." *Journal of Diversity Higher Education* 4 (4): 250–261.

López-Gavira, R., and A. Moriña. 2015. "Hidden Voices in Higher Education: Inclusive Policies and Practices in Social Science and Law Classrooms." *International Journal of Inclusive Education* 19 (4): 365–378.

Lourens, L., and H. Swartz. 2016. "Experiences of Visually Impaired Students in Higher Education: Bodily Perspectives on Inclusive Education." *Disability & Society* 31 (2): 240–251.

Luna, L. 2009. "'But How Can Those Students Make It Here?': Examining the Institutional Discourse about What It Means to Be 'LD' at an Ivy League University." *International Journal of Inclusive Education* 13 (2): 157–178.

Madriaga, M., K. Hanson, H. Kay, and A. Walker. 2011. "Marking-out Normalcy and Disability in Higher Education." *British Journal of Sociology of Education* 32 (6): 901–920.

Mcguire, J. M., S. S. Scott, and S. F. Shaw. 2006. "Universal Design and Its Applications in Educational Environments." *Remedial and Special Education* 27 (3): 166–175.

McLean, P., M. Heagney, and K. Gardner. 2003. "Going Global: The Implications for Students with a Disability." *Higher Education Research & Development* 22 (2): 217–228.

Michalko, R. 2001. "Blindness Enters the Classroom." *Disability and Society* 16 (3): 349–359.

Nolan, C., C. Gleeson, D. Treanor, and S. Madigan. 2015. "Higher Education Students Registered with Disability Services and Practice Educators: Issues and Concerns for Professional Placements." *International Journal of Inclusive Education* 19 (5): 487–502.

Oliver, M. 1990. *The Politics of Disablement*. Basingstoke: MacMillan and St Martin's Press.

Olney, M. F., and K. F. Brockelman. 2003. "Out of the Disability Closet: Strategic Use of Perception Management by Select University Students with Disabilities." *Disability and Society* 18 (1): 35–50.

O'Neil, L. N., M. J. Markward, and J. P. French. 2012. "Predictors of Graduation among College Students with Disabilities." *Journal of Postsecondary Education and Disability* 25 (1): 21–36.

Orr, A. C., and S. Bachman-Hammig. 2009. "Inclusive Postsecondary Strategies for Teaching Students with Learning Disabilities: A Review of the Literature." *Learning Disabilities Quarterly* 32 (3): 181–196.

Peters, S. 2010. "The Heterodoxy of Student Voice: Challenges to Identity in the Sociology of Disability and Education." *British Journal of Sociology of Education* 31 (5): 591–602.

Phipps, L., A. Sutherland, and J. Seale, eds. 2002. *Access All Areas: Disability, Technology and Learning*. Oxford: ALT/TechDis.

Pino, M., and L. Mortari. 2014. "The Inclusion of Students with Dyslexia in Higher Education: A Systematic Review Using Narrative Synthesis." *Dyslexia* 20 (4): 346–369.

Quick, D., J. Lehmann, and T. Deniston. 2003. "Opening Doors for Students with Disabilities on Community College Campuses: What Have We Learned? What Do We Still Need to Know?" *Community College Journal of Research and Practice* 27: 815–827.

Quinlan, M. M., B. R. Bates, and M. E. Angell. 2012. "'What Can I Do to Help?': Postsecondary Students with Learning Disabilities' Perceptions of Instructors' Classroom Accommodations." *Journal of Research in Special Educational Needs* 12 (4): 224–233.

Redpath, J., P. Kearney, P. Nicholl, M. Mulvenna, J. Wallace, and S. Martin. 2013. "A Qualitative Study of the Lived Experiences of Disabled Post-transition Students in Higher Education Institutions in Northern Ireland." *Studies in Higher Education* 38 (9): 1334–1350.

Reed, M., and K. Curtis. 2012. "Experiences of Students with Visual Impairments in Canadian Higher Education." *Journal of Visual Impairment and Blindness*, July: 414–425.

Richardson, J. T. E. 2010. "Course Completion and Attainment in Disabled Students Taking Courses with the Open University UK." *Open Learning: The Journal of Open, Distance and e-Learning* 25 (2): 81–94.

Riddell, S., and E. Weedon. 2014. "Disabled Students in Higher Education: Discourses of Disability and the Negotiation of Identity." *International Journal of Educational Research* 63: 38–46.

Ryan, J. 2007. "Learning Disabilities in Australian Universities: Hidden, Ignored, and Unwelcome." *Learning Disabilities* 40: 436–442.

Seale, J. 2010. "Doing Student Voice Work in Higher Education: The Potential Contribution of a Participatory Framework." *British Educational Research Journal* 36 (6): 995–1015.

Seale, J. 2013. *E-Learning and Disability in Higher Education: Accessibility Theory and Practice.* 2nd ed. New York: Routledge.

Seale, J., E. A. Draffan, and M. Wald. 2010. "Digital Agility and Digital Decision-making: Conceptualising Digital Inclusion in the Context of Disabled Learners in Higher Education." *Studies in Higher Education* 35 (4): 445–462.

Sheridan, L., and S. Kotevski. 2014. "University Teaching with a Disability: Student Learnings beyond the Curriculum." *International Journal of Inclusive Education* 18 (11): 1162–1171.

Stein, K. F. 2013. "DSS and Accommodations in Higher Education: Perceptions of Students with Psychological Difficulties." *Journal of Postsecondary Education and Disability* 26 (2): 145–161.

Stodden, R. A. 2015. "Supporting Students with Disabilities in Higher Education in the USA: 30 Years of Advocacy." OUJ International Symposium 2015, Tokyo, Japan. Accessed August 28, 2016. http://www.ouj.ac.jp/eng/sympo/2015/report/pdf/speech_3_2015e.pdf

Summers, J. A., G. W. White, E. Zhang, and J. M. Gordon. 2014. "Providing Support to Postsecondary Students with Disabilities to Request Accommodations: A Framework for Intervention." *Journal of Postsecondary Education and Disability* 27 (3): 245–260.

Venville, A., A. Street, and E. Fossey. 2014. "Student Perspectives on Disclosure of Mental Illness in Post-compulsory Education: Displacing Doxa." *Disability & Society* 29 (5): 792–806.

Vickerman, P., and M. Blundell. 2010. "Hearing the Voices of Disabled Students in Higher Education." *Disability and Society* 25 (1): 21–32.

Wagner, M., L. Newman, R. Cameto, N. Garza, and P. Levine. 2005. "Changes over Time in the Early Post-school Outcomes of Youth with Disabilities: A Report of Findings from the National Longitudinal Transition Study (NLTS) and National Longitudinal Transition Study-2." Accessed August 28, 2016. http://www.nlts2.org/reports/2005_06/nlts2_report_2005_06_execsum.pdf

Webster, D. 2004. "Giving Voice to Students with Disabilities Who Have Successfully Transitioned to College." *Career Development and Transition for Exceptional Individuals* 27 (2): 151–175.

Wray, M. 2012. "Comparing Disabled Students' Entry to Higher Education with Their Non-disabled Peers-barriers and Enablers to Success." *Widening Participation and Lifelong Learning* 14 (3): 87–101.

Wright-Mills, C. 1959. *The Sociological Imagination.* London: Oxford University Press.

# Index

ableism assumptions 160
academic activism 155–156; ableism assumptions 160; dimensions of difference 161; giving voice to disabled students 155; labelling 159–160; privileging voices of disabled students 156–157; privileging voices of relevant stakeholders 157–158; sensitivities to tensions around construction of disability 158–159; social model of disability critiques 164–165; UDL critique 162–164
academic burnout: tiredness 21–22
Academic Self-Efficacy Scale 23
academic self-efficacy *see* ASE
academic staff *see* faculty
access: applications 99; disclosure link 121–122; improving 4–5; Republic of Ireland initiatives 56–57; support services 65–68
accessible curriculum and assessment 101–102
accommodations *see* reasonable accommodations
achievement: ASE correlation 29; hope as predictor 21; inclusive learning environments 105
*Action Group on Access to Third Level* report 56
activating teaching and evaluation methods: ASD functioning and participation problems 84
additional curriculum 107
ADHD (Attention Deficit/Hyperactivity Disorder): definition 36; SOC and symptom severity 20–21
ADHD students functioning and participation problems: analysis 42; classical *versus* alternative teaching and evaluation methods 48; counselling sessions with student counsellors 49; differences in student reports and student counsellors reports 47; effective reasonable accommodations 41–42, 45–46; environmental characteristics influence 37–38; frequency of functioning and participation problems measure 41; frequency of occurrences 43; functioning and participation in higher education 37; higher education performance 36; implementation of reasonable accommodations 48; limitations 48–49; personal characteristic influence 36–37; problems experienced 47; reasonable accommodations 38; reluctance to use accommodations 50; social problems 47; study participants 39–40; teaching and evaluation methods 41; during teaching and evaluation methods 44–45
AHEAD (Association for Higher Education Access & Disability) 112
Allan, J.: academic activism 155–156
alternative teaching and evaluation methods and ADHD functioning and participation problems 48
anticipatory adjustments barrier 104–105
Antonovsky, A.: SOC 20
applications: accessibility 99
ASD (autistic spectrum disorder) 56; definition 72; higher education participation rates 57, 73; inefficient study skills 84; reasonable accommodations 73, 81
ASD functioning and participation problems 73–74; analysis 78; communication 82–84, 87; comparison with students without a disability 83; effective reasonable accommodations 81–82; environmental characteristics 86–87; frequency of experienced problems 78–79; frequency of occurrences 82–83; ICF framework 74; mapping problems before selecting and implementing effective reasonable accommodations 86–87; measures 76–78; perceived effectiveness of reasonable accommodations 85; social interactions 83–84, 87; study limitations 86; study participants 75–76; study procedures 76; during teaching and evaluation methods 79–81, 83–84
ASD student transitions: accessing support 65–68; accommodation/transport offers 65; analysis 62–63; disclosing disabilities 65–68; early transition planning 67; effectiveness of

# INDEX

supports 66–67; per-transition heightened pressures 64–65; secondary school support and knowledge in transition planning 63–64; self-determination 58–59; social challenges 59–60; social interaction in the classroom 68; social isolation 59, 67; student attrition and failure in first year 58–59; study participants 61; study procedures 61–62; study research questions 60–61; support services 59; transfer to post-secondary education 58–60
ASE (academic self-efficacy) 18; defined 20; measuring 23; predictors 25, 29
ASE and LD students study: analysis 24–25; ASE measures 23; ASE predictors 29; direct/indirect effects of LD on ASE 27–28; educational implications 30–31; hierarchical regression analysis for predicting ASE 27; hope measures 23–24; limitations 29; male *versus* female scores 26; mediation analyses 25–27; past experiences role shaping present contextual conditions 28; Pearson correlations among variables 27; predictors of ASE 25; SOC scale 24; students with *versus* without learning disabilities scores 26; study participants 22–23; tiredness measure 24
assessments: accessibility 101–102; UDL 163–164
assistive technology: funding 99
Association for Higher Education Access & Disability (AHEAD) 112
Attention Deficit/Hyperactivity Disorder *see* ADHD
autistic spectrum disorder *see* ASD
awareness of mental health: academic staff 119–120

bachelor's thesis evaluation method 54
barriers: ableism assumptions 160; accessible curriculum and assessment 101–102; application accessibility 99; disabled student participation in policies and provisions development 157; DSO 100; external agencies 99–100; funding equipment 99; inadequate support services for mental health 113; inclusive learning 107–108; independent access to information 104; infrastructure 102; insufficient PowerPoint notes 148; labelling 159–160; lack of understanding 156; lack of whole campus approach to mental health 122–123; negative attitudes 156; participation 104–105; preparedness for higher education 102–103; proving disabilities 159; self-advocacy 103; social model of disability 164; stigma of disclosing disability 113; student perceptions 6–7; faculty attitudes 6; study materials 148; support plan implementation 100–101

belonging in inclusive education 130–134; dynamism 133; groundedness 131–132; reciprocity 132; self-determination 134; subjectivity 131
Bioecological Model of Inclusive Education 95–96; chronosystems 97, 102–104; exosystems 97–98; macrosystems 97–98; mesosystems 97–102; microsystems 96, 99–102
Bioecological Systems Theory of Human Development *see* BST
BIS (Business, Innovation and Skills) new DSA proposal 92
bootstrapping: LD students ASE study 24
breaking the silence within teaching 155
Bronfenbrenner, Urie: BST 95
BST (Bioecological Systems Theory of Human Development) 95
burnout: academic 21–22; disability coordinators 143

chi square statistics: functioning and participation problems of ADHD students in higher education 42
chronosystems 97, 102–104
classical teaching and evaluation methods: ADHD functioning and participation problems 48; ASD functioning and participation problems during 80, 83–84
classroom social interactions: ASD challenges 59–60
closed book exams evaluation method 54
communication problems: ASD students 82–84, 87
comprehensive lecture notes for DPP PowerPoint presentations 150–152
construction of disabilities: ableism 160; dimensions of difference 161; labelling 159–160; sensitivities 158–159
Convention of the Rights of People with Disabilities: access obligation for higher education, professional training, adult education and lifelong learning 4–5
coping skills: ASD students 80–81, 84
COR (Conservation of resources) theory 19
culture outside physical environment 97–98
cultures of silence 155
curriculum: accessibility 101–102

DARE (Disability Access Route to Education) 57
Debrand and Salzberg proposal 11
dedicated services for academic and mental health supports 120–121
digital agility 160
digital capital 108
dimensions of difference 161
direct/indirect effects of LD on ASE through SOC, agency and paths 27–28

# INDEX

disabilities: social model definition 138
disability coordinators: burnout 143; changing nature of disabilities 142–143; coordinator terminology 139; flexibility 141–143; good practices 141–142; interest and internal motivations for job choice 141; personal experiences with disability 141; practice and education-research paths 143–144; students disabled during university life 143; study overview 139–140; system-related suggestions 144; time 142–143; variability 139
Disability Officers 56
disabled educators 158
disabled students: access initiatives in Republic of Ireland 57; higher education participation rates 57; labelling 159–160; participation in policies and provisions development 157; privileging voices of 156–157; transition planning success factors 57
disclosing disabilities 9–10; access support 121–122; post-transition 65–68; stigma 113; stigmatisation 156–157
diversity: inclusive education 3; students 4
DPP PowerPoint presentation approach 149–151; benefits 150–151; comprehensive lecture notes 150–152; lecture handouts 149, 152; limitations 152
DSA (Disabled Student Allowance) 91; equipment funding 99
DSOs (Disability Support Offices) 91, 100
dual academic and mental health support services 120–121
dual PowerPoint approach *see* DPP PowerPoint presentations
dynamism: sense of belonging 133
dyslexia 159

early engagement with mental health topics during whole campus services 118–119
early transition planning 67
ECTS (European Credit Transfer System) 38
effective reasonable accommodations: ASD functioning and participation problems 81–82; functioning and participation problems 45–46; mapping problems before selecting and implementing 86–87; measuring 77; perceptions of ASD students 85; support services 66–67
enablers: DSO 100; external agencies 99–100; independent access to information 103–104; infrastructure 102; whole campus approach to mental health 122–123
environmental characteristics: ASD functioning and participation problems 74, 86–87; influence on academic functioning of students 37–38; social model of disability 164
Equality Act 91, 97, 138–139, 151

equipment: funding 99
ethics: inclusion as ethical project 135
European Credit Transfer System (ECTS) 38
*European Strategy 2010–2020:* improving access and educational inclusion 5
exam deferrals: ASD students 85
excursion teaching method 54
exosystems 97–98
extended examination duration: ASD students 85
external agencies: support services 99–100

facilitators: student perceptions 6–7; whole campus approach to mental health 114–115, 122
factors outside learners immediate environment 98
factors outside physical environment 97–98
faculty: mental health awareness 119–120; self-perceptions of attitudes 10–11; students perceptions of attitudes 6; training and sensitisation towards disabilities 10–11
failures: student transfers to higher education 58–59
flexibility: disability coordinators 141–143
Freire, P.: cultures of silence 155
frequencies: functioning and participation problems of ADHD students 41–43; functioning and participation problems of ASD students 78–79, 82–83
functioning and participation problems of ADHD students: analysis 42; classical and alternative teaching and evaluation methods 48; counselling sessions with student counsellors 49; definition 36; differences in student reports and student counsellors reports 47; effective reasonable accommodations 41–42, 45–48; environmental characteristics influence 37–38; frequency 41–43; ICF framework 37; limitations 48–49; personal characteristics influence 36–37; problems experienced 47; reluctance to use reasonable accommodations 50; social problems 47; during teaching and evaluation methods 41, 44–45
functioning and participation problems of ASD students 73–74; analysis 78; communication 82–84, 87; comparison with students without a disability 83; effective reasonable accommodations 81–82, 85; environmental characteristics 86–87; frequency of experienced problems 78–79, 82–83; ICF framework 74; mapping problems before selecting and implementing effective reasonable accommodations 86–87; measures 76–78; social interactions 83, 87; study limitations 86; study participants

75–76; study procedures 76; during teaching and evaluation method 79–81, 83–84
Fund for Students with Disabilities 56
funding: assistive equipment 99

giving voice to disabled students 155
government policies: inclusive learning environments for VI students 98
groundedness in sense of belonging 131–132

Healey and colleagues materials 11
heightened pressures during per-transition phase 64–65
hidden disabilities: student perceptions 9–10
Higher Education Opportunity Act 128
higher education participation rates 57
Hobfoll, S.E.: Conservation of resources (COR) theory 19
hope 21; LD scores lower than non-LD peers 21; measuring 23–24; predicting achievement 21; predictor of ASE 29

IAUCC (Irish Association for University and College Counselling Service) 113
Iceland: education system 126; inclusive higher education 127–128
Iceland vocational diploma programme 127: belonging 130–134; details 128–130; dynamism 133; groundedness 131–132; limitations 134–135; reciprocity 132; self-determination 134; student mentor support 135; subjectivity of belonging 131
IEPs (Individual Education Plans) 58
immediate environments: factors outside 98; interacting factors 99–102
implementing: support plans 100–101
*Inclusion of students with disabilities in tertiary education and employment* review 57
inclusive definition 128
inclusive education 127–128; accessible curriculum and assessment 101–102; application accessibility 99; approaches for VI students 98; belonging 130–134; Bioecological Model of Inclusive Education 95–96; definition 3; diversity 3; DSO 100; as ethical project 135; external agencies 99–100; funding equipment 99; Iceland policies 128; improving 4–5; inclusion definition 128; independent access to information 103–104; infrastructure 102; institution preparedness 105, 108; need for support 5; preparations for higher education 102–103; self-advocacy 103; support plan implementations 101–102; technology 108; US policies 128
inclusive learning for VI students: accessible curriculum and assessment 101–102;

achievement 105; analysis 94; applications 99; approaches to inclusion 98; barriers 107–108; Bioecological Model of Inclusive Education 95–96; DSA funded equipment 99; DSO 100; Equality Act 97; external agency support 99–100; government policies 98; independent access to information 103–104; infrastructure 102; institution preparedness 105, 108; learner preparedness for transitioning into higher education 106–107; longitudinal qualitative study 92–94; moving towards more inclusive practice 98; participation 104–105; preparation for higher education 102–103; progressive mutual accommodations 106–107; self-advocacy 103; societal attitudes 98; study participants 94; support plan implementations 100–101; technology significance 108; terminology 94; value 105
independent access to information 103–104
independent learners: motivations 150
Individual Education Plans (IEPs) 58
individualised learning agreements 121
individualised support for mental health 120–121
inefficient study skills: ASD students 84
infrastructure: inclusive learning 102
institutions: preparedness for inclusive learning 105, 108
insufficient PowerPoint notes barrier 148
intellectual disabilities *see* students with intellectual disabilities
internship teaching method 54
interventions: increasing retention 9
invisible disabilities 9–10
IPA (Interpretative Phenomenological Analysis) 138
Ireland: AHEAD 112; HSE *Mental Health in Ireland: Awareness and Attitudes* report 112; IAUCC 113; Mental Health Act 111; My World Survey 112; students with disabilities higher education participation rates 112; whole population approach to mental health 111–112
Ireland mental health support in higher education: academic staff awareness 119–120; disclosure and access to support 121–122; dual academic and mental health support 120–121; early engagement with mental health topics during whole campus services 118–119; focus group procedures 117–118; inadequate support services on campus 113; individualised learning agreements 121; semi-structured interviews 118; specialised supports 115–116, 120–121; stigma and disclosure of mental health difficulties 113; study limitations 122; study

# INDEX

overview 116–117; whole campus approach effect on inclusion experiences 122–123; whole campus approach to mental health 114–115, 122

Irish Association for University and College Counselling Service (IAUCC) 113

labelling 159–160
lack of understanding: stigmatisation of disabled students 156
LD (learning disability): lower hope scores than non-LD peers 21; lower SOC than peers without LD 20; predictor of lower ASE 29
LD students and ASE: analysis 24–25; ASE measures 23; ASE predictors 29; direct/indirect effects of LD on ASE 27–28; educational implications 30–31; hierarchical regression analysis for predicting ASE 27; hope measures 23–24; identification 19; limitations 29; male *versus* female scores 26; mediation analyses 25–27; past experiences role shaping present contextual conditions 28; Pearson correlations among variables 27; predictors of ASE 25; resiliency 19; SOC scale 24; students with *versus* without learning disabilities scores 26; study participants 22–23; tiredness measure 24
Leaving Certificate exams 57
lecture handouts for DPP PowerPoint presentations 149, 152
lecture teaching method 54

macrosystems 97–98
MANOVA: LD students ASE study 24–25
mapping problems before selecting and implementing effective reasonable accommodations 86–87
master's thesis evaluation method 54
meaningful participation 130
measuring: ASE 23; effective reasonable accommodations 77–78; functioning and participation problems of ASD students in higher education 77; hope 23–24; SOC 24; teaching and evaluation methods 77; tiredness 24
mediation model: LD students ASE study 24–27
medical model 5
mental health: My World Survey 112; whole population approach 111–112
Mental Health Act 111
Mental Health Commission of Ireland (MHCI) 111
*Mental Health in Ireland: Awareness and Attitudes* report 112
mental health support in higher education: academic staff awareness 119–120; disclosure and access to support 121–122; dual academic and mental health support 120–121; early engagement with mental health topics during whole campus services 118–119; focus group procedures 117–118; inadequate support services on campus 113; individualised learning agreements 121; semi-structured interviews 118; specialised supports 115–116, 120–121; stigma and disclosure of mental health difficulties 113; study limitations 122; study overview 116–117; whole campus approach effect on inclusion experiences 122–123; whole campus approach to mental health 114–115, 122
Merriam-Webster dictionary: tiredness definition 21
mesosystems 97–102
MHCI (Mental Health Commission of Ireland) 111
microsystems 96, 99–102
motivations: independent learners 150; UDL 163
multiple-choice exams evaluation method 54
My World Survey 112

negative attitudes: stigmatisation of disabled students 156
NLN (National Learning Network) support services 115–116
normality: disclosing/not disclosing disabilities 9–10
note-takers: DPP PowerPoint presentations benefits 150–151

occupational opportunities: expanding 12
OECD (Organisation for Economic Co-operation and Development): *Inclusion of students with disabilities in tertiary education and employment* review 57
one-to-one supports for academic and mental health 120–121
open book exams evaluation method 54
opening up to the other: ableism assumptions 160; dimensions of difference 161; labelling 159–160; sensitivities to tensions around construction of disability 158–159
opportunities: provided by higher education 12
oral exams evaluation method 54

participation: barriers 104–105; higher education rates 57, 112; meaningful 130; *see also* functioning and participation problems of ADHD students; functioning and participation problems of ASD students
past experiences: perceptions of present contextual conditions and demands in college 28
peer-evaluation teaching method 54
personal characteristics influence on academic functioning of students 37–38

# INDEX

personal functional and participation problems of ASD students 73
personal resources: direct/indirect effects on ASE 27–28; impact on ASE risk factors 28; predictors of ASE 25
physical environment: factors and culture outside 97–98
policy development: disabled student participation 157
political voices of research *see* academic activism
portfolio evaluation method 54
post-transition phase for ASD students 65–67
PowerPoint presentations for SEN: DPP approach 149–150; UDL 148–149
practical exams evaluation method 54
practical teaching method 54
predictors: ASE 25, 29
preparations for higher education 102–103
pre-transition phase for ASD students 63–65
process evaluation teaching method 54
progression support: Republic of Ireland policies 56
progressive mutual accommodations 106–107
proving disabilities 159
provision development: disabled student participation 157
psychological stress: resources 19

Qualifications Act 56

ready-made solutions critiques: social model of disability 164–165; UDL 162–164
reasonable accommodations: DARE initiative in Republic of Ireland 57; defined 38, 73; Equality Act 15, 151; equal participation chances 81; functioning and participation problems 45–46; mapping problems before selecting and implementing 86–87; progressive mutual 106–107; reluctance to use 50; *see also* effective reasonable accommodations
reciprocity in sense of belonging 132
relevant stakeholder voices 157–158
Republic of Ireland: access initiatives 56–57; addressing SEN/people with disabilities inequalities 56; DARE 57; Disability Officers 56; Fund for Students with Disabilities 56; higher education participation rates 57; Qualifications Act 56
Republic of Ireland ASD student transition experiences: accessing support 65–68; accommodation/transport offers 65; analysis 62–63; disclosing disabilities 65–68; early transition planning 67; effectiveness of supports 66–67; pre-transition heightened pressures 64–65; secondary school support and knowledge in transition planning 63–64; social interaction in the classroom 68; social isolation 67; study participants 61; study procedures 61–62; study research questions 60–61

resiliency: LD students 19
resources: conservation of (COR) 19
retention 9
Ryan, J.: self-determination theory 19

Scotland: Teachability proposal 10–11
Seale, J.: digital capital 108
secondary school support and knowledge in transition planning 63–64
self-advocacy: encouraging 157; inclusive learning 103
self-determination 19; ASD students 58–59; sense of belonging 134
self-evaluation teaching method 54
SEN (special educational needs): 55–57
SEN PowerPoint presentations: benefits 150–151; comprehensive lecture notes 150–152; DPP approach 149–150; lecture handouts 149, 152; limitations 152; UDL 148–149
sensitisation towards disabilities: faculty perceptions 10–11
sensitivities: tensions around construction of disability 158–159
SHS (State Hope Scale) 23
Snyder's Hope Theory 21
SOC (sense of coherence) 20–21; ADHD symptom severity 20–21; direct/indirect effects on ASE 27–28; LD lower SOC than peers without LD 20; measuring 24; predictor of ASE 29
social interactions: ASD students 59–60, 68, 80, 83–84, 87; inclusion 12; students with intellectual disabilities belonging 130–134
social isolation: ASD students 59, 67
social model of disability 5; critique 164–165; definition 138
societal attitudes: inclusive learning environments for VI students 98
sociological imagination 155–166
socratic gadflies: ableism assumptions 160; dimensions of difference 161; labelling 159–160; privileging voices of disabled students 156–157; privileging voices of relevant stakeholders 157–158; sensitivities to tensions around construction of disability 158–159; social model of disability critiques 164–165; UDL critique 162–164
special educational needs (SEN) 55–57
specialised supports for mental health 115–116, 120–121
State Hope Scale (SHS) 23

# INDEX

stigmatisation 156–157
Student Central 116
student counsellors 39; support 49–50
students with intellectual disabilities inclusive education: belonging 130–134; dynamism 133; groundedness 131–132; Iceland vocational diploma programme 128–130; meaningful participation 130; reciprocity 132; self-determination 134; student mentor support 135; subjectivity of belonging 131; US policies 128
study material barriers 148
subjectivity: belonging in inclusive education 131
success: ASE predictors 29; first year successful transition effect on 9; technology assistance 108
support services: academic staff awareness of mental health 119–120; accessing 65–68; ASD students 59; disclosure link to accessing 121–122; dual academic and mental health 120–121; effectiveness 66–67; external agencies 99–100; facilitators 6–7; Iceland vocational diploma programme 135; inadequate mental health 113; individualised learning agreements 121; need 5; plan implementations 100–101; specialised supports for mental health 115–116, 120–121; student counsellors 39, 49–50; *see also* disability coordinators

Teachability proposal in Scotland 10–11
teaching and evaluation methods: classical *versus* alternative 48; functional and participation problems of ASD students 79–84, 87; functioning and participation problems of ADHD students 44–45; listing of 54; measuring 77
technology: inclusive learning success 108; UDL 163
textbooks: alternative formats 101
time: disability coordinators 142–143
tiredness 21–22; definition 21; measuring 24
training faculty towards disabilities: faculty perceptions 10–11; universal design for learning 11–12
transition to higher education for ASD students 58–60; accessing support 65–68; accommodation/transport offers 65; analysis 62–63; disclosing disabilities 65–68; early transition planning 67; effectiveness of supports 66–67; pre-transition heightened pressures 64–65; secondary school support and knowledge in transition planning 63–64; self-determination 59; social challenges 59–60; social interaction in the classroom 68; social isolation 59, 67; student attrition and failure in first year 58–59; study participants 61; study procedures 61–62; study research questions 60–61; support services 59
transitioning process: difficulties and ideas for improvement 8–9; early planning 67; first year criticality for retention and success 9; preparations 102–103; Republic of Ireland policies to support 56; secondary school support and knowledge 63–64; student preparedness 106–107; success factors 57
two-mode partitioning: functioning and participation problems of ADHD students in higher education 42; functioning and participation problems of ASD students in higher education study 78

UCAS (Universities and Colleges Admissions Service) website access 99
UDL (Universal Design for Learning) 11–12; ADHD student accommodation 50; assessments 163–164; critique 162–164; PowerPoint presentations 148–149; student motivations 163; technology 163
UK: additional curriculum 107; BIS new DSA proposal 92; Equality Act 91, 97, 138–139, 151; Healey and colleagues materials 11; inclusion services and responsibilities 91–92
UK disability coordinator experiences: changing nature of disabilities 142–143; flexibility 141–143; good practices 141–142; interest and internal motivations for job choice 141; personal experiences with disability 141; practice and education-research paths 143–144; students disabled during university life 143; system-related suggestions 144; time 142–143
UK inclusive learning environments for VI students: accessible curriculum and assessment 101–102; achievement 105; analysis 94; applications 99; approaches to inclusion 98; barriers 107–108; Bioecological Model of Inclusive Education 95–96; DSA funded equipment 99; DSO 100; Equality Act 97; external agency support 99–100; government policies 98; independent access to information 103–104; infrastructure 102; institution preparedness 105, 108; learner preparedness for transitioning into higher education 106–107; longitudinal qualitative study 92–94; moving towards more inclusive practices 98; participation 104–105; preparation for higher education 102–103; progressive mutual accommodations 106–107; self-advocacy 103; societal attitudes 98; study participants 94; support plan implementations 100–101; technology significance 108; terminology 94; value 105
UniLink 115–116, 120

# INDEX

Universal Design for Learning *see* UDL
Universities and Colleges Admissions Service (UCAS) website accessibility 99
University of Gloucestershire: Healey and colleagues materials 11
University of Strathclyde: Teachability proposal 10–11
U.S.: Debrand and Salzberg proposal 11; Higher Education Opportunity Act 128; IEPs 58
Utah State University: Debrand and Salzberg proposal 11

value: inclusive learning experiences 105
VI (visual impairment) inclusive learning environments: accessible curriculum and assessment 101–102; achievement 105; analysis 94; applications 99; approaches to inclusion 98; barriers 107–108; Bioecological Model of Inclusive Education 95–96; DSA funded equipment 99; DSO 100; Equality Act 97; external agency support 99–100; government policies 98; independent access to information 103–104; infrastructure 102; institution preparedness 105, 108; learner preparedness for transitioning into higher education 106–107; longitudinal qualitative study 92–94; moving towards more inclusive practices 98; participation 104–105; preparation for higher education 102–103; progressive mutual accommodations 106–107; self-advocacy 103; societal attitudes 98; study participants 94; support plan implementations 100–101; technology significance 108; terminology 94; value 105
voices: disabled students 156–157; relevant stakeholders 157–158
voices of change 155

websites: tiredness definition 21; UCAS accessibility 99
whole campus approach to mental health 114–115, 122; early engagement with mental health topics during whole campus services 118–119; effect on inclusion experiences 122–123
whole population approach to mental health 111–112
Wright-Mills, C.: sociological imagination 165–166
writing papers evaluation method 54